The Last Days of Mankind

Karl Kraus

KARL KRAUS

The Last Days of Mankind

A TRAGEDY IN FIVE ACTS

Abridged and edited by
FREDERICK UNGAR
Introduction by the editor

Critical analysis by Franz H. Mautner

FREDERICK UNGAR PUBLISHING CO.
NEW YORK

TRANSLATED FROM THE GERMAN
Die letzten Tage der Menschheit
BY ALEXANDER GODE AND SUE ELLEN WRIGHT

Copyright © 1974 by Frederick Ungar Publishing Co., Inc.
Printed in the United States of America
Library of Congress Catalog Card Number: 73-91749
Designed by Irving Perkins
ISBN 0-8044-2484-5

For sale in the United States only

Contents

Introduction   ix

The Last Days of Mankind

Preface   3

ACT I

SCENE 1:	The Ringstrasse promenade in Vienna, where an excited crowd has gathered	7
SCENE 2:	In front of a bridge in South Tyrol	16
SCENE 3:	On the far side of the bridge	17
SCENE 4:	The Optimist and the Grumbler conversing	17
SCENE 5:	At the Ballhausplatz	20
SCENE 8:	A street on the outskirts of Vienna	23
SCENE 10:	At the Café Pucher	26
SCENE 11:	Two Draft Dodgers meet; a Neue Freie Presse Subscriber and a Patriot conversing	29
SCENE 14:	An interview at the home of the actress Elfriede Ritter, just returned from Russia	44
SCENE 22:	The Optimist and the Grumbler conversing near the War Ministry	50
SCENE 24:	Conrad von Hötzendorf, the Chief of Staff, in his quarters	52
SCENE 26:	A command post on a mountaintop on the southwestern front	55

v

SCENE 27:	At the Vatican, where Pope Benedict is praying	58
SCENE 28:	At the office of the Neue Freie Presse, where chief editor Benedikt is dictating	59
SCENE 29:	The Optimist and the Grumbler conversing	60

ACT II

SCENE 7:	At an artillery emplacement	73
SCENE 10:	The Optimist and the Grumbler conversing	75
SCENE 16:	A command office	80
SCENE 17:	At Anton Gruesser's restaurant	81
SCENE 26:	The Subscriber and the Patriot conversing	89
SCENE 29:	The Optimist and the Grumbler conversing	91

ACT III

SCENE 2:	In front of the Austrian artillery positions	97
SCENE 5:	In front of a locked German bookstore in Hermannstadt	98
SCENE 13:	Before a criminal court in Heilbronn	98
SCENE 14:	The Optimist and the Grumbler conversing	100
SCENE 15:	A Protestant church	103
SCENE 16:	Another Protestant church	104
SCENE 17:	Another Protestant church	105
SCENE 18:	Pilgrims' chapel	107
SCENE 21:	A physician's consulting room in Berlin	108
SCENE 22:	An office at a command post	109
SCENE 37:	The Subscriber and the Patriot conversing	111
SCENE 40:	Near the Wahnschaffes' villa at the German spa Gross-Salze	114
SCENE 41:	The Optimist and the Grumbler conversing	123
SCENE 42:	At the gate of a villa during the Battle of the Somme	127
SCENE 43:	A room, fronting on the Ringstrasse, of the Ministry of War	127

ACT IV

SCENE 2:	The Optimist and the Grumbler conversing	129
SCENE 3:	A railroad station near Vienna	130
SCENE 5:	Two Poets conversing	132
SCENE 6:	Students' drinking bout	133
SCENE 7:	Physicians' meeting in Berlin	134
SCENE 11:	A divisional command	143
SCENE 20:	A banquet in Sofia for newspaper editors	144
SCENE 22:	In the Wahnschaffes' parlor	147
SCENE 24:	The Subscriber and the Patriot conversing	150
SCENE 28:	A movie theater	151
SCENE 29:	The Optimist and the Grumbler conversing	153
SCENE 30:	A court-martial	161
SCENE 32:	A military court at Kragujevac	165
SCENE 34:	A police station	166
SCENE 37:	German headquarters	167
SCENE 39:	In company commander Hiller's dugout	169
SCENE 44:	Army training camp at Vladimir Volynski	170
SCENE 45:	Count Dohna-Schlodien surrounded by press representatives	171

ACT V

SCENE 2:	The Optimist and the Grumbler conversing	173
SCENE 6:	The base at Fourmies	174
SCENE 7:	A mass rally at the Busch Auditorium in Berlin	175
SCENE 11:	General war conference of the Social Democratic Party caucus	178
SCENE 14:	A battlefield near Sarrebourg	179
SCENE 17:	The Subscriber and the Patriot conversing	180
SCENE 18:	The Optimist and the Grumbler conversing	183
SCENE 33:	The Optimist and the Grumbler conversing	183
SCENE 34:	In the village of Postabitz	186
SCENE 37:	An Austrian rear-echelon drill field, after the winter offensive in Transylvania	187

SCENE 38:	*The press service at Hofburg*	190
SCENE 40:	*A side street, a soldier and his daughter walking*	191
SCENE 41:	*Army command headquarters*	192
SCENE 53:	*A deserted street*	193
SCENE 54:	*The Grumbler at his desk*	194
SCENE 55:	*Love feast at a corps command. A series of apparitions appear*	205

Critical Analysis by Franz H. Mautner   239

Introduction

Karl Kraus is still largely unknown in English-speaking countries, although his name, which has begun to appear with increasing frequency in the cultural journals, conveys a certain sense of importance. That Kraus is so little known may stem from the fact that he has remained untranslated, indeed, that those familiar with his work believe it to be untranslatable—more of that later. It is nonetheless a puzzling situation: Kraus was a major influence in the intellectual life of Vienna, whose seminal thinkers and artists have profoundly changed twentieth-century thought. Among his contemporaries were such men as Freud, Wittgenstein, Buber, Hofmannsthal, Schnitzler, Klimt, Kokoschka, Mahler, Schönberg. There were many more in Austria, among them Rilke and Kafka. On some of these men Kraus's influence was fundamental. Indeed, critic George Steiner recently wrote that without Kraus "Schönberg's musical development might well have been different and Wittgenstein's philosophy nonexistent."

Difficult to classify into any literary, philosophical, or political category, Karl Kraus stands unique in world literature, a writer *sui generis.* Many critics and scholars believe him to be the greatest satirist since Swift; he is also one of the greatest aphorists. His tragedy *The Last Days of Mankind,* presented here in abridged form to an English readership for the first time, is a work of great ethical and aesthetic significance. It has no equal in its passionate opposition to war. For this drama, seven professors of the Paris Sorbonne nominated for the Nobel Prize in Literature not a fellow countryman, but Karl Kraus, their world-war "enemy" of only a few years before. So did Thomas Masaryk, first president of the Czechoslovak Republic. (To substantiate his nomination, Kraus was compared with Aristophanes, Juvenal, Swift, and Gogol.)

I vividly remember the profound impression made on me when as a young man of twenty I first attended one of Kraus's public readings; I missed only a few of his later readings.

On such occasions the hall was filled with a capacity audience electrified by intellectual and emotional excitement. After the hall lights were extinguished, and with only a lamp lit over the green-covered table, Kraus emerged from behind the folding screen and walked with a few quick steps to the table and sat down. The first impression was of some shyness; but when he started to read, his passionate condemnation of the war, of everything that was corrupt in Austria, and the force of his conviction, compelling in its sincerity, had a powerful impact upon his audience. But he himself was also carried away by the emotion of his visionary fervor. His clenched right fist trembled with emotion under the lamp's glaring light. And the mastery of his diction was further enhanced by the mastery of his recitation—he had all technical means at his disposal.

As one contemporary writer described it: "For an hour and a quarter he wields the rod of his word. Now his voice is hoarse with quiet wrath, now it sounds melodious, as if he were weaving in a stanza from a folk song, now it rises to a roaring thunderstorm, in which one can hardly distinguish word from scream; at another moment it cuts the air like blows from glittering weapons."

Austria's cultural flowering was in striking contrast to the social and political decay and disintegration that finally led to the dissolution of the Austro-Hungarian empire at the end of World War I. Unwilling to deal with the social and political problems in a time of rising demands for national self-determination and mass democracy, trying in vain to control the centrifugal forces of the many nationalities that tore the empire apart, conscious of the gathering storm but unable to ward it off, the monarchy tottered to its doom.

Kraus, like Freud, Schnitzler, and others among his notable contemporaries, came from a well-to-do Jewish family. He was born on April 28, 1874, in Jičín, Moravia. When he was three, his father, a prosperous paper manufacturer, moved the family to Vienna. Kraus's school and university years coincided with the heyday of the Burgtheater, the foremost German stage, and the lively literary life that characterized turn-of-the-century Vienna. From both, Kraus received decisive impressions. He entered the University of Vienna to study law, but actually attended mainly lectures in philosophy and literature without ever working toward a degree. His strong inclination toward the stage led him to attempts to become an actor, which, however, were unsuccessful. But his dramatic gifts evolved later into his uncommon accomplishments as a reader of his own works and those of others, mainly Shakespeare, Goethe, Nestroy, Raimund, and Hauptmann. He also sang excerpts from the much-admired Offenbach operettas, most effectively despite his untrained voice.

A keen observer of the contemporary scene and endowed with an extraordinary talent for satirizing well-known figures, Kraus was in violent opposition to the pervading corruption of the spirit in all domains of public life—in politics, the administration of justice, in literature and art.

At eighteen, the aspiring writer began contributing to various Austrian and German periodicals and newspapers, including Moriz Benedikt's famous daily *Neue Freie Presse*. He wrote mainly, but not exclusively, book and theater reviews with a satirical edge. The satire was still playful, but the cub was sharpening his claws. In 1896 he published *Die demolierte Literatur* (The Demolished Literature), in which he lampooned most of the Viennese writers then in vogue. Two years later appeared *Eine Krone für Zion* (A Crown for Zion), in which Theodor Herzl and Zionism were his targets. (He later was to regret the attack on Herzl.) Both pamphlets created sensations and made his name known.

In 1898, Kraus became editor of the magazine *Die Waage* (The Scales), for which he wrote critical pieces on politics and culture. His position as editor gave him an inside view of the extent to which political, financial, and social considerations inhibit truth in journalism. A man of independent means, he decided to escape all restrictions on his writing by establishing his own publication, in which he could unleash his biting attacks not only on the cliques that dominated Austrian cultural life but also on the bankers and cartels shielded by a corrupt press. This was to be the task of his life. *Die Fackel* (The Torch), founded in 1899, was to be his principal weapon.

When Moriz Benedikt heard about Kraus's plan to publish his own magazine, he offered him the position on *Neue Freie Presse* left vacant by the death of Daniel Spitzer, the witty writer of the celebrated column "Wiener Spaziergänge" (Strolls through Vienna). Kraus did not hesitate long. "There are two beautiful things in the world: to belong to the staff of the *Neue Freie Presse* and to despise it. I did not doubt for a moment what my choice had to be."

Kraus's decision to become an independent publisher was an event of decisive importance for both his literary career and Viennese cultural life. The effect of *Die Fackel*'s first issue, dated April, 1899, in which he announced his uncompromising hostility to all that was corrupt in Austrian life, was sensational.

In it Kraus wrote: "May *Die Fackel* provide light for a country on which, unlike the empire of Charles V, the sun never rises." The enormous excitement generated by the first issue caused Kraus to send it back to the presses twice in quick succession to meet reader demand. The magazine delighted his readers and infuriated his victims. Inflated reputations were deflated with a brief reference, sometimes only a relative clause. His mordant wit and extraordinary polemical skill made him a formidable adversary, and those who were his targets often considered it the better part of wisdom not to engage the enemy. The aptness of his epithets stuck to his victims as if they had been born with them.

In its first twelve years, *Die Fackel* contained contributions by statesmen (Masaryk, Lamasch), public figures (Liebknecht, Viktor Adler), and writers (Strindberg, Wedekind, Oscar Wilde, Heinrich Mann, Peter Altenberg, Trakl), whose views or work Kraus esteemed and wanted to further. From 1911 to the time of his death on June 12, 1936, *Die Fackel* was written entirely by Kraus himself. It was, in a sense, an autobiographical diary.

The target for Kraus's most corrosive prose was journalism, which he attacked with a persistence that suggests that he considered such activity the central purpose of his life. He saw the press as the embodiment of intellectual venality, as a menace to peace already sorely imperiled, as the instrument of life's trivialization. His attacks, however, were not primarily directed at journalism's sinister political influence, but rather at its perversion of culture and its corruption of language. Measuring everything by absolute standards, condoning no compromise, however trivial, he was bound to regard the journalist, who works under the pressure of day-to-day contingencies rather than ultimate principles, as the embodiment of everything evil.

And it must be noted here that the Viennese press of Kraus's time was an example of journalism in its ugliest form. The founder of *Die Presse*, an earlier incarnation of Moriz Benedikt's *Neue Freie Presse*, openly declared that ideally no line printed in his paper should be without direct or indirect financial return to the publisher. The *Neue Freie Presse* was the leading newspaper of the monarchy. It had a very high literary standard and, as the covert mouthpiece of the government, was the most powerful.

Because of its entanglement with industrial and banking interests, the *Neue Freie Presse* had enormous influence, and even the government was sometimes dependent on the paper's good will. Wickham Steed, the *London Times* correspondent, said with much truth that the emperor was the most powerful man in the country next to Moriz Benedikt. (Benedikt appears in *The Last Days of Mankind* in Act I, Scene 28, and again in the Epilogue [not included in this abridgment] as the Lord of the Hyenas.)

The newspapers reacted to Kraus's attacks by surrounding him with a wall of silence. For example, Peter Altenberg's funeral was not reported because Kraus delivered a eulogy at it. There were even attempts to prevent Kraus from renting concert halls. No bookstore would carry *Die Fackel* during the first twenty years of its publication. Kraus accepted the challenge. "I shall make this silence audible! It would be a poor retort not to speak about it." In a lighter vein he noted that "if a comet were to graze my head . . . the papers would not report its appearance."

It was a gallant fight Kraus fought against the enslavement of man's sexual drives by state and church. In passionate indignation he came to the aid of unprotected life and spoke out powerfully against its oppressors. Many of his polemical essays later appeared in book form under the titles *Sittlichkeit und*

Kriminalität (Morality and Criminality) and *Die chinesische Mauer* (The Chinese Wall).

The climax of Kraus's work was the epic drama *The Last Days of Mankind*. Max Reinhardt and Erwin Piscator tried unsuccessfully to obtain Kraus's permission to stage the play; the work, however, is meant to be read. The imagination of the reader must provide the stage. Kraus stated in his preface that the play is "intended for a theater on Mars," since a performance would require ten full evenings according to the way we measure time on earth.

Written during World War I, this drama appeared in special issues of *Die Fackel* in 1918 and 1919 before being published as a book (1922) in a revised and amplified form. "This book will have to be read by those who want to work against war," wrote the pacifist and Nobel Peace Prize winner Alfred H. Fried. "I count it among the noblest creations of the mind. It belongs to those books of mankind that are of eternal value. . . . Its translation seems impossible. Commentaries to this work will have to be written to assure its world-wide dissemination. This will be well worth the effort."

Kraus was one of the very few who never succumbed for a moment to the chauvinistic poison that filled the air in those war years. The only writer of rank to stand firm against those Austrians who were embracing the war, he challenged with absolute courage the powers that be, championing abused humanity at the risk of his life. In Berlin in 1916, when the tide of war enthusiasm was running high, he read in public his sketch "Ein Kantianer und Kant" (A Kantian and Kant), in which he contrasted the author of *Toward Perennial Peace* with Kaiser Wilhelm II, who liked to fancy himself as fashioned in the Kantian mold. He dismissed the ruler of Germany as a "second-class stage hero," and he considered a desire for a German victory as high treason against the spirit.

Kraus's satirical tragedy evolves, through the poetic power of its creator, into an apocalyptic warning of an impending, world-engulfing disaster. It represents a vast fresco of events at the front as well as behind the lines and back home.

To a large extent the text consists of quotations—words that were actually spoken or written. It is, in a way, the first documentary drama. Kraus was convinced that the self-unmasking by way of quotation was more devastating than any other technique. In scenes of biting scorn and in gigantic visions of horror, he portrayed the monstrousness of war. In the eyes of many, a more powerful denunciation of war has never been written. The lack of unity of time, place, or action makes the unity of the idea only the more compelling.

As Walter Muschg, the Swiss literary historian, wrote: "With the outbreak of war in 1914, Kraus's art transcended itself. From being Viennese it rose to become universal, from being literary it rose to become religious. The heritage of high Jewish spirituality, dormant in Kraus in his younger years, came to life. . . . Kraus is a spirit who acts under higher orders."

In its condemnation of war, *The Last Days of Mankind* is a testament for the ages. Many distinguished critics consider it unique in world literature.

The material misery of society was not Kraus's primary concern. What mattered most for him was society's spiritual and moral misery. Fundamentally conservative, he did not want to see society reorganized along socialist lines, but he considered the existence of communism useful as a threat, and only as such. He saw through its life-desecrating cynicism, but for him, communism had value as a warning to us where our smugness might lead. Kraus's own views are expressed in the voice of the Grumbler, the dominant figure in debates with the Optimist that run through *The Last Days of Mankind*.

Our social structure is basically the same today as it was in Kraus's time. If he were alive today, he would fight the same enemies, although they would have different names and use different rhetoric. He would blame them for the same sins—for their responsibility for war, for their stultifying and dehumanizing influence, for their essential betrayal of the trust placed in them. In a truly prophetic vision in his Epilogue, Kraus anticipated the development of atomic armament and its threat for all mankind. For all these reasons, the play is as timely today as it was when Kraus wrote it.

His was a warning voice calling upon his contemporaries not to be so completely absorbed in acquisition that they confused life's purposes with its means. He blamed man for destroying imagination, "the real backbone of life," the faculty that must be strengthened to make war impossible. He wrote: "In this time, in which things happen that could not be imagined and in which what no longer can be imagined must happen—for if it could be imagined, it could not happen. . . ."

Kraus in the war years was for many an Austrian the last refuge of spiritual values. He saved many from despair and preserved their faith in mankind, particularly the faith of those on the battlefront to whom *Die Fackel* sometimes found its way. He awakened human responsibility in many, offering the example of an idealism that could not be diverted from the demands of conscience.

Kraus's conception of language is of central importance in understanding both the man and his work. He saw the ubiquitous divorce of language and meaning as a major modern dilemma. His relationship to language was of a magic and religious character: the word as magic substitute for the thing, the linking together of words as a formula possessing magic power. Language for him was not just a means of communication, but rather creative in itself. Kraus firmly believed that there is a pre-established harmony of word and world, and that the cosmos of one is reflected in the other.

He had the gift of letting the spirit of language, as it were, think for him, and he would follow it into its labyrinths like a somnambulist. "I have drawn out of language many a thought I did not have or could not put into words." It is the divining rod that finds the springs of thoughts, the key to bringing order into chaos.

Because he considered language a direct index of morality, Kraus elevated it to man's essential concern, to which every other consideration should be subordinated. In its use of language he saw the cultural strength or weakness of a nation and the carrier of its spirit. Kraus firmly believed that purification of language would work to purify ethics. To support this conviction, he more than once quoted Confucius in his readings: "If concepts are not right, words are not true; if words are not true, works are not achieved; if works are not achieved, morality and the arts do not thrive; if morality and the arts do not thrive, justice miscarries; if justice miscarries, the nation does not know where to put its feet and hands. Therefore, disorder in words must not be tolerated."

Kraus championed the honor of language by dishonoring the culpable speaker. Purity of language was thus to him the measure of a man's integrity. There were many whose ears he trained to discern the hollow ring of vacuous phrases, of cant and deceit, of the shamelessness and perfidy that assaulted them from the columns of the daily press, particularly in time of war. And there were many whom he strengthened in the integrity of their conduct. "He taught us how to read," wrote Karel Čapek, "how to appraise accurately sense and nonsense in printed words, their contradictions, their frightening recurrence. Whoever has gone through the school of the red paperbound issues of *Die Fackel* has completed, as it were, a course in moral philology. He is the greatest taskmaster of reading that ever lived."

Kraus's approach to life was aesthetic and ethical, that is, not necessarily practical or rational. His yardstick was the absolute;

no compromise that would conflict with his moral sense was acceptable. Such a view precludes objectivity, the weighing of pros and cons, the consideration of circumstances that would, if not justify, at least tolerate certain behavior. No doubt Kraus was often unjust in his attacks, however pure his motive. Because of this he was not only loved and admired, but also hated and condemned.

Unable to identify long with any political party, Kraus varied his allegiance with the ethical demands of the issue being decided, alternately heaping scorn on all sectors of the political spectrum. Some who were discredited by his attacks reproached him with the negative character of his criticism, which they claimed "could only destroy but not build up." But, to be sure, the great satirist must see values as absolutes in themselves. His endeavor to eradicate the worthless must be inspired by a desire to make room for the worthwhile; profound faith in positive values and affirmative truth is actually the prerequisite for his creativity.

Karl Kraus died when Austria was facing the menace of National Socialism at its western borders—this was two years before the forced Anschluss. His last work, written during the outbreak of barbarism in neighboring Germany, was not published until 1952. Through an analysis of language and speech, *Die dritte Walpurgisnacht* (The Third Walpurgis Night) portrays the horrors of the Hitler era and its diabolical nature.

A poet of a high order, Kraus left behind an extensive body of poetry; it is to be found in the nine-volume *Worte in Versen* (Words in Verse). Many of his poems are cerebral, their content frequently identical with his militant prose. Yet among them are poems of great lyrical power in which beauty of language and emotional content join harmoniously.

The usual distinctions between a writer's life and work do not apply in the case of Karl Kraus, whose life *was* his work. Writing at night and sleeping until late in the day, he sacrificed most of his private life. He never married, but his deep and lasting friendship with Sidonie Nadherny von Borutin, at whose family estate near Prague he often spent the summer months, is reflected in their correspondence, recently published abroad.

Although Kraus condemned his time, and although he believed prophetically that the dangers inherent in modern civilization were threatening an ultimate apocalypse, his work is nevertheless a profession of faith in man and in the worth of life. He never doubted that his work would endure and that through it he would "live on." In this, too, he has proved to be prophetic.

While still a publisher in Vienna, I had the privilege of issuing the eulogy by the composer and distinguished writer Ernst Krenek (later a professor of music at Vassar College). He said: ". . . that book shown in evidence on Judgment Day, so that justice may be administered to this world from it, will have many pages covered by the tiny hieroglyphs of his handwriting. Untiring and yet powerless in the face of what assaulted him in such profusion, he kept the minutes of delusion and disintegration in which the testimonies of an entire age were recorded. . . . In dreamland the judge awakened to become poet and he spoke about God's beauty and God's grace . . . it became clear that he was such a stern, such an inexorable judge, because he suffered so much by being turned away from that dreamland of beauty, forced back into 'this world of deluded figures.'"

The word *Ursprung* (source) occurs in Kraus's writing every so often. In his work it has a special meaning, one central to his thinking. In the last lines of his poem "Dying Man," God speaks to him, that is, Kraus, thus:

> Walking in darkness you did see the light.
> Now you are here and look into my face.

> You looked behind yourself and sought my garden.
> You stayed at the source. The source, it is the goal.
> You, unsurrendered to life's sullying game,
> No longer do you have to wait, my child.

What is meant is readmittance to the forfeited world of a pristine age, the world of the first day on which God gave to man his first law, the world that was lost through man's sins. It is for the poet to re-create that world in his poetry. This Kraus does also in his satire, in which he destroys the world as it is and so preserves the world of the source. He must destroy the world because only then can he feel sure of living in the ideal world of *Ursprung* and believe fully in it. He must take away our belief in *this* world to give us back our belief in the other. Satire thus forms a union with poetry, which also points to the ideal, although by other means. Kraus saw in both satire and poetry a moral task and a work of atonement for a sinful world, from whose sinning he did not exclude himself.

A word should be said about the abridgment of this work and about the translation problems it posed. The present edition is less than one-third of the original work's almost eight hundred pages. To make this great drama accessible to the American reader, entire scenes and parts of scenes had to be omitted. Only through such omissions could this translation be presented in such a manner as to put the fewest obstacles possible in the reader's way.

Despite these substantial omissions, however, the essence and unity of the original have been preserved. Professor Mautner's critical essay following Act V will supply information about some of the omitted text and also add to the reader's understanding and enjoyment of the work.

Kraus has been considered untranslatable, and in a sense, and for a considerable part of his work, this is true. In translation, much of the brilliance of Kraus's style is unavoidably lost: the ingenious play on words, the double meanings, the special connotations of words and phrases. Only now and then could some of this be preserved. Translating dialect and jargon was, as a matter of course, not attempted; this means the loss of the very funny contrast between the Austrian and the German idioms, all of which, as elements of characterization and ambiance, play such an important part in this work. Kraus also coined many words which are not to be found in any dictionary; their meanings are not always obvious. Compounding these difficulties is the fact that there are no English equivalents for many German terms, reflecting the different structures of the Austrian/German and American societies, systems of government, administration of justice, the military, etc.

Like those in whose memories Kraus's intricate ironies and witticisms continue to echo, I am aware of what has been lost in translation. It is to be hoped that enough has been retained to make this publication worthwhile. By issuing this important work for English readers, I may in some measure have paid my emotional and intellectual debt to Karl Kraus.

FREDERICK UNGAR

The Last Days of Mankind

Preface

The performance of this drama, whose scope of time by earthly measure would comprise about ten evenings, is intended for a theater on Mars. Theatergoers in this world would not be able to endure it. For it is blood of their blood, and its contents are from those unreal, inconceivable years, those years that no waking consciousness can apprehend, that are inaccessible to any memory and preserved only in a gory dream, those years in which operetta figures enacted the tragedy of mankind.

The action, leading into a hundred scenes and hells, is impossible, fissured, and hero-less, just as that other action was. The humor is but the self-reproach of one who did not go mad at the thought of having witnessed and yet survived the events of this time with his mind intact. Except for him who reveals to posterity the shame of such sharing, no one has a right to this humor. The present generation, which permitted the things recorded here to happen, should place the obligation to weep before the right to laugh. The most improbable deeds reported here really happened. The most improbable conversations that are carried on here were spoken word for word. The most glaring inventions are quotations. Sentences whose insanity is indelibly imprinted on the ear grow into a refrain that stays with one forever. A document is a dramatis persona; reports come to life as personae; personae breathe their last as editorials; the feuilleton acquires a mouth that speaks itself in a monologue. Intonations race and rattle through time and swell to become the chorale of the unholy action. People who had lived among mankind and who survived it are the perpetrators and spokesmen for a generation that possesses not flesh but blood, not blood but printer's ink; as such they are stripped down to shadows and puppets and reduced to their busy lack of substance.

This gives no one the right to regard this tragic carnival as a local affair. Even what happens on the Sirk Corner* is determined from a cosmic point of view. Whoever has weak nerves, even if they are strong enough to bear the time, should absent himself from this play. It is not to be expected that a present, in which all this could happen, take this horror that has become word for anything other than a joke, particularly where it resounds from the homey depths of the most loathsome dialects. It is not to be expected that a present time take those events which it has just lived through, which it has outlived, as anything other than an invention, one whose subject has been declared taboo. For greater than the outrage of the war is that of people who do not want to hear any more about it; to be sure, they tolerate that it is, but not that it was. For those who survived the war, the war has gone out of fashion; and although the masks go through Ash Wednesday, they do not want to be reminded of each other. How understandable is the sobering up of an epoch that was never capable of profound experience and is incapable of realizing what it had experienced! It cannot be shaken even by its own collapse, perceiving the atonement no more than the deed, but having a strong enough sense of self-preservation to stop its ears to the phonograph recordings of its heroic melodies, and enough readiness for self-sacrifice to strike them up again should the occasion

---

*Meeting place and promenade across the street from the Vienna Opera House.

arise. For that there will be war again appears least incomprehensible to those for whom the slogan, "There's a war on now," both made possible and covered up every dishonor. But the admonition "Now the war is over!" disturbs the well-earned rest of the survivors.

They fancied that, clad in knightly armor, they would conquer the world market—the goal to which they were born; now they have to settle for the less lucrative business of selling their knightly armor to the junk dealers. In such a mood let anyone speak to them of war! And it may be feared that even some future generation, sprung from the loins of so depraved a present, may, in spite of its greater distance, lack the greater power of comprehension. Nonetheless, such total confession of guilt for belonging to this mankind must be welcome somewhere and of use at some time. And "even while men's minds are wild," let Horatio's message to Fortinbras be heard:

> And let me speak to the yet unknowing world
> How these things came about: so shall you hear
> Of carnal, bloody, and unnatural acts,
> Of accidental judgments, casual slaughters,
> Of deaths put on by cunning and forced cause,
> And in this upshot, purposes mistook
> Fall'n on the inventors' heads. All this can I
> Truly deliver.

Act I

SCENE 1

Vienna. The Ringstrasse promenade at the Sirk Corner. Flags fly from the buildings. Rousing cheers for troops marching by. General excitement. The crowd breaks up into small groups.

FIRST NEWSBOY: Extra-a-a! Extra-a-a-a!
SECOND NEWSBOY: Extra-a-a! Bo-o-oth official reports!
A DEMONSTRATOR (*breaking away from a group that is singing the "Prince Eugen" march. His face heavily flushed, he has shouted himself hoarse*): Down with Serbia! Down with Serbia! Hurrah for the Hapsburgs! Hurrah! Hurrah for S-e-r-bia!
AN INTELLECTUAL (*noticing the mistake, pokes him sharply in the ribs*): Do you know what you are saying?
DEMONSTRATOR (*first bewildered, then pulling himself together*): Down with S-e-r-bia! Down with the Serbians! Hurrah! Down with the Hapsburgs! S-e-r-b-i-a!

(*In a thronging second group including a Streetwalker, a Hoodlum walking right behind her is trying to snatch her purse.*)

HOODLUM (*shouting incessantly*): Hurrah! Hurrah!

STREETWALKER: Keep your hands off me, you bastard! Hands off, or I'll—

HOODLUM (*giving up*): Why aren't you cheering? You call yourself a good Austrian? What you are is a whore. Remember that!

STREETWALKER: And you're a purse snatcher!

HOODLUM: What a slut! There's a war on and don't you forget it! You're a whore, that's what you are.

FIRST PASSER-BY: Keep it down, why don't you? Keep it down!

CROWD (*getting interested*): It's a whore. What did she say?

SECOND PASSER-BY: If I heard her right, she made a crack against our hereditary ruling house.

CROWD: Let's get her! Let's give it to her! (*The girl succeeds in making her escape through a house with a rear exit.*) Oh, let her go! We're not that kind of people. Hurrah for the Hapsburgs!

FIRST REPORTER (*to his colleague*): There's a variety of moods here. What's going on?

SECOND REPORTER: We'll see.

(*Two Army Contractors have climbed up on one of the benches that line the Ringstrasse.*)

FIRST ARMY CONTRACTOR: We can see them better from here. How beautifully they march by. Our brave boys!

SECOND ARMY CONTRACTOR: Bismarck is quoted in today's *Presse*. He says that our people are just kissable.

FIRST ARMY CONTRACTOR: Did you hear they've taken even Eisler's oldest boy?

SECOND ARMY CONTRACTOR: That's unheard of. Rich people like that! Couldn't they have done something about it?

FIRST ARMY CONTRACTOR: I hear they're trying to now. He'll probably go up and fix it.

SECOND ARMY CONTRACTOR: And if worse comes to worse—you'll see, now he'll buy that car the boy's had his heart set on.*

FIRST ARMY CONTRACTOR: And that's another way you can get hurt.

AN OFFICER (*to three other officers*): Hello, Novotny. Hello, Pokorny. Hello, Povolny. Well, Povolny, you're the one who knows politics. What have you got to say?

SECOND OFFICER (*carrying a cane*): If you ask me, it's all because of the encirclement.

THIRD OFFICER: You know—well, of course.

FOURTH OFFICER: That's just how I see it. God, what a night I had. Did you see Schönpflug's newest cartoon? It's a classic.

THIRD OFFICER: You know, the paper said the whole thing is incapable.

SECOND OFFICER: Inescapable, you mean.

THIRD OFFICER: Yes, of course—inescapable. I must have read it wrong. How are things with you?

FOURTH OFFICER: Well, you know, I've got a chance for a desk job at the War Ministry.

FIRST OFFICER: Good work. Then you will be coming in with us. Listen, last night while I was taking in the Mela Mars show at the Apollo, I ran into Novak of the Fifty-ninth. He told me he'd heard they've put me in for the silver medal.

NEWSBOY: *Tagblatt*! Great victory near Scha-a-abaa-atz!

FOURTH OFFICER: Congratulations! (*Turns to look at a passing girl.*) Say, did you see that? A tasty morsel that. (*Goes after her.*)

* Possession of an automobile was rare in Austria at that time, and a young man who brought one into the army with him could expect to be assigned to a soft job.

OTHERS (*calling after him*): See you then at Hopfner's.
A GIRL: My Poldl's promised me a Serb's liver for our supper. I've sent that letter in to the editor of the *Reichspost*.
A VOICE: Hurrah for the *Reichspost*! Our Christian daily!
ANOTHER GIRL: I sent in a letter too! My Ferdy'll bring me the kidneys of a Russian.
AN INTELLECTUAL (*to his Girl Friend*): Here in this very spot you could delve deeply into the soul of the people, if we only had more time. What time is it? This morning's editorial says, "living is a joy." Brilliant, when he says that all the glory of classical greatness sheds its radiance upon our time.
GIRL FRIEND: It's half past. Mother said I'll catch it if I get home after half past.
INTELLECTUAL: Come on, stay. Look at the people. There's a ferment in the air. Just watch the uplift!
GIRL FRIEND: Where?
INTELLECTUAL: I mean of the soul. How ennobled the people are! As the editorial says, "every man a hero." Who would have believed times could have changed so—and we with them.

(*A horse-drawn cab pulls up in front of a house.*)

PASSENGER: How much do you get?
CABBY: The gentleman knows.
PASSENGER: No, I don't. How much do you get?
CABBY: Well, just what the fare is.
PASSENGER: What is the fare?
CABBY: Well, just what you give to the others.
PASSENGER: Can you change this? (*Hands him a ten-kronen gold piece.*)
CABBY: Change it? I wouldn't take even the whole thing! It could be French money.

A Concierge (*walking over to them*): What? A Frenchman? Well, what do you know? He could be a spy! We'll give it to him! Where did he come from?

Cabby: From the East Terminal.

Concierge: Ah, from Saint Petersburg!

Crowd (*which has collected around the cab*): A spy! A spy! (*The Passenger disappears into the house with a rear exit.*)

Cabby (*shouting after him*): What a shady bastard!

Crowd: Oh, let him go. No reprisals! That's not right. We're not like that!

An American Representative of the Red Cross (*to his companion*): Just look at these people. How enthusiastic they are!

Crowd: Two Englishmen! Speak German! May God punish England! Let 'em have it! We're in Vienna! (*The Americans escape into the house with a rear exit.*) Oh, let 'em go. We're not like that!

A Turk (*to another Turk*): Regardez l'enthousiasme de tout le monde.

Crowd: Two frogs! Speak German! Let 'em have it! We're in Vienna! (*The Turks escape into the house with a rear exit.*) Oh, let 'em go. We're not like that! Listen, that was Turkish. Don't you see they're wearing fezzes. They're our allies. Catch up with them and let's sing the "Prince Eugen" march for them.

(*Two Chinese enter. They keep silent.*)

Crowd: Some Japs are here! Japs still in Vienna! The bastards should be strung up by their pigtails.

First: Leave them alone. Those are Chinks!

Second: You're a Chink yourself!

First: Maybe you are!

Third: All Chinks are Japs!

FOURTH: Are you a Jap maybe?
FIFTH: Now then, now then! What are you doing? Haven't you read the paper? (*Unfolds a newspaper*). Just look, here it says, "Such excesses of patriotism can in no way be tolerated. Furthermore, they are liable to harm tourist traffic." How is tourist traffic supposed to develop if this kind of thing goes on!
SIXTH: Bravo! He's right. If we want to increase the tourist traffic—that's hard, it's not easy to do—
SEVENTH: Shut up! War's war, and if somebody jabbers American or Turkish or something—
EIGHTH: Right! There's a war on, and this is not the time to fool around.

(*A lady with a trace of a moustache appears.*)

CROWD: Ah, look at that! We weren't born yesterday. A spy in disguise! Arrest her! Lock her up, quick.
A LEVEL-HEADED MAN: Just a minute, gentlemen—just consider—she could have gotten a shave.
ONE OF THE CROWD: Who?
LEVEL-HEADED MAN: If she were a spy.
SECOND: He forgot to. And so he's trapped himself.
SHOUTS: Who? —He! —No, she!
THIRD: That's just one of those tricks spies have.
FOURTH: They let their beards grow so that we won't notice that they're spies.
FIFTH: Don't be so dumb. That's a female spy, and she's stuck on a beard so that we won't catch on.
SIXTH: It's a female spy trying to pass herself off as a man.
SEVENTH: No, it's a man passing himself off as a female spy.
CROWD: In any case he's a shady character who should be taken to the precinct. Grab him!

(The lady is led away by a policeman. One hears the singing of "The Watch on the Rhine.")

FIRST REPORTER (*notebook in hand*): This was no flare-up of intoxicated momentary enthusiasm, no noisy outburst of morbid mass hysteria. With genuine manliness Vienna accepts the fateful decision. Do you know how I would sum up its mood? Its mood might be summed up in the words: far from haughtiness and far from weakness. Far from haughtiness and far from weakness—this phrase, which we have coined to describe the dominant mood of Vienna, cannot be repeated too often. Far from haughtiness and far from weakness. Well, what do you think of my stuff?

SECOND REPORTER: What should I say? Brilliant!

FIRST REPORTER: Far from haughtiness and far from weakness. Thousands upon thousands of people have marched through the streets today arm in arm; rich and poor, young and old, high and lowly. Everyone's bearing showed that he was fully aware of the solemnity of the situation but also proud to feel throbbing in his own body the pulsebeat of the great era about to break upon us.

VOICE FROM THE CROWD: Kiss my ass!

FIRST REPORTER: Listen to the "Prince Eugen" march and the Austrian national anthem being played over and over again, and with these two, as a matter of course, "The Watch on the Rhine," in keeping with the Nibelung troth.* Today Vienna has stopped working earlier than usual. Oh, and don't let me forget. We must especially describe how the public was massing in front of the War Ministry. But most of all, we must not forget to bring out—guess what?

* Loyalty to the death. A reference to the medieval Nibelung saga, used by Wagner as the basis for the operas in his *Ring* cycle.

SECOND REPORTER: How could I not know? We must not forget to bring out that hundreds upon hundreds of people massed on the Fichtegasse in front of the building of the *Neue Freie Presse.**

FIRST REPORTER: A great mind you've got! Yes, that's what the boss likes. But what do you mean "hundreds upon hundreds?" Did you count them? Why don't you say "thousands upon thousands?" What do you care since they are massing anyway? Then they roared thundering cheers—to Austria, Germany, and the *Neue Freie Presse*. The sequence wasn't exactly flattering for us, but still it was very nice of the enthusiastic crowd. All evening they stood pressed tightly and were massing on the Fichtegasse unless they had something to do in front of the War Ministry or on the Ballhausplatz.†

SECOND REPORTER: I can't imagine where people get the time.

FIRST REPORTER: The time is so great that there's time left over for it.

SECOND REPORTER: The big thing now is street scenes. From every street curb where there's a dog demonstrating he‡ wants a street scene. He called me in yesterday and told me I should observe human interest scenes. But that's exactly what I find disagreeable. I hate getting mixed up in a crowd. Yesterday I had to join in singing "The Watch on the Rhine." Let's get away from here. Things might start getting out of control. Just look at them. I know this mood. All of a sudden you're caught up in it, and before you know it, you're singing the national anthem.

FIRST REPORTER: God forbid! You're right. I can't see any sense

---

* The most influential newspaper in Vienna.
† Location of the Foreign Ministry.
‡ Moriz Benedikt, chief editor and co-owner of the *Neue Freie Presse*.

in our sticking around either. I don't see why, it's only a waste of time. We should be writing about it, instead we're just standing around. By the way, it's very important to describe the people's firm resolve and how here and there somebody separates himself from the crowd to make a donation. You can make a great story out of that. Yesterday he called me in and said we had to stimulate the people's appetite for war—and for the newspaper too—both can be done at the same time. The details are very important, you know, the nuances—and especially the Viennese flavor. For example you have to mention that as a matter of course all class distinctions have been cast aside, and immediately at that. They waved from automobiles, even from horse-drawn carriages. I saw a lady in a lace gown stepping out of her car and hugging a woman with a faded kerchief on her head. It's been that way ever since the ultimatum. Everybody of one heart and one mind.

COACHMAN's VOICE: Drive on, you damn rascal.

SECOND REPORTER: You know what I've observed? I've noticed how groups have been forming.

FIRST REPORTER: Well?

SECOND REPORTER: And a student made a speech about how everybody must do his duty.

FIRST REPORTER: I can only state that a mood of utmost earnestness is spreading all over the city, and this earnestness, relieved by high spirits and an awareness of experiencing a historical moment, is expressed in every countenance: in those of the men already called to the colors and of those who for the time being are staying home—

VOICE: Kiss my ass!

FIRST REPORTER: —and in the countenance of those privileged to share in this exalted task. Gone is the easygoing nonchalance, the hedonistic thoughtlessness. The keynote now is proud dignity and the confrontation of fate with cheerful earnestness. The physiognomy of our city has changed suddenly. Nowhere is there a trace of uneasiness or gloominess, nowhere fidgety nervousness or troubled minds sicklied o'er with the pale cast of thought. But neither is there frivolous underestimation of the event or foolish, unthinking chauvinism.

CROWD: Hurrah, a German! Down with Serbia!

FIRST REPORTER: Look here, Mediterranean temperament controlled and held in check by German earnestness.

(*Scene change.*)

SCENE 2

South Tyrol, in front of a bridge. An automobile is being stopped. The driver shows his pass.

MILITIAMAN: Good morning, gentlemen! May I ask—

GRUMBLER: At last a friendly person for a change. All the others flare up so easily; they immediately point their rifles at you—

MILITIAMAN: Yes, it's because of a Russian automobile, filled with gold, you know—

GRUMBLER: But a driver can't stop an automobile in a second, it rolls on a few meters—and the results can be tragic.

MILITIAMAN (*in a rage*): Yes—if one doesn't stop, we blast everything to smithereens—blast everything to smithereens—blast everything to smithereens—

(*The automobile drives on.*)

(*Scene change.*)

SCENE 3

On the far side of the bridge. Troops are swarming around the automobile. The driver is showing his pass.

A SOLDIER (*rifle poised*): Stop!

GRUMBLER: But the car is stopped! Why is this man in such a furious rage?

CAPTAIN (*in a rage*): The man is doing his duty! As long as he's in a furious rage at the enemy in the field, it'll be all right!

GRUMBLER: Yes, but we didn't—

CAPTAIN: War is war! And that's all there is to it!

(*The automobile drives on.*)

(*Scene change.*)

SCENE 4

The Optimist and the Grumbler conversing.

OPTIMIST: You can consider yourself lucky. In Styria, a Red Cross nurse was shot to death because her car kept rolling a few more feet.

GRUMBLER: The slave has been given power. It won't agree with him.

OPTIMIST: In times of war, regrettably, sometimes the lower echelons unavoidably exceed their authority. But in times such as these all other considerations must be subordinated to one thought—to be victorious!

GRUMBLER: The power that's been given to the slave won't suffice to cope with the enemy—but it will be enough to destroy the state.

OPTIMIST: Militarism means increasing the state's authority by exercising force, so that—

GRUMBLER: —the means will lead to its eventual disintegration, the dissolution of the state. In wartime, everybody becomes his fellow man's superior. The military men become the superiors of the state, which sees no way out of this unnatural constraint but corruption. If the statesman allows the military man to control him, he has fallen under the spell of a grade-school idol which has had its day and which, in our day, can be allowed to rule over life and death only at our peril.

OPTIMIST: I don't see that your gloomy predictions are justified. Just as you did in peacetime, you are obviously drawing overall conclusions from unavoidable accompanying symptoms. You're starting from accidental nuisances, and making them out to be symptomatic. Our time is far too great to bother with trifles.

GRUMBLER: The trifles will grow with the times!

OPTIMIST: This knowledge, that we are living in an era of such tremendous events, will prompt even the most limited among us to rise above themselves.

GRUMBLER: The small thieves who have not yet been hanged will grow up to be big thieves—and then they will get off scot-free.*

OPTIMIST: What even the most insignificant among us will gain from the war is—

GRUMBLER: Filth.

OPTIMIST: Yes, you—you who have seen filth in everything,

* Refers to the German proverb: "Small thieves are hanged, the big ones get off scot-free."

Act I, Scene 4

must now sense that your time is up! Go right on grumbling in your corner as you've always done—the rest of us are marching onward into an era of spiritual uplift! Don't you see that a new time, a time of greatness, has dawned?

GRUMBLER: I knew the time when it was still this small (*gestures*), and it will be small again.

OPTIMIST: Can you be negative even now? Don't you hear this exultation? Don't you see this enthusiasm? Can a feeling heart refuse to abandon itself to it? Only yours could. Do you really think that this mighty emotion of the masses will bear no fruit, that this magnificent beginning will be without a sequel? Those who are rejoicing today—

GRUMBLER: —will be lamenting tomorrow.

OPTIMIST: What does individual sorrow matter? As little as an individual life. Man's vision has at last been raised aloft again. No longer do we live merely for material gain, but also—

GRUMBLER: —for medals.

OPTIMIST: Man does not live by bread alone.

GRUMBLER: He must also make war in order not to have it.

OPTIMIST: There will always be bread! But we live by the hope of final victory, which is not to be doubted, and because of which—

GRUMBLER: —we'll starve to death.

OPTIMIST: Oh, what little faith! How ashamed you will be some day! But don't shut yourself off when there is rejoicing! The soul's gates have been thrown wide open. The memory of these days, in which people back home share in the sufferings and deeds of our glorious frontline fighters—though only by receiving daily war reports—will leave upon the souls of men—

GRUMBLER: —no scars!

OPTIMIST: The people will learn from this war only—

GRUMBLER: —not to refrain from war in the future.
OPTIMIST: The shot is out of the barrel and for mankind—
GRUMBLER: —gone in one ear and out the other!

(*Scene change.*)

SCENE 5

At the Ballhausplatz.

COUNT LEOPOLD FRANZ RUDOLF ERNEST VINZENZ INNOCENZ MARIA: That ultimatum was first-rate! At last! At last!
BARON EDUARD ALOIS JOSEF OTTOKAR IGNAZIUS EUSEBIUS MARIA: By God! But—they came within a hair's breadth of accepting it.
COUNT: That would have rattled me terribly. Luckily we had those two little paragraphs in it, our investigation on Serbian soil and all that—well, they didn't go for that one. Now they've only themselves to blame, those Serbs.
BARON: If you stop to think, it's because of two little paragraphs, for such a trifle, that the world war has broken out! Actually, it's terribly funny.
COUNT: But we couldn't do without them, we had to insist on those two little paragraphs. Why did those Serbs take it into their heads not to accept those two little paragraphs?
BARON: Well, it was clear from the beginning, that they wouldn't accept them.
COUNT: We knew that beforehand. That Poldi Berchtold* is quite a guy, no question about that. All society people

---

* Leopold (Poldi) Berchtold, Austrian Foreign Minister at the outbreak of the war.

are in complete agreement about it. Tremendous! I tell you—the elation! At last! At last! You couldn't bear it any longer. You felt hemmed in at every step. It'll be a different kind of life now! This winter, as soon as there's peace, I'll wangle myself the Riviera.

BARON: I'll be satisfied if we wangle ourselves the Adriatic.

COUNT: Don't make jokes. The Adriatic is ours. Italy is not going to make a move. Let me tell you, after peace has been concluded—

BARON: When do you think there will be peace?

COUNT: In two weeks—at the latest, three, I guess.

BARON: Don't make me laugh.

COUNT: Well, what else? Serbia we'll finish off just like that, my friend—you'll see how well our people fight. The mere élan of our Sechser Dragoner regiment! Some of them are said to be at the front already. Our artillery is first-rate. A real precision outfit!

BARON: Well, and Russia?

COUNT: The Russians will be glad to be left alone. Leave it to Conrad,* he knows why he is letting them get into Lemberg. As soon as we are in Belgrade the tide will turn. I'm telling you, the Serbs will get a terrible beating. Everything else will work out by itself.

BARON: Then, when do you believe, seriously—

COUNT: In three, four weeks, we'll have peace.

BARON: You have always been a terrific optimist.

COUNT: Okay then, when?

BARON: Can't be done under two or three months. You'll see. If everything goes well, in two. But believe me, it would have to go very well for that.

COUNT: Well, I can't quite go along with that, that would

---

* Conrad von Hötzendorf, Chief of Staff.

really be awfully boring! Wouldn't work, if only because of the food supplies. The other day Frau Sacher told me—now really, you don't think that that business with the food regulations will last, do you? Even at Demel's they are starting with this "sticking-it-out" routine. A fine state of affairs, a man is willing to cut down wherever possible, but for any length of time—Ridiculous, I won't buy that! Or do you feel otherwise?

BARON: You know my opinion. I don't have much faith in our home front. After all, we are no Krauts even if we have to accept their—only yesterday I talked to Putzo Wurmbrand, you know, the one who goes with that Maritschl Palffy, he is Krobatin's right-hand man and a first-rate patriot—he says when you start a defensive war—you know he is just set on this matter of the war being defensive—

COUNT: Well, isn't this a defensive war? You're a dyed-in-the-wool defeatist. Why don't you stop it? Have you forgotten how hard-pressed we were? Are you forgetting the encirclement? Yes, and are you perhaps suggesting that we were not forced to have the Serbs attack us at Temeš-Kubin in order to—

BARON: How come?

COUNT: How come? Go on, don't act as if—you know very well that a Serbian attack at Temeš-Kubin was necessary—I mean—we had to strike—

BARON: Why, sure, that's understood.

COUNT: Well then, would there otherwise have been any need for that attack—it was exactly like the German false report that Nuremberg had been bombed. If you don't mind then—If this is not a defensive war, I'd like to know what would be.

BARON: Did I say otherwise? As you know, I was outspokenly for a showdown from the very beginning, especially since it is the last one anyway. It doesn't make any difference to me what you call it. Defensive war—that sounds almost as if you had to apologize for it. I say, war is war.

(*Scene change.*)

SCENE 8

A street on the outskirts of Vienna. One sees a milliner's shop, a Pathéphone company, the Café Westminster, and a branch of the dry-cleaning establishment of Söldner & Chini. Four young men enter, one of whom carries a ladder, strips of paper, and glue.

FIRST: We got another one! What does this say? "Salon Stern, Modes et Robes." We'll paste over all of that one!*
SECOND: Well, but the name can stay, so people know what kind of business it is. Hand me that, we'll do it this way. (*He pastes and reads aloud.*) "Salo Stern Mode." There. That's what it should be. That's German. Let's go on.
FIRST: "Pathéphone"—just look at that, what the hell is that? Is that French?
SECOND: No, that's Latin, that can stay, but there I read: "Musical compositions, German, French, English, Italian, Russian, and Hebrew."
THIRD: Now what? What do we do with that?
FIRST: That's got to go, all of it!

* At the outset of World War I the Central Powers attempted to eliminate all words of foreign, particularly French, origin from everyday usage. This was especially difficult (if not absurd) in Austria, where French had always had enormous influence on speech at all levels of society.

SECOND: Well, do it like this. (*He pastes over and reads aloud.*) "Musical compositions, German—Hebrew." That's what it should be.

THIRD: Yes, but what's this? Just take a look at that! It says "Café Westminster." Seems to me that's even an English word!

FIRST: Wait, we can do that only after talking to the owner. That's a coffeehouse, the owner could be a very important person and we'd wind up in trouble. Let's call him out—wait! (*He goes inside and returns instantly with the Proprietor, who is obviously quite perturbed.*) You understand, of course—it's a patriotic sacrifice—

PROPRIETOR: That's most unfortunate—but if the gentlemen are from the volunteer committee—

FOURTH: Well, why did you ever give your establishment that name at all—that wasn't foresighted of you.

PROPRIETOR: But gentlemen, who could have foreseen that—now I am embarrassed myself. You see, I gave it that name because, as you know, we are right next to the West Terminal, where the English lords usually arrive during the tourist season. The idea was to make them feel at home right away—

FIRST: Now listen, did you ever have an English lord in your place?

PROPRIETOR: And how! Those were great times, Jesus Christ!

FIRST: Then I congratulate you. Look here, right now none of them can come here anyway.

PROPRIETOR: Thank God. May God punish England—but look, the name has become so familiar, and after the war, when, God willing, the English customers will come back—Look, I think you really should take this into consideration.

FIRST: Look, my dear man, the voice of the people can't take that kind of thing into consideration, and the voice of the people, as you might know—

PROPRIETOR: Yes, of course, how would a man like me not know that—after all, we are more or less a people's coffeehouse, but, what am I going to call the place?
SECOND: Don't worry, we won't do much harm. We'll work that out in no time—and painlessly at that. (*He scratches out the i.*)
PROPRIETOR: But—what would the name be afterward?
SECOND: There! Now you have the painter put an ü in there,
PROPRIETOR: An ü? Café Westmünster?
SECOND: An ü. It's the same thing and it's German. Great! Nobody can tell the difference, but it's clear to everyone that it's something quite different. Well, what do you say?
PROPRIETOR: Ah, excellent, excellent! I'll send for the painter right away. Thank you, gentlemen, for your forbearance. This will remain as long as the war is on. For the time it will do. Afterward I would rather—for what would the lords then say, their eyes would pop out!

(*Two guests come from the café taking leave of one another. One says: Adieu! The other says: Addio!*)

FIRST: What's that I heard? Frenchmen and Italians come to your place? One says Adieu and the other even Addio? You seem to have a rather international crowd, there are quite a few things suspect—
PROPRIETOR: But look, if somebody says Adieu—
SECOND: But didn't you hear the first one say Addio? That is the language of the sworn enemy.
THIRD: The perfidious traitor!
FOURTH: The one who broke faith at the River Po!
FIRST: Yes sir, the traitor was our sworn enemy!
SECOND: Our sworn enemy who broke the faith!
THIRD: At the River Po!
FOURTH: At the River Po! Keep that in mind!
FIRST (*calling after him*): You English dago at the River Po!

SECOND: Now we've taught them what happens when you use foreign words. Let's go on.

THIRD: Just look here, we're in luck today. Söldner & Chini! That's the same mixture we had with that coffeehouse owner. Söldner, that's an Englishman, as everybody knows, and Chini, that's an Italian!

FIRST: May God punish England and destroy Italy—we'll paste over all of that one. Dry cleaners? Clean it off. I am so mad I could bust. Tomorrow the whole district has to be clean of foreign words, and if I catch another one, I'll tear his guts out.

(*The second pastes over the panel.*)

(*Scene change.*)

SCENE 10

In the Café Pucher.

OLD BIACH (*reaching for the* Neue Freie Presse): Fantastic!

THE OTHERS: What is it?

OLD BIACH: See, this impresses me. For two weeks now, he has been using the front page to celebrate the fiftieth anniversary of the paper. The battle of Lemberg and all his impressions come after that. In this way one can see at least that there are also happy events in Austria. After all, this is an event the likes of which never happened before. The bastion of German-liberal sentiment, civilization, and culture, it's terrific! Just look at the names of all these important people who have sent their congratulations—wait a minute—three, four, no, five full pages. They all vie in congratulating him, the highest dignitaries are not abashed to do so.

IMPERIAL COUNCILLOR*: Today *I* wrote him—just watch, tomorrow it will be printed!

OLD BIACH (*excited*): If you wrote, I will write, too. It's no small honor, in such company—

DOCTOR [probably of law]: One thing strikes me as funny, though: in printing all the thousands and thousands of congratulations he receives, he always prints the entire address: To the Honorable Moriz Benedikt, Publisher of the *Neue Freie Presse*, Vienna, I, Fichtegasse 11. I cant help but feel it's a little vain of him. He could at least drop the "honorable." And wouldn't it be enough if he gave the address only twenty times?

HIS BUSINESS PARTNER: Don't say that. You can never hear that often enough.

IMPERIAL COUNCILLOR (*almost simultaneously*): I can't agree with you. He simply doesn't want to change anything. This is how they wrote to him and this is how he publishes it. He is right.

OLD BIACH: What did he say? What did he say?

BUSINESS PARTNER (*reassuringly*): But—nothing—Lemberg is still in our hands.

IMPERIAL COUNCILLOR: Do you know what impresses me most? I am not impressed by what is printed on the front page, and not by what is printed in the middle pages, but by what is on the back pages! Do you remember, on the day of the anniversary, the hundred congratulatory ads from the banks, each one a full page? Right in the midst of the moratorium, they all had to shell out the cash until it hurt. Sure enough, the press is a power that can't be shaken—but when it does the shaking down, the plums fall from the trees.

* Honorary title awarded to businessmen in recognition of a long and successful career.

OLD BIACH: What do you want? This man's genius in his field is unmatched in all of Austria. He has imagination and feeling and intelligence and convictions, in addition, he is a great money-grabber before the Lord.

IMPERIAL COUNCILLOR: Do you know, Herr Biach, who your language reminds me of?

OLD BIACH: Who does it remind you of? Who should it remind you of?

IMPERIAL COUNCILLOR: Of himself with all the many "ands."

OLD BIACH: And so what? Does that surprise you? One cannot help but be under his spell. Did you read, the other day, in the evening edition "Lay Questions and Lay Answers"? Terrific, wasn't it? He is his true self, especially when he writes in the evening edition. There he repeats everything all over again. Then they said Lemberg is still in our hands, he said, "What strikes us most in this statement is the word 'still,' the eye fastens on to it and one can imagine what it means." All this he gives us, and then still some! "It was reported yesterday—it is reported today"—you just can't get those phrases out of your head. He speaks like one of us, only more clearly. It is hard to say whether he speaks as we do or we speak as he does.

IMPERIAL COUNCILLOR: Well, and the editorial, is that a small feat? The very first sentence—who can imitate him? "The Brodsky family is one of the richest in Kiev." Period. Right away, you are in the midst of things. Then he jumps around, speaks of Talleyrand, what he had said at dinner, and before you know it, he's talking about the Hungarian Compromise.

OLD BIACH: I am particularly impressed when he says "one can imagine." Or when he starts talking about imagination —that fascinates me, we can see everything immediately, as if he were right in the midst of the powder smoke, God forbid! And we right along with him. But he seems to attach the greatest value to mood and impressions, and it is fascinating when he tells how passions have been aroused. As far as I am concerned, I enjoy it most when he imagines how they toss and turn restlessly at night, especially Poincaré and Grey, and even the Tsar, and how worries gnaw at them because the walls are beginning to crumble. "And perhaps at this moment there is already . . . and perhaps at this moment they have already . . . and perhaps . . . and perhaps . . ."—that is high drama! I have been told he dictates his articles. I tell you, my imagination revels in the idea that when he dictates, the chandeliers in his office tremble.

DOCTOR: I happen to know, however, because once I personally carried a complaint about the garbage collector and the flies up to his office—

OLD BIACH: What is it you know?

DOCTOR: That there aren't any chandeliers there.

OLD BIACH (*excited*): What else do they have there? Leave me alone, Doctor, you are an old killjoy! So he has floor lamps! It doesn't matter—the chandeliers still tremble. A person like me still has illusions.

(*Scene change.*)

SCENE 11

Two Draft Dodgers meet.

FIRST DRAFT DODGER: Well, still in Vienna? Weren't you drafted?

SECOND DRAFT DODGER: I went up and got it fixed. But what are you doing in Vienna? Weren't you drafted?

FIRST DRAFT DODGER: I went up and got it fixed.
SECOND DRAFT DODGER: Of course.
FIRST DRAFT DODGER: Of course.

(*Enter Subscriber to the* Neue Freie Presse *and a Patriot.*)

PATRIOT: Healthy young people. Have you noticed? A whole army corps of them could be put together on the Ringstrasse.
SUBSCRIBER: That's really infuriating. For shame, draft dodgers in France!
PATRIOT: All in all, isn't the sorry state of the enemy countries something? The way things are going!
SUBSCRIBER: You're telling me! Speaking of France, for example, haven't they just announced that they're going to draft rejects? Can you imagine it—drafting rejects!
PATRIOT: As though it weren't enough that they're drafting them; they're even sending them to the front! I read an article on "The Induction of Former Rejects in France."
SUBSCRIBER: And what do you think of the abuses in the French Army Quartermaster Corps?
PATRIOT: War matériel has been contracted at shocking prices.
SUBSCRIBER: Dubious price discrepancies have been reported in purchases of canned goods and ammunition.
PATRIOT: Exorbitant prices have been paid for cloth, linens, and flour.
SUBSCRIBER: Large profits have been realized by certain middlemen! They work with middlemen!
PATRIOT: Where?
SUBSCRIBER: In France, of course.
PATRIOT: Scandalous.
SUBSCRIBER: And this is brought up in open sessions of parliament!
PATRIOT: As if that would be possible here! Fortunately we have—
SUBSCRIBER: No parliament, you mean—

PATRIOT: No. A clear conscience, I was going to say.
SUBSCRIBER: And what about Russia? It's highly significant that they've even had to call the Duma into session. The government must accept being spoken to in plain language.
PATRIOT: That sort of thing would be out of the question here. Fortunately we have—
SUBSCRIBER: A clear conscience, I know.
PATRIOT: No parliament, I was going to say.
SUBSCRIBER: And what do you say to this year's harvest?
PATRIOT: I can only say: Poor crops in Italy. Crop failure in England. Unfavorable crop prospects in Russia. Uneasiness over crops in France. And what do you say to the exchange rate, eh?
SUBSCRIBER: What can I say? The fall of the ruble speaks a language that cannot be misunderstood.
PATRIOT: Why, if you compare with it our Austrian krone, for example—
SUBSCRIBER: The lira's in a bad way, too. It's dropped thirty percent.
PATRIOT: The krone has only dropped twice that—fortunately. And England. What do you say to that?
SUBSCRIBER: I say this: in England potato prices have risen tremendously.
PATRIOT: Yes. It even turns out that they're lower over there now than they are here in peacetime. Gives you some idea, doesn't it?
SUBSCRIBER: And what about the treatment of our civilian internees? Have you read how they have to suffer? You know how well we're treating the Russian prisoners of war.
PATRIOT: Yes, and in return, of course, they behave with the greatest impudence. I've been told that up in the Brenner Pass in Tyrol we let them dig trenches just to give them something to do. And what do you suppose they do? They refuse. Of course we make short shrift of them. We bring

up a firing squad from Innsbruck and then ask them again if they're ready to dig the trenches. No, they say. Rifle at the ready, we say. Why not? Aren't we within our rights? To hell with international law! War's war. But being good-natured, we're still patient and ask them one more time—the rebels. No, they say. Take aim, we say. Then of course—you should have seen them all put their hands up. Yes, they're ready to dig trenches. All of a sudden, let me tell you, they can't wait to dig trenches. That is, all except four of them. Well, those of course were shot. It goes without saying. Among them was a lieutenant—just listen to this—

SUBSCRIBER: I'm listening.

PATRIOT: Probably the ringleader. He had the nerve to stand up and make a speech against Austria. Listen—

SUBSCRIBER: I'm listening.

PATRIOT: Our men—the Austrians, I mean—like the kindhearted fellows they are, were too excited when it came to firing, and they just couldn't hit them. The captain himself had to take a hand and shot the bastards down with his service revolver. Well, what do you say to the kind of liberties those Russians take with us?

SUBSCRIBER: With us here? Why not talk about the insolent way they treat their Austrian prisoners? In case you haven't read yet what's in today's paper, I've got it right here. Listen to this. "Russian Troops Illegally Force War Prisoners to Participate in Hostilities." From army press headquarters it is reported that, since the Russians were driven out of Galicia, hardly a day has gone by without the disclosure of some hitherto unreported infringement of international law by Russian troops, so that there is hardly a single clause in the Hague Convention that cannot be shown to have been trampled underfoot by the Russians.

PATRIOT: Very good!

SUBSCRIBER: Just listen to this—

PATRIOT: I'm listening.

SUBSCRIBER: Recent police investigations in the formerly occupied areas of Galicia have shown that during the entire occupation, by order of the Russian commanding officers, all able-bodied men and women were, if necessary, in addition to being given other types of work, conscripted specifically for the digging of trenches—

PATRIOT: What do you say to that!

SUBSCRIBER: —for which purpose they were marched as far as the Carpathian Mountains. The Russian authorities are, of course, not troubled by the fact that the enemy is expressly prohibited by the Hague Convention from imposing on the peaceful inhabitants of occupied areas the rendering of services that are in effect directed against their own country.

PATRIOT: Of course, they're not troubled! The bastards!

SUBSCRIBER: Just listen—

PATRIOT: I'm listening.

SUBSCRIBER: It is therefore no small wonder that the Russians, as has similarly been ascertained, are also making improper use of captured members of the Austrian Army in the building of military installations to be used against us—

PATRIOT: Incredible! Exactly the same case!

SUBSCRIBER: —although this too contravenes the clause in the Hague Convention prohibiting prisoners of war from being employed in work that is in any way connected with the war effort.

PATRIOT: That's just like the Russians. Nobody else in the world is like that! And probably none of the poor Austrian soldiers dared to refuse.

SUBSCRIBER: Well, can you imagine the chutzpah of that Russian lieutenant?

PATRIOT: That was an excellent article by Professor Brockhausen, the one in which he said that in this country defenseless war prisoners have never been mocked, not even verbally.

SUBSCRIBER: He was right. That appeared in the paper the same day as the Lemberg City Commandant's statement that Russian prisoners being transported through the streets had been abused and attacked with sticks by a segment of the population. He explicitly stated that such conduct was unworthy of a civilized nation.

PATRIOT: He admitted that we *are* a civilized nation.

SUBSCRIBER: Of course. But there's really no point on which we don't distinguish ourselves from the enemy—who, after all, are nothing but the scum of humanity.

PATRIOT: For example, in the civilized way we speak even when referring to our enemies, who are really the filthiest bastards on God's earth.

SUBSCRIBER: And above all, unlike them, we're always humane. For example, the leading article in the *Presse* shows concern even for the fishes and marine creatures in the Adriatic. These are good days for them, it says, because they're getting so many Italian corpses to feed on. It's really carrying humanitarianism to extremes to think of the fishes and marine creatures in the Adriatic in these callous times when even human beings are going hungry.

PATRIOT: Yes, he sometimes overdoes it. But he really lets them have it. And it's not only in wartime humanitarianism that we're ahead of them, it's also in something else much more valuable: staying power. Over there defeatism is rampant. They'd be glad to see an end to it. Here—

SUBSCRIBER: Yes, I've noticed that too. For instance, there's discouragement in France.

PATRIOT: Listlessness in England.

SUBSCRIBER: Despair in Russia.

Act I, Scene 11

PATRIOT: Contrition in Italy.
SUBSCRIBER: In fact, the moods in the Allied countries in general—
PATRIOT: The walls are crumbling.
SUBSCRIBER: Worry is gnawing at Poincaré.
PATRIOT: Grey's down in the mouth.
SUBSCRIBER: The Tsar tosses and turns in bed at night.
PATRIOT: Anguish in Belgium.
SUBSCRIBER: That's a relief! Demoralization in Serbia.
PATRIOT: That makes one feel good! Despair in Montenegro.
SUBSCRIBER: We can take courage! Consternation among the Allies.
PATRIOT: What a lift that gives one! Misgivings in London, Paris, and Rome. Really, you have only to look at the headlines. There's no need to read any further, since the situation is immediately apparent. You see how badly things are going for them and how well we're doing. We have moods, too, but of a different kind, thank God!
SUBSCRIBER: With us there is joy, confidence, jubilation, hope, and satisfaction. We're always in good spirits, why shouldn't we be? We have every reason to be.
PATRIOT: Sticking it out, for example—we revel in it.
SUBSCRIBER: There's nobody as good at it as we are.
PATRIOT: The Viennese is an especially first-rate stick-it-outer. People here put up with all their hardships as if they were pleasures!
SUBSCRIBER: Hardships? What hardships?
PATRIOT: I mean, if there were any hardships.
SUBSCRIBER: Unfortunately there aren't any!
PATRIOT: That's right. There aren't any. But tell me this— if people have no hardships—why do they have to stick it out?
SUBSCRIBER: I can explain that. There are in fact no hard-

ships, but we take them joyfully in our stride. That's the trick of it. We have always done that well.

PATRIOT: That's right. Standing in line, for example, is great fun. People practically stand in line just to stand in line.

SUBSCRIBER: The only difference between now and before is that now there's a war on. If it weren't for the war, you'd really think it was peacetime. But war is war, and now you *have* to do a lot of things you only *wanted* to do before.

PATRIOT: Precisely. Nothing's changed here. And if they do reexamine the army rejects once in a great while, you really ought to see these men. They just can't wait to get to the front—our boys up to fifty.

SUBSCRIBER: The higher age brackets haven't even been called up yet.

PATRIOT: Did you see this? "Nineteen-Year-Olds Drafted in Italy." The headline alone tells the whole shocking truth.

SUBSCRIBER: No, I must have missed that. What do you say! Such youngsters! In Austria they have to be a bit more mature than that. If I'm not mistaken, we're calling up the fifty-year-olds—only for noncombat zones of course. There are still plenty of forty-nine-year-olds at the front.

PATRIOT: In France they're already up to the forty-eight-year-olds.

SUBSCRIBER: Men with gray hair! All the younger ones seem to have been called up already. In March we're going to trot out our seventeen-year-olds. That will really be a joy.

PATRIOT: Surely, those are the best years. Do you know what also makes the difference? Equipment. For that's the main thing. With us this is simply a matter of course. We don't make any fuss about that. Did you see in today's paper: "Italians Worried about Warm Mountain Clothing for the Troops"?

SUBSCRIBER: The things they worry about!

PATRIOT: Here we don't fret over things of that sort. Nothing

Act I, Scene 11

to it! You place the order with the army contractor and that's all there is to it. You've heard the story of the wool blankets, haven't you?

SUBSCRIBER: No.

PATRIOT: There you have an excellent example of the way everything works itself out in this country. Feiner and Company signed a contract with Germany for a million and a half wool blankets. That's about the number our War Ministry thought they were going to need for the Carpathian Mountains this winter. But the Ministry didn't take the matter too seriously since they were counting on final victory long before then. But when the situation got really serious after all, the word went out, all right, but first the customs formalities had to be complied with. The Minister of Finance couldn't be induced to release the goods until that was done, even though the Minister of War insisted that the wool blankets were needed. What can I say—the problem was shunted back and forth between the War Ministry and the Finance Ministry for six months, all through the battle for the Carpathian Mountains. Then the firm got into the act, and Katzenellenbogen from Berlin—you know, our troubleshooter, especially in dealing with the War Ministry—stepped in personally. He went up to see the Minister of Finance and told him to his face that it couldn't be done. The Minister of Finance said he couldn't settle this problem on the spot. So Katzenellenbogen, forceful as he is, you know his energy, well, Katzenbellenbogen told him first that the firm was going bankrupt and second that the wool blankets were rotting. They were lying outdoors in the rain and the cold, and all of them had just about had it.

SUBSCRIBER: All of whom?

PATRIOT: The wool blankets, of course, because they were being kept outdoors.

SUBSCRIBER: Who?

PATRIOT: The blankets of course. Why are you asking? So he told him categorically first that the company was going bankrupt, second that the blankets were rotting, and thirdly, after all, the soldiers needed them. The Minister of Finance shrugged his shoulders and said he couldn't do anything. The file had to be finished first. First the customs duty, then the blankets.

SUBSCRIBER: So why didn't the War Ministry pay it?

PATRIOT: What a question! The Minister of War took the position that he couldn't do it. The file had to be processed first.

SUBSCRIBER: The file on the customs duty? Isn't that the Finance Minister's business?

PATRIOT: No, the file on the authorization of funds to pay the duty.

SUBSCRIBER: Oh, I see. Well, and what happened then? I can't wait to—

PATRIOT: What happened then? Katzenellenbogen went back and said straight to his face: Your Excellency, he said, the War Ministry won't give in. Let me tell you something, he said. In business, if a customer can't pay at the moment, but if you check up on him and find out that he's financially sound, then it's customary to give him credit. Your Excellency, I'd like to tell you something. Check up on the War Ministry. You'll find it's all right. Why be close-minded? Give them credit. Well, that made sense to the Minister of Finance. They gave them credit and the blankets were released.

SUBSCRIBER: Well, everything was then in shipshape order after all?

PATRIOT: So far, yes. But by then it was March. Well, what can I tell you? When they pulled out the blankets, they were completely ruined. So they got refugees to stitch them together by twos and finally, when April came round and everything seemed to be going pretty well—though unfortunately the blankets cost twice the price at which they were ordered because all that labor had to be paid for after all, and patching a million and a half blankets together is no joke—well, by the time they'd got them all done, what do you suppose came to light?

SUBSCRIBER: What?

PATRIOT: It turned out that the soldiers didn't need the blankets any longer. In the first place it was no longer so cold in the Carpathian Mountains by then, and in any case most of the men already had frostbitten feet, anyway. Now, I ask you: do we worry about blankets?

SUBSCRIBER: The Italians do. Serves them right. What do you say to the rise in food prices in Italy?

PATRIOT: I haven't read anything about that. I only read about a poor harvest in Italy.

SUBSCRIBER: Aren't you confusing that with the crop failure in England?

PATRIOT: That's another story, and it has to be distinguished from the food shortage in Russia.

SUBSCRIBER: That's just it. It's the same everywhere. And casualty lists, for example, they have all started publishing them.

PATRIOT: Yes, just as we do here. They copy everything—

SUBSCRIBER: Excuse me. What do you mean by that? Have we—

PATRIOT: On the contrary, here they have now introduced the daily British casualty list.

SUBSCRIBER: I noticed that, too, and I also noticed that our own list appears only once in a blue moon.

PATRIOT: Well, you're not suggesting that we fake lists and invent names for them? At the most we've had maybe eight hundred wounded in the past year.

SUBSCRIBER: In Italy they don't publish any lists at all. That looks more than suspicious. They simply can't admit the hecatombs they've suffered.

PATRIOT: Speaking of Italy, did you see this: "Italian General Relieved of His Command"? For incompetence demonstrated at the front. Further dismissals are imminent.

SUBSCRIBER: Whew! Would you believe that! Have you ever heard of a general in this country—

PATRIOT: Well, actually yes—

SUBSCRIBER: For incompetence?

PATRIOT: For that too!

SUBSCRIBER: But at least he didn't have an opportunity to prove it at the *front*!

PATRIOT: Not that. You're quite right there. By the way, do you know there already are draft dodgers in Italy?

SUBSCRIBER: Where else? And they just got into the war! But do you know what else they've introduced? Censorship. By the way, so far as freedom of opinion is concerned, they're all in a bad way. I've been told that you don't dare open your mouth over there.

PATRIOT: The most their papers are allowed to say is that our military position is a lot better than their own. Oh well, the truth simply can't be suppressed. The British military analysts describe the situation of the Allies as hopeless.

SUBSCRIBER: What are things coming to when they permit that? Whatever would happen to anyone who said that sort of thing here?

PATRIOT: If he said that the situation of the Allies was hopeless?

SUBSCRIBER: No, if he said that the situation of the Central Powers was hopeless. He'd be hanged—and quite rightly, too. No one here would have that nerve.

PATRIOT: Why should he anyhow? He'd be lying. There you are! Even in England they do tell the truth—that is, when they are forced to admit that things are going badly.

SUBSCRIBER: Fine patriots they must be there! Recently someone over there wrote that Britain deserves to be annihilated by Germany. He really had to pay for that. Do you know how long he got? Fourteen days!

PATRIOT (*clutching his head*): Imprisonment for criticism in England! How do you like that? Fourteen days!

SUBSCRIBER: No, the fine English gentlemen certainly don't like that kind of talk. They can't take the truth. But then no journalist in this country would ever let himself get carried away like that.

PATRIOT: And are things any better in France? Not the least bit. Didn't you see this in today's paper: "Imprisonment for Disseminating the Truth in France"? Now really! Just because someone told the truth. A lady in fact—she said Germany was prepared for war but France wasn't. So if you tell the honest truth to their face for once—

SUBSCRIBER: No. Those who are in power in France can't take that. Waging war, yes. They like that well enough. Attacking Germany, their peaceful neighbor, out of the blue—that's what they like.

PATRIOT: Golden words. Germany is waging a defensive war. Not a living soul in Germany was prepared for war. The big industrialists were virtually stunned.

SUBSCRIBER: That goes without saying. And when that poor soul in France told such a simple truth in plain words that even a layman can understand—

PATRIOT: Just a minute, you've got that wrong. The woman was convicted because she—

SUBSCRIBER: Well, because she told the truth!

PATRIOT: Yes, but after all she did say that Germany *was* prepared for war—

SUBSCRIBER: But the truth is that Germany was *not* prepared for war.

PATRIOT: Yes, but she said Germany *was* prepared for war.

SUBSCRIBER: But that's a lie.
PATRIOT: But she was convicted because she spoke the truth—
SUBSCRIBER: Well, why was she convicted?
PATRIOT: Well, because she said Germany *was* prepared for war.
SUBSCRIBER: But how can she be convicted for that in France? For that she should be convicted in Germany.
PATRIOT: How's that again? Just a minute. No. Or—yes—listen, this is how I explain the matter to myself. She did tell the truth, of course, but in France—you know what they're like over there—she was convicted because she had lied.
SUBSCRIBER: Just a minute. You're all mixed up. I think it's more like this—she had lied and they convicted her because in France they can't take the truth.
PATRIOT: That's it! That's the way it must have been. After all, it's in their blood. Over there people let themselves get carried away and say things—
SUBSCRIBER: Of course. You can read how they tell their government the truth in the newspapers over there and the pack of lies they tell about us. That's perversity! If you believed what the London press writes about us you'd think Britain was done for.
PATRIOT: But look, who believes it? Here people just don't see things that way. The mentality, I've been told, is totally different over there. Thank God! Our newspaper editors—you can safely say that—show even more patriotic spirit than our soldiers.
SUBSCRIBER: By the way, do you know who's going to come here today? Guess! The greatest living writer, Hans Müller.
PATRIOT: No! You can tell Hans Müller from me that he writes exactly what's in my heart. What's he like personally? That interests me. The words that can describe his style are *sunny* and *sweet*. The way he gave that serviceman a

kiss right there in the street in Berlin—sweet is not the word for it. And then the prayer in church at the end of his column calling on God to bless our allied arms! He's my special favorite. Of all those who write about the war, none of them, not even Roda Roda or Felix Salten, catches the shoulder-to-shoulder spirit as he does. When he first started his frontline column "Cassianus in the Trenches," it was so genuine, so enthusiastic, one really believed he was out there at the front. Only later I learned by sheer chance that he was in Vienna. He even wrote it right here in Vienna! The way he brings it off! Talented! I'd love to know what he's like personally.

SUBSCRIBER: Personally—that's hard to say. At the moment he's very worried. The day after tomorrow he has to report for his army physical. Poor fellow.

PATRIOT: Oh? And how come he's worried?

SUBSCRIBER: Well, about the physical.

PATRIOT: Worried? Because he's afraid they may not take him?

SUBSCRIBER: I don't understand you. He's worried, of course, because he's afraid they *will* take him.

PATRIOT: Oh, don't kid me! Hans Müller? The Hans Müller who would let himself be torn to bits for the fatherland? You don't say so! I've never heard of any other man about whom you felt so sure he would live and die for the Nibelung troth. On the contrary, I thought that was why he came back from Germany, because he couldn't wait, because he wanted to volunteer. He'd be on top of the world, I thought, if they took him—and ready to kill himself if they didn't.

SUBSCRIBER: Why? You heard yourself that the frontline column came out of Vienna. Just that impressed you—how he managed to write from the front lines right here in Vienna.

PATRIOT: I thought he wrote his frontline column because his feelings were wounded at being rejected—just to show

them. He wanted to prove to them the kind of frontline writing he'd be capable of if he really was at the front. I can't believe what you're telling me. You must be confusing him with somebody else.
SUBSCRIBER: He'd be happy if they confused him with somebody else during the physical day after tomorrow.
PATRIOT: Listen, this is really annoying! I can only think that you're not properly informed. Anyone who has written the way Hans Müller has written—so genuinely, so enthusiastically—is bound to be happy to be taken.
SUBSCRIBER (*agitated*): Well then, must they take everybody? Must everybody be happy? May a person have no other worries? Isn't it enough that he's enthusiastic? No, he's got to serve in the army, too! Müller of all people! What a soft heart you have! It's as though you can't wait to see him drill. But you're worrying unnecessarily, and let's hope he is, too. And if they do take him—fortunately Hans Müller has a reputation today. They'll use him as his talents deserve.

(*Scene change.*)

SCENE 14

The home of Elfriede Ritter, an actress, who has just returned from Russia. Half unpacked trunks. Reporters Fuechsl, Feigl, and Halberstam snatch at her arms and crowd about her.

ALL THREE (*at one time*): Did the knout leave welts? Show us! We need the facts, the details. How were you treated in Moscow? What are your impressions? You must have suffered horribly, really you must!

FUECHSL: Tell us about how they treated you like a prisoner!
FEIGL: Give the *Abendblatt* the story of your visit.
HALBERSTAM: Tell the *Morgenblatt* what the trip home was like.
ELFRIEDE RITTER (*smiling*): I'm most grateful for your sympathetic interest, gentlemen. And deeply touched to find that my beloved Viennese have kept a warm spot in their hearts for me. Let me thank you with all my heart for having taken the trouble to come and see me personally. It's not that I mind postponing my unpacking, but with the best will in the world, there isn't anything I can say except that it was very, very interesting, that nothing at all happened to me—let me see, what else—that the trip home was perhaps wearisome, but by no means a hardship, and (*coyly*) that I am happy to be in my beloved Vienna again.
HALBERSTAM: Interesting—a wearisome journey—in other words, she admits—
FEIGL: A hardship, she said.
FUECHSL: Wait a minute, I wrote the lead back in the office. Hold it a second— (*Writing.*) Rescued from the ordeal of Russian captivity, at the end of a wearisome journey filled with hardships, actress Elfriede Ritter wept tears of joy at the thought of finally being back in her beloved Vienna.
ELFRIEDE RITTER: (*wagging her finger admonishingly*): Doctor* Fuechsl, Doctor Fuechsl, that's not what I said. On the contrary, I said that I had no reason to complain—absolutely none.
FUECHSL: Aha! (*Writing*) Today, the actress looks back upon her torments with a kind of ironic detachment.
ELFRIEDE RITTER: Now really, Doctor Fuechsl, I really must say—this is outrageous—

* Top journalists were assumed to have a doctorate in law or philosophy.

FUECHSL (*writing*): But as the visitor prompts her memory, indignation grips her again. In agitation, Elfriede Ritter relates how every opportunity to complain about her treatment was denied her.

ELFRIEDE RITTER: Now, Doctor Fuechsl, what are you trying to do? After all, I can't say—

FUECHSL: She cannot even say—

ELFRIEDE RITTER: Now, really. I truly can't say—

HALBERSTAM: See here now, what do you know about what people can or cannot say? Listen to me, my dear Fräulein Ritter, the public is hungry for news—do you hear! I tell you, you can say a great deal. Maybe you can't in Russia, but here, thank God, we have freedom of speech. Here, thank God, you can say anything you want—about the way things are in Russia. Did any newspaper in Russia give you the kind of attention we're giving you here? Well, then.

FEIGL: Fräulein, be sensible! Do you think that a little publicity will hurt you just as you're about to begin a return engagement? Come, now!

ELFRIEDE RITTER: But gentlemen—I really can't—you're dragging things in by the hair—if you had only seen—nobody, neither people in the streets nor in government offices— if there had been the slightest cause for complaint, because of harassment or anything like that, do you think that I would keep silent?

FUECHSL (*writing*): Still trembling with agitation, Fräulein Ritter tells how street mobs dragged her along by the hair, how she was harassed by the authorities at the slightest complaint, and how she was terrorized into keeping silent about it all

ELFRIEDE RITTER: Doctor Fuechsl, you're joking, aren't you? I can even tell you that the police were very helpful. Why, whenever they could they practically took me by the hand. I could go where I pleased and come home when I pleased. I assure you that if I had felt like a prisoner for even one moment—

FUECHSL (*writing*): The actress relates how she once tried to go out, and how the police immediately took her by the hands and dragged her home again. She literally led the life of a prisoner.

ELFRIEDE RITTER: Now I really am angry. Gentlemen, it's not true. I protest.

FUECHSL (*writing*): She becomes quite angry at the thought of these experiences, of her hopeless protests—

ELFRIEDE RITTER: Gentlemen! It's not true!

FUECHSL (*looking up*): Not true? What do you mean, not true, with me taking down every word you say?

FEIGL: You mean to say that something we want to print isn't true?

HALBERSTAM: That's the first time anybody's ever said things like that to me. That's really interesting!

FEIGL: She may even insist that the paper print a retraction.

FUECHSL: Don't fuss now—that can hurt you.

FEIGL: Don't ruin your career!

HALBERSTAM: When is she supposed to get a new part?

FUECHSL: If I tell the director about this, Berger will get the role of Gretchen—that I guarantee!

FEIGL: So this is the way you thank people, after Fuchs has given you such great reviews. Believe me, you don't know the kind of man Fuchs is. If he ever hears about this, you'd better just watch out at the next opening.

HALBERSTAM: I can tell you that Wolf has got a grudge against you as it is, ever since you acted in his play. Anyway, Wolf hates Russia. All he needs to hear now is that you've got no complaints against Russia, and he'll tear you limb from limb.

FUECHSL: That's nothing! And Löw? Don't monkey around with Löw. An actress has to know how to get along in the world and that's all there is to it!

FEIGL: On the other hand, let me tell you a secret. It would do you no end of good not only with the public—but even with the press—to have been mistreated in Russia.

HALBERSTAM: Think it over. Even though you're from Berlin you've caught on fast to how we do things here. This city has always been good to you. Why, we welcomed you with open arms and—

FUECHSL: I can only tell you that such matters are not to be fooled around with. What! A person, a first-class actress, returns from Russia and has nothing to say about the sufferings she endured there? Ridiculous! Believe me, your very life as an artist is at stake.

ELFRIEDE RITTER (*wringing her hands*): But—but, my dear doctor, I really thought—I—please—I only—wanted to tell the truth—forgive me—please—please—please, forgive me—

FEIGL (*irate*): You call that the truth? I suppose, then, that we're liars?

ELFRIEDE RITTER: I mean—I'm sorry—I really did believe it was true—but—gentlemen—if you—think—it isn't true—I mean, you're journalists—you must know better—you understand—as a woman I just don't have the right perspective—do I? Good God—you understand—there's a war on—people like me are so easily intimidated—I was so happy to get out of enemy territory in one piece—

HALBERSTAM: Now, you see! If you try to remember, little by little—

ELFRIEDE RITTER: How true, Doctor Halberstam, how true. I was so overwhelmed with joy at being in dear old Vienna again—everything seemed to be rosier—but just for a moment, of course—then anger and indignation welled up in me again—

HALBERSTAM: So, you see, we knew right from the first moment that you'd—

FUECHSL (*writing*): Anger and indignation still grip the artist as she recalls the torments she endured, and as soon as her unhappy memories have given way to the first outburst of joy at being back in Vienna —(*Turning to her.*) Well, is that now the truth?

ELFRIEDE RITTER: Yes, gentlemen, that's the truth. You know, I was still under the impact of—I was so intimidated, so—

FUECHSL: Hold it a minute. (*Writing.*) Still thoroughly intimidated, she hardly dared to speak openly about it. In the land of freedom she still sometimes falls prey to the fear that she is in Russia, where she was so infamously made to feel the absence of personal freedom, freedom of opinion, and freedom of speech. (*Turning to her.*) Well, now, is that the truth?

ELFRIEDE RITTER: Really, Doctor Fuechsl, the way you sense my innermost feelings—

FUECHSL: Now you see!

HALBERSTAM: Well, she admits that she went through—

FEIGL: She suffered!

FUECHSL: What do you mean, suffered? She endured real torments!

HALBERSTAM: Well, I guess we've got everything, we might as well go. After all, we're not here for the fun of it.

FUECHSL: Of course! I'll finish it up at the office. And—we won't have to worry about retractions, will we? That would be all we'd need.

ELFRIEDE RITTER: What an idea! Doctor Fuechsl. It was lovely of you to come to see me. Come again soon. Good-by, good-by. (*Calling.*) Grete! Gre—te!

FEIGL: She's really quite sensible after all. Bye-bye, dear. (*To the others, as he goes.*) She went through hell and didn't have the courage to tell anyone—poor thing.

(*Elfriede Ritter sinks into an armchair, then gets up and starts to unpack her luggage.*)

(*Scene change.*)

SCENE 22

The street in front of the War Ministry. The Optimist and the Grumbler conversing.

OPTIMIST: You are simply putting on blinders so as not to see what abundant generosity, what spirit of self-sacrifice the war has inspired!

GRUMBLER: No, it's just that I don't close my eyes to all the dehumanization and vileness it took to achieve that result. If you have to set fire to a house just to find out whether two decent tenants will come to the rescue of ten tenants, while eighty-eight shady tenants seize the opportunity to do something underhanded, then it would be a mistake to delay the work of the fire brigade and police with eulogies on the goodness of human nature. Surely, there was no need to prove the goodness of the good, and it was impractical to bring about a situation through which the wicked become still more wicked. At best war teaches us an object lesson by increasing contrasts. It may well be of value in preventing war from being waged in the future. The only contrast not sharpened by war is the one between health and sickness.

OPTIMIST: In that the healthy stay healthy, and the sick remain sick?

GRUMBLER: No, in that the healthy get sick.

OPTIMIST: But it's also true that the sick get healthy!

GRUMBLER: Are you thinking of war's well-known ability to steel our souls? Or the proven fact that the shells used in this war have blasted millions of cripples to health, saved hundreds of thousands of consumptives, and restored the same number of syphilitics to society?

OPTIMIST: No—thanks to the accomplishments of modern medical science, we have succeeded in curing a great many who became ill or were wounded in the war—

GRUMBLER: —in order to send them back to the front for a postcure. But these sick people are cured not by the war but in spite of it, and in order to be exposed again to the war.

OPTIMIST: Well, yes—there just is a war on. But most importantly, our modern medicine has succeeded in preventing the spread of typhus, cholera, and the plague.

GRUMBLER: That too is due not so much to war as to a power that opposes war. But this power would have a still easier task if there were no war. Or is it an argument in favor of war that war has provided the opportunity of making some small progress in coping with its attendant phenomena? Shame on a science that takes pride in its ingenuity in making artificial arms and legs but lacks instead the power to prevent altogether and as a matter of principle the splintering of bones. The science that today dresses wounds stands morally no higher than the one that invented shells. War is a moral force compared with a science that is not only content to patch up the damage war has done, but does so for the purpose of making its victim fit to fight again. Yes, God's ancient scourges such as cholera and plague, horrors of the wars of a distant past, are awed by medical science and desert the field of battle. But syphilis and tuberculosis are this war's faithful allies, and lie-ridden humanitarianism will not be able to make a separate peace with them. These diseases keep pace with compulsory military service, and with a technology that races along in armored tanks and in clouds of poison gas. We shall no doubt see that each era gets the epidemic it deserves. To every age its own plague!

(*Scene change.*)

SCENE 24

In the Chief of Staff's quarters. Conrad von Hötzendorf alone. His arms crossed, weight on one leg, pensive.

CONRAD (*raising his eyes to heaven*): If only Skolik were here now!
A MAJOR (*entering*): Your Excellency, reporting respectfully, Skolik is here.
CONRAD: Skolik? Who's he?
MAJOR: Oh, the court photographer Skolik from Vienna, the man who at the time of the Balkan War took that fine photograph in which Your Excellency is immersed in the study of the map of the Balkans.
CONRAD: Oh yes, I now remember dimly.
MAJOR: No, not dimly, sir, quite clear, Your Excellency, and well lighted.
CONRAD: Yes, yes, I remember; yes, that was glorious.
MAJOR: He claims that Your Excellency sent for him.

CONRAD: Well, I wouldn't actually say "sent for him," but I did drop him a hint because the man does do some nice work. He writes that he can't begin to meet the demands of the illustrated magazines, the picture was such an extraordinary success at the time, in short—

MAJOR: He also asked whether he couldn't get a group shot of the generals this time.

CONRAD: I wouldn't like that. Let them get their own photographers.

MAJOR (*with a smirk*): He says they don't have heads, so he'll take only shoulder shots.

CONRAD: That's something else again. All right, let Skolik in! Wait a minute—should we try it again, studying that map of the Balkans—that was quite extraordinary—but I think, for a change, maybe the Italian—

MAJOR: That would certainly be more fitting now.

(*Conrad von Hötzendorf spreads out the map and tries several different poses. As the photographer and the Major come in, he is already preoccupied studying the map of the Italian war theater. The photographer bows deeply. The Major positions himself next to the table. He and Conrad gaze fixedly at the map.*)

CONRAD: Now, what is it? Can't a person have a minute—I was just in the process—

(*The Major winks at the photographer.*)

SKOLIK: Only one little feature shot, Your Excellency, if I may.

CONRAD: Here I am, working in the cause of world history and there—

SKOLIK: Actually, I'm supposed to do—for *Interest*—and so—

CONRAD: I see, as a remembrance of this era—

SKOLIK: Yes, and also for *The Week*.

CONRAD: But I may end up getting my picture among those of our generals, I know that all too well, I'd much rather—

SKOLIK: Oh, no, Your Excellency, you need not be at all concerned on that score. With the immortal name that Your Excellency enjoys, it goes without saying that Your Excellency should appear all by himself. The others, they'll be all together, with the caption, Our Illustrious Army Commanders, or something like that; individually they would rate picture postcards, at the most.

CONRAD: Well now, not bad, not bad—but, my dear friend, at the moment I'm unfortunately—couldn't you come a little bit later, to be exact, I'm—I'll let you know in confidence, and strictly off the record (you must not tell anybody), I'm just now studying the map of the Balkans—uh, what am I saying, of Italy—

(*The Major winks at the photographer, who is about to step back.*)

SKOLIK: How fortunate!—this is a moment of the greatest presence of mind, one I mustn't miss. I can see the caption now: General of the Army Conrad von Hötzendorf, with his aide-de-camp Major Rudolf Kundmann, studying the map of the Balkans—uh, what am I saying, of the Italian war theater. Would you permit it to read like this, Your Excellency?

CONRAD: All right, for all I care—just because Kundmann would like it, he can hardly wait—

(*He stares incessantly at the map, as does the Major, who hasn't budged an inch. Both adjust their moustaches.*)

CONRAD: Will it take long?

SKOLIK: Only a historical moment, if you please—

CONRAD: Should I continue studying the map of the—er, uh, yes, of Italy?

SKOLIK: Free and easy. Just be nonchalant, Your Excellency, just continue your study of the map—that's it—relax—completely unaffected—that's it—no, that'd be a bit unnatural, in the end one might think it was posed—Major, sir, if you please, a little bit further back—your head—that's good—no, Your Excellency, more relaxed—and bold, more bold, please!—it is really to be—that's it—indeed a permanent histri—uh, historical souvenir of the great period—that's exactly right, just like that!—only yet—a little bit—tha-a-at's it—Your Excellency, let's have a fiend-ly expression!—hold it! Now— I thank you!

(*Scene change.*)

SCENE 26

Southwestern front. A command post on a mountaintop more than fifteen hundred meters high. The table is decorated with flowers and war trophies.

OBSERVER: Here they come now.
SCHALEK[*] (*at the head of a group of war correspondents*): I see they made preparations to give us a formal reception. Flowers! They are probably meant for my colleagues, and the trophies for me! Thank you, my good men. We've forged ahead to this command post, it doesn't amount to much, but no matter. We have to be content that it is at least within view of the enemy. Unfortunately, the commander could not grant my ardent request to visit an exposed point, because, he said, it might stir up the enemy.

[*] Alice Schalek, the first female war correspondent accredited by the Austrian War Ministry.

A RIFLEMAN (*spits and says*): Morning, madam.

SCHALEK: Good Lord, how interesting! There he sits, like a picture, if you didn't know he was alive, you'd say he was painted by Defregger—what am I saying, by Egger-Lienz! It seems to me that he even has a wily, furtive twinkle in his eye! The common man in person! Let me tell you, my good men, what we experienced as we pressed forward to reach you. Well, the road in the valley that's usually so busy is now under the uncontested control of the War Correspondents' Corps. Up on the ridge, I felt, for the very first time, something like satisfaction when I saw a hotel in the Dolomites transformed into military quarters. Where are they now, those painted signorinas fluttering with lace, where is the Italian hotelkeeper? Not a trace of them left! Aaah—makes me feel good! The officer who was our guide had to think for a while which peak might be most suitable for us. He suggested one that was least under enemy fire, my colleagues agreed, of course, but I said, no, I won't go along with that; and so we finally have come up here. That's the least we could do! Now I want you to answer just one question: How is it that before the war I never saw all those splendid figures that I now meet every day? The common man is really a sight worth seeing! In the city—God, how dull! Here, everybody is an unforgettable figure. Where is the officer?

OFFICER (*from within*): Busy.

SCHALEK: That doesn't matter. (*The Officer emerges. She starts drawing tight-lipped responses to her demand for details. She then asks*): Now where is the lookout? You must have a lookout, musn't you? Every place I went, they had a lookout for me in the observer's dugout, two inches wide, between the moss-camouflaged shelter. Ah—there it is! (*She steps up to the observer's lookout.*)

OFFICER (*shouting*): Get your head down! (*She ducks.*) Those guys over there have no way of knowing where we observers are sitting—the tip of a nose could give us away. (*The male war correspondents in the group get out their handkerchiefs and cover their noses.*)

SCHALEK (*aside*): Cowards! (*The guns begin to operate.*) Thank God, we came just in time. Now a show is beginning—now you tell me, lieutenant, whether an artist's art could make this spectacle more gripping, more passionate. Those who stay at home—let them go on calling the war the shame of the century—even I did as long as I was back home—but those who are out here are gripped by the fever of actual experience. Isn't it true, lieutenant, you who are right in the midst of the war, you might as well admit it, that many of you wouldn't even want the war to end!

(*The sound of hissing projectiles is heard overhead.*)

SCHALEK: Sss! That was a shell.

OFFICER: No, that was shrapnel. Don't you know the difference?

SCHALEK: Apparently it's difficult for you to understand that my ears do not yet separate the finer sound nuances. But I have learned so much since I have been out here, I'll learn that too. —It seems the show is over. What a pity—it was first-rate!

OFFICER: Are you satisfied?

SCHALEK: Satisfied? Satisfied is not the word for it! Patriotism, you idealists may call it. Hatred of the enemy, you nationalists. Call it sport, you moderns. Adventure, you romantics. You who know the souls of men call it the joyous thrill of power. I call it humanity liberated.

OFFICER: What do you call it?

SCHALEK: Humanity liberated.

OFFICER: Yeah—if you could only get a furlough, once in a blue moon!

SCHALEK: But for that you are compensated by deadly peril every hour of the day—that's what I call living! Do you know what interests me most of all? What goes on in your mind, what kind of sentiments do you have? It is amazing how easily men at an altitude of fifteen hundred meters can get by not just without women's help, but without us women altogether.

A RUNNER (*enters*): Beg to report, sir, Sergeant Hofer is dead.

SCHALEK: How simply the simple man makes his report! He is white as a sheet. Call it patriotism, hatred of the enemy, sport, adventure, or the joyous thrill of power—*I* call it humanity liberated. I am gripped by the fever of this experience! Lieutenant, just tell me now, what goes on in your mind, what do you feel?

(*Scene change.*)

SCENE 27

The Vatican. The voice of Benedict as he prays.*

—in the holy name of God, our heavenly Father and Lord, for the sake of the blessed Blood of Jesus, which was the price of human salvation, we implore you, who were appointed by Divine Providence to be rulers of the warring nations, finally to put an end to this terrible slaughter that has been dishonoring Europe for a year. It is the blood of brothers that is being shed on land and at sea. The most

---

* Pope Benedict XV.

beautiful regions of Europe, this garden of the world, are sown with bodies and ruins. In the eyes of God and man you bear the horrifying responsibility for peace and for war. Listen to our plea, to the fatherly voice of the Vicar for the eternal and highest Judge, to Whom you will have to make your accounting. The fullness of riches with which God the Creator has provided the nations in your charge certainly allows you to continue this struggle. But at what price? Let the thousands of young lives answer who daily draw their last breaths on the battlefields—

(*Scene change.*)

SCENE 28

In the chief editor's office. The voice of Benedikt as he dictates.

And the fishes, lobsters, and sea spiders of the Adriatic have for a long time not had it so good as now. In the southern Adriatic they helped themselves to the crew of the *Leon Gambetta* almost to the last man. The dwellers in the mid-Adriatic found nutriment in those Italians whom we could not rescue from the vessel *Turbine.* In the northern Adriatic the creatures of the sea are feasting at an ever more abundant table. The armored cruiser *Amalfi* has joined the *Medusa* and the two torpedo boats. The sample collection of maritime booty, which so far has been limited to maritime small craft, has been significantly augmented. And more bitter than ever must be the taste of the Adriatic, whose bottom is covered more and more with broken hulks of Italian ships. And over its blue waters wafts the decomposition of the fallen liberators of the Karst plateau.

(*Scene change.*)

SCENE 29

The Optimist and the Grumbler conversing.

OPTIMIST: You cannot deny that the war, aside from the way it fortifies those who constantly have to look death in the eye, has also brought with it a spiritual uplift.

GRUMBLER: I don't envy death now that so many poor devils have to look into his eyes; these are men who are elevated to a metaphysical level only by the universal gallows duty, and even then not always.

OPTIMIST: The good become better and the bad become good. War purifies.

GRUMBLER: It deprives the good of their faith, if not of their lives, and it makes the bad worse. The contrasts of peacetime were great enough.

OPTIMIST: Do you perhaps want to deny the enthusiasm with which our brave soldiers go into the field, and the pride with which those remaining at home follow them with their eyes?

GRUMBLER: Certainly not; I only contend that our brave soldiers would sooner change places with those proudly following them with their eyes than those proudly following them with their eyes would change places with our brave soldiers.

OPTIMIST: Do you want to deny the great solidarity that the war has produced, as if with one magic stroke?

GRUMBLER: The solidarity would be still greater if no one had to march to the front and all might proudly follow with their eyes.
OPTIMIST: The German Kaiser said, "There are no political parties any more; now there are only Germans."
GRUMBLER: That may be right for Germany; but perhaps in other places human beings have a still higher ambition. One should gradually accustom oneself to interpreting what we call British envy, French thirst for revenge, and Russian rapacity as an aversion to the iron tread of sweaty German feet.
OPTIMIST: So you don't believe that it is simply a case of a premeditated surprise attack?
GRUMBLER: But yes! Yes, I do.
OPTIMIST: So how——?
GRUMBLER: As a rule a surprise attack is made against the party who is attacked, less often against the one who attacks. Or let us call it a surprise attack that came as something of a surprise to those attacking, and an act of self-defense that took the attackers a little bit by surprise.
OPTIMIST: You seem to find that funny.
GRUMBLER: In all seriousness, I take this European alliance against central Europe as the last profound effort of which Christian civilization is capable.
OPTIMIST: Thus you are obviously of the opinion that it was not central Europe but rather the allies that acted in self-defense. What if, however, as may happen, they are not capable of successfully carrying through this self-defense of a surprise attack?
GRUMBLER: Then this traders' war will be decided for the present in favor of those who had less religion, in order to change after a hundred years into an outright religious war.
OPTIMIST: How do you mean that?

GRUMBLER: I mean that then the Judaized Christianity of Europe will surrender to the command of the Asiatic spirit.

OPTIMIST: And how would the Asiatic spirit force it to that?

GRUMBLER: With massive quantity and a developed technology by which alone the infernal spirit of central Europe can be gotten the better of. The quantity China already has, the other weapon she will procure for herself in good time. And in time China will see to it that she is Japanized. She will proceed as England, on a smaller scale, is proceeding today, in that she will have to become militaristic in order to take the teeth out of militarism.

OPTIMIST: But England is not keeping militarism within bounds.

GRUMBLER: I hope she does. And that she will not be done in herself, if she succumbs to militarism; and that she will not purchase material victory at the cost of spiritual impoverishment. Otherwise Europe will be Germanized. Militarism is perhaps a system by which a European people is conquered after it has conquered through it. The Germans had to be the first to give up their better selves in order to be the most powerful military nation on earth. Let's hope that the same doesn't happen to others, especially the English, who until now have been saved from compulsory military service by a nobler drive for self-preservation. The present self-defense, which demands general conscription, is only a desperate measure of dubious success. England could defeat itself in the process of defeating Germany. The only race strong enough to survive the technological life does not live in Europe. That's the way I see it at times. May the Christian God grant that it be otherwise!

OPTIMIST: Aha, your Chinese, the race most unfit for war!

GRUMBLER: Certainly, today they lack all the achievements of modern times, for perhaps in a remote era unknown to us they already lived through them and have managed to preserve their inner lives. They will easily attain these achievements again as soon as they need them in order to disabuse Europeans of them. They will also deal in military tomfoolery, but to a moral purpose. That's what I call my kind of religious war that has character.

OPTIMIST: What idea will it help triumph?

GRUMBLER: The idea that God created man not as consumer or producer but rather as human being. That the means of life should not be the goal of life. That the stomach should not outgrow the head. That life is not exclusively based upon the profit motive. That the human being is allotted time in order to have time and not to arrive somewhere faster with his legs than with his heart. What is alive in the instinct of even the most enslaved mankind, is its longing to protect the freedom of the spirit against the dictatorship of money, to protect human dignity against the autocracy of acquisitiveness.

OPTIMIST: The Germans are after all also the people of poets and thinkers. Does German education not contradict the materialism that you allege?

GRUMBLER: German education has no content, but is merely a house decoration with which the people of judges and hangmen ornament their emptiness.

OPTIMIST: The people of judges and hangmen? You call them that? The people of Goethe and Schopenhauer?

GRUMBLER: Goethe and Schopenhauer would, with more justice and severity than *Le Matin* does, reproach today's Germans with everything that they had in their hearts against their own German contemporaries. Today they would be lucky if, as undesirable nonaliens, they were fortunate enough to escape over the border. Goethe was able to derive nothing but the feeling of emptiness from the emotionally exalted state of his people during the wars of liberation. We would be fortunate if colloquial and journalistic German were still at the level at which Schopenhauer found it contemptible. No people lives further from its language, thus from the source of its life, than the Germans. What Neapolitan beggar is not closer to his language than the German professor to his! Yes, but this people is more educated than any other, and since without exception its Ph.D.'s—unless they've managed to get into the press corps—know how to handle gas bombs, it rushes to give its field commanders Ph.D.'s. What would Schopenhauer have said to a faculty of philosophy that awards its highest honor to an organizer of mechanical death? Educated they are; British envy has got to concede that to them, and they know everything there is to know about everything. Their language is merely good enough to meet primitive needs. Today people write the stunted artificial pidgin language of sales jargon and abandon their classics to the pitiless barbarism of the hucksters. At a time when no human being divines and feels the soul of words any more, the German people find compensation in deluxe printings, bibliophily, and similar obscenities of an aestheticism that is as genuine a stigma of barbarism as is the bombardment of a cathedral.

OPTIMIST: But I don't quite understand what you are saying about the German language. After all, you're the one who acts as if you were betrothed to the German language and, in your treatise against Heine you claimed its superiority over the Romance languages. Now you evidently think differently.

GRUMBLER: Only a German would find that I think differently now. It is precisely because I am betrothed to her that I think this way. I am also faithful to her. And I know that a victory, which God may spare us, would be the most complete betrayal of man's spiritual nature.

Act I, Scene 29

OPTIMIST: But you do see the German language as the more deeply profound?
GRUMBLER: Yes, but far beneath its level are those who speak it.
OPTIMIST: And in your opinion don't the other languages rank far below the German language?
GRUMBLER: Yes, but those who speak them rank far above.
OPTIMIST: Are you then in a position to establish a tangible connection between language and the war?
GRUMBLER: Yes: those who speak a language that is the most congealed into set phrases and stock terminology have the tendency and the readiness to find, in accents of conviction, blameless in themselves everything that they find blameworthy in others.
OPTIMIST: And is this supposed to be a quality of the German language?
GRUMBLER: For the most part yes. The language itself is now a manufactured product like other products whose sale absorbs the lives of those who speak German today.
OPTIMIST: And aren't the others also out for business?
GRUMBLER: But their lives aren't swallowed up by it.
OPTIMIST: The English make a business of war and have always had only mercenaries do their fighting for them.
GRUMBLER: That's because the English are not idealists; they don't want to stake their lives on their business.
OPTIMIST: But our soldiers are fighting for the fatherland.
GRUMBLER: Yes, they really are, and luckily, they're doing it with willing enthusiasm, because otherwise they would be forced to do it. The English are no idealists. They are so honest that, if they want to do business, they don't call it fatherland; they are said not even to have a word for it in their language; they don't drag in ideals when the export market is in danger.

OPTIMIST: They are traders.

GRUMBLER: And we are heroes. They don't want to be forced by any cutthroat competitors to work longer than six hours because they want to reserve the rest of the day for those interests for which God created the British—God or sport. The interest in God is a turning away from the world of commerce even if only hypocritically, because at any rate it's an idea that leads far away from daily labor. And that is the important thing. In contrast to this, the German works twenty-four hours a day. By applying to his daily work—as an ornament, as a trademark, as packaging—aspects of his spiritual, intellectual, artistic, and other concerns, he fulfills all those obligations that he would neglect if he had to attend to each separately. He doesn't want to pass anything up. And this mixture of inner things with the necessities of life—this is the unfortunate element in which German genius flowers and fades.

OPTIMIST: The cause of the war, as everybody knows, is that Germany wanted to have her place in the sun.

GRUMBLER: That is well known, but people don't yet know that, if this place is indeed won, the sun will go down. As a grumbler, I am obliged to look at the dark side of everything and to fear that that nation will be victorious that has preserved the least individuality—in other words, the Germans. However, mostly I'm an optimist, but of a kind quite different from you. And when I am, I hope with confidence that it will come out well, and I realize that all these victories are nothing but a wanton loss of time and blood for the sake of postponing the inevitable defeat. I fear our victory and hope for our defeat. In the past, war was a tournament of the few, and now it involves the multitude. It used to be a contest between the strong, now it is a battle of machines.

OPTIMIST: The development of weapons cannot possibly lag behind the technical achievements of modern times.

GRUMBLER: No, but the imagination of modern times has lagged behind the technical achievements of mankind.
OPTIMIST: Yes, but does one wage war by imagination?
GRUMBLER: No, for if we still had imagination, we would no longer wage war.
OPTIMIST: Why not?
GRUMBLER: Because then the stimulus of a phraseology left over from a decrepit ideal would not befog our brains. Because we would be able to imagine even the most unimaginable horror and would anticipate how quickly the road is traversed from the colorful phrases and all the flags of enthusiasm to the field-gray* of misery. Because the prospect of dying of dysentery for the fatherland or of having one's feet get frostbitten would no longer set ringing oratory into motion. Because we would at least know with certainty that in setting out for the front we would get full of lice for the fatherland. And because we would know that man has invented the machine only to be overpowered by it, and because we would not outdo the madness of having invented it with the worse madness of letting ourselves be killed by it. Had we imagination, we would know that it is a crime to expose life to chance, and a sin to degrade death to chance. That it is folly to build armored ships if one builds torpedo boats to outwit them. Folly, to make mortars if, as a defense against them, one digs trenches in which only the man who first sticks his head out is lost. Folly, to chase mankind into mouseholes, in flight before his own weapons, and henceforth to let mankind enjoy peace only under the earth. If we had imagination instead of newspapers, then technology would not be the means for making life harder, and science would not strive to annihilate life.

* The color of the front-line uniform.

OPTIMIST: But when you speak of a war of multitudes, aren't you demonstrating your own conviction about the necessity of war itself? For you thus admit that for a time war will also solve the problem of overpopulation.

GRUMBLER: That it does thoroughly. Concern about overpopulation might give way to concern about depopulation. The legalization of abortion would have eliminated those concerns more painlessly than a world war, without bringing it on.

OPTIMIST: Prevailing moral opinion would never consent to that!

GRUMBLER: I never thought it would, since prevailing moral opinion only consents to having fathers—whom chance had not been able to kill off—slink through the world as starving cripples and mothers bear children for aerial bombs to tear apart. With regret and yet it happens. Rather rich experience in this area could have brought those who order murder from the air, and those who are entrusted with its execution, to the final awareness that although their intention is to hit an arsenal, they must unavoidably hit a bedroom instead, and in place of a munitions factory, a girls' school. Repeated experience should have taught them that this is the result of those attacks they afterward boastingly recall as a successful bombing mission.

OPTIMIST: All in all, it is a permissible means of war, and now that man has conquered the skies—

GRUMBLER: —the scoundrel immediately uses the opportunity to make the earth unsafe, too. Read the description of the ascent in a balloon in Jean Paul's *Kampanertal.* These five pages could no longer be written today because the guest of the air no longer cherishes a veneration for the heavens —instead, an intruder into the air, he uses the safe distance from the earth to assault it. Man takes revenge on himself for any progress he makes. He immediately employs against life precisely those things that should sustain life. He makes it difficult for himself with just those things that should make life easier. Ascent in an air balloon is an act of devotion; ascent in an airplane is a danger for those who are not on board.

OPTIMIST: But surely also for the bomb-dropping flyer himself.

GRUMBLER: Oh, yes, but not the danger of being killed by those whom he will kill, and he can more easily elude the machine guns that lie in wait than the defenseless ones below can elude him. He also more easily eludes the honest combat between two equally armed murderers: honest, insofar as the desecration of the element in which it takes place admits this evaluation. The aerial bomb, however, is always—even if "the courageous one" handles it—the arming of cowardice; it is as wicked as the U-boat, which demonstrates the principle of armed perfidy, that kind of perfidy that lets the dwarf triumph over the armed giant. The infants whom the flyer kills are, however, not armed, and even if they were, they would hardly be able to reach the flyer as unfailingly as he can reach them. The greatest disgrace of this war is that the single invention that brought mankind closer to the stars has served solely to prove his earthly wretchedness even in the air, as if it weren't sufficiently widespread on earth.

OPTIMIST: And the infants who are starved?

GRUMBLER: The governments of the Central Powers have the option of saving their infants from this fate by weaning their adults from their patriotic primers. Even assuming that enemy rulers share equal guilt with our own for the blockade, the bombardment of enemy infants as reprisal represents a notion that does all honor to German ideology, an intellectual shelter, in which I, by the German God, would not like to live!

OPTIMIST: It cuts me to the quick to hear you speak this way

—but this really means that you insist on seeing as small, a time that must appear great to even the most nearsighted. May God grant you larger ideas. Perhaps they will come to you tomorrow during Mozart's "Requiem." Come with me, the net proceeds go to the War Assistance Fund—

GRUMBLER: No, the poster is enough for me—but what sort of strange drawing is that? A church window? If my nearsightedness doesn't deceive me—a mortar! Is it possible? Yes, who has succeeded in reconciling both worlds? Mozart and mortar! What a concert arrangement! Who has made such a felicitous combination? No, one must not weep about it. Only tell me, would such a betrayal of God be possible even in the culture of the Senegal Negro, whom the enemy has called in to help against us?

OPTIMIST (*after a pause*): I think you are right. But God knows, only you see it that way. It eludes the likes of us, and therefore we see the future in a rosy light. You see it, and therefore it is there. Your mind's eye invokes it and then your eyes see it.

GRUMBLER: Because they are nearsighted. They perceive the contours and imagination does the rest. And my ear hears noises that others don't hear, and these noises disturb the music of the spheres for me, something else others don't hear. Think that over, and then if you still don't come to a conclusion by yourself, call me. I like to converse with you, you supply the key words for my monologues. I would like to go before the public with you. As of now I can only say to them that I am remaining silent, and if possible, what I am remaining silent about.

OPTIMIST: What for instance?

GRUMBLER: For instance: That this war, if it doesn't kill the good, may perhaps create a moral island for the good, who were good even without it. That the war, however, will transform the whole surrounding world into a great rearguard of deceit, debility, and the most inhuman betrayal of God, in that evil keeps working on beyond the war and because of it, becoming fat behind pretended ideals and waxing on sacrifice! That in this war, the war of today, culture does not renew itself, but rather saves itself from the hangman by committing suicide. That the war has been more than sin; that it has been a lie, a daily lie, out of which printer's ink flowed like blood, the one nourishing the other, streaming out in several directions, a delta toward the great sea of insanity. That this war should be ended not by peace, but rather by a war of the cosmos against this rabid planet!

OPTIMIST: You are an optimist. You believe and hope that the world is coming to an end.

GRUMBLER: No, it is only running its course like my nightmare, and when I die, it will all be over. Sleep well!

(*Exit.*)

Act II

SCENE 7

At an artillery emplacement.

ARTILLERY OFFICER: What do you know, our good chaplain is coming from his infantry post to see us. That's nice of him!
CHAPLAIN ANTON ALLMER: God be with you, you brave fellows! God bless your weapons! Are you pounding away at the enemy?
OFFICER: It's going very well, reverend.
CHAPLAIN: With God's help, I'd also like to try a gun for once.
OFFICER: Fine, reverend. Let's hope you hit a few Russians.

(The chaplain fires a gun.)

CHAPLAIN: Zap!
CRIES: Bravo!

OFFICER (*to his men*): What a good, noble priest! And a son of our beautiful Styria. I must send that to the Graz *Volksblatt*! (*To the chaplain.*) The Styrian regiment is pleased and proud of its chaplain and courageous fellow fighter for leading the way with a good example.
CRIES: Good for him!
OFFICER: Now that the reverend has fired, our weapons are blessed.

(*Schalek approaches.*)

SCHALEK: What sort of position is this? Is this supposed to be a position? I've seen better positions before.
OFFICER: Please be indulgent—in the short time—
SCHALEK: Lieutenant, you know what? I'd like to shoot a little bit.
OFFICER: I'd be glad to let you, madam, but unfortunately, it's impossible right now, it could rouse the enemy. At the moment there's a lull in the fighting and we're happy—
SCHALEK: Oh, please don't make a fuss—so the chaplain can and I can't? When I've come all this way just for that reason? As you know, I report only from personal experience—keep in mind that I absolutely must finish my story—it's for the Sunday edition!
OFFICER: Yes—well—but I can't take any responsibility—
SCHALEK: But I can! Give it to me. Okay, how is it fired?
OFFICER: Like this—

(*Schalek fires. The enemy answers fire.*)

OFFICER: See what's happened!
SCHALEK: What do you want? At least it's been interesting, hasn't it?

(*Scene change.*)

SCENE 10

The Optimist and the Grumbler conversing.

OPTIMIST: One thing, at any rate, I can affirm with a clear conscience: Since the declaration of war I have not met so much as one young man in Vienna, who was still there, and if he was still there, was not feverishly impatient not to be there any longer.
GRUMBLER: I don't get around much. But my phone is on a party line. Before the war I could listen in on every conversation in the area—about a poker game setup, a prospective business deal, and some eagerly desired sex. I could do all this effortlessly, without so much as having to ring for the operator. My sole connections with the outside world are the wrong ones. Ever since the outbreak of the war, which has in no way improved the national telephone service, the conversations concern yet another problem, and every single day, whenever I am called to the telephone to listen to other people talk to each other, which is at least ten times every day, I hear conversations such as these: "Gus went up and got things fixed." "And how is Rudi doing?" "Rudi went up, too, and he also got things fixed." "And what about Pepi? Has he already gone off to the front by any chance?" "Pepi has lumbago. But as soon as he can get out of bed he, too, is going to go up and get things fixed."
OPTIMIST: Watch your words.
GRUMBLER: Why? I could prove it.
OPTIMIST: From your point of view you ought to welcome the getting away of each and every one.

GRUMBLER: Yes, every single one. If I consider the compulsion to die a disgrace, privileged treatment in the face of death merely sharpens the disgrace into feeling that only as a suicide can one go on living in this country.

OPTIMIST: But there have to be exceptions, after all. Literature, for instance. The fatherland needs not only soldiers—

GRUMBLER: —but also lyric poets who give them the courage which they themselves do not possess.

OPTIMIST: But the higher purpose has most decidedly made our poets grow. You cannot possibly deny that they, too, have been steeled by the war.

GRUMBLER: In most of them, it has mobilized the greed for profit, in the few with character, only their stupidity.

OPTIMIST: Ah, yes, in times such as these all poets are swept along—

GRUMBLER: —to sing the deeds of those who desecrate creation.

OPTIMIST: Look at Kernstock—

GRUMBLER: I'd rather not.

OPTIMIST: A poet of Christian mildness, a religious man even by profession.

GRUMBLER: Yes, I admit, he has been steeled to an extraordinary degree. I am thinking in particular of the verses with which he exhorts his Styrian lads to squeeze blood-red wine from Dagos and Frogs.

OPTIMIST: Or think of Brother Willram—

GRUMBLER: Unfortunately my memory doesn't fail me. Isn't he the Christian poet to whom blood is a red flowering and who dreams of a springtime of blood.

OPTIMIST: In every country the church implores God to bestow His blessing upon the weapons of its own people—

GRUMBLER: —and strives to increase them still further. Admittedly we cannot expect the church to implore God to bestow His blessings upon the weapons of the enemy, but it could at least have brought itself to curse its own. Then the churches of the warring nations would have understood each other better. Now it is possible that the Pope deplores the war but speaks of "rightful national aspirations," and that on the very same day the Archbishop of Vienna blesses the war that is being waged as a defense against "ruthless national aspirations." Yes, if inspiration had been stronger than the aspirations, these would not exist—and neither would the war.

OPTIMIST: It's just that the international of the churches was a still greater failure than the red international.

GRUMBLER: The only international that has proved itself is the press . . .

OPTIMIST: It is gratifying to see that you recognize its power—

GRUMBLER: What is a Benedict against—

OPTIMIST: What do you have against—

GRUMBLER: But I am speaking of the Pope. What can a sermon in favor of peace accomplish against an editorial in favor of the war. And since all sermons are in favor of the war—

OPTIMIST: I'll admit that. In Bethlehem the world's salvation was decided in another manner.

GRUMBLER: Bethlehem in America is correcting the mistake that was made nineteen centuries ago.

OPTIMIST: In America? What do you mean?

GRUMBLER: Bethlehem is the name of the largest cannon foundry in the United States.

OPTIMIST: This then is the name of the place from which Germany's enemies are being supplied with weapons!

GRUMBLER: By Germans.

OPTIMIST: You're joking. Carnegie is at the head of the steel trust.

GRUMBLER: Schwab is at the head.
OPTIMIST: You mean the enemies are now being supplied by German-Americans?
GRUMBLER: By German nationals.
OPTIMIST: Who says so?
GRUMBLER: Those who know. The *Wall Street Journal*, which is supposed to be at least as knowledgeable as our own financial journals, ascertained that twenty percent of the steel trust shares are in German hands, not in German-American hands, but in the hands of German nationals. More than that. Here, why don't you read what a German socialist newspaper says about it: "While it has been learned that several authentic Anglo-American manufacturers have turned down orders from the French and British governments, the socialist *Leader*, published in Milwaukee, has listed the names of several German-Americans who publicly embrace the cause of Germany loudly and zealously—

(*A group of young men with paper lanterns passes, singing the song: "Dear Fatherland, You Need Not Worry."*)

—while the factories they direct produce bullets, rifles, and other war matériel for Britain and France. Yes, and that's not the worst: in the United States branches of native German companies are a party to these transactions! That being the case, does one still have the right to find fault with the strange neutrality of America, which, after all, has no reason to forgo these gigantic profits for the sake of our beautiful eyes?"

OPTIMIST: As far as politics is concerned, I say nothing succeeds like success. For that reason the sinking of the *Lusitania* will make a considerable impression.
GRUMBLER: Such an impression it has indeed made. In the whole world, so far as it is still capable of revulsion. But also in Berlin.

OPTIMIST: Even in Berlin?
GRUMBLER: This can also be proved only by proofs. (*He reads aloud.*) "At the moment the ship went under, hundreds of people jumped into the sea. Most of them were torn away by the eddy. Many held onto pieces of wood torn loose by the explosion . . . in Queenstown tragic things could be observed. Wives were seeking their husbands, mothers calling for their children, middle-aged women roaming about with hair dripping with water, young women aimlessly wandering about, pressing their children to their breasts. One hundred and twenty-six bodies were already lying in a heap, among whom were men, women, and children of every age. Two poor little children held themselves tightly embraced in death. It was a pitiful, unforgettable sight." This should impress you.
OPTIMIST: Well, but as to Berlin?
GRUMBLER: Berlin. In a nightclub on the very day after the catastrophe a film showing all this was offered. The program read: "Poland: the sinking of the *Lusitania*. True to nature. At this time of the program, smoking permitted."
OPTIMIST: That is certainly in bad taste.
GRUMBLER: No, it is in style.
OPTIMIST: Well, I cannot take a sentimental view of the *Lusitania* incident.
GRUMBLER: Nor can I—only criminally.
OPTIMIST: The people were warned.
GRUMBLER: The warning against the danger was the threat of a crime; consequently, the murder was preceded by blackmail. To exonerate himself, the blackmailer can never claim that he had previously threatened to commit the crime he then did commit. If I threaten to kill you in case you refuse to do, or not to do, something on which I have no claim, I am extortioning, not warning. After the deed I am a murderer, not an executioner.

OPTIMIST: The deed was not noble but useful. The *Lusitania* carried weapons on board, weapons that were intended for German soldiers.

GRUMBLER: German weapons.

(*Scene change.*)

SCENE 16

A command office.

A MEMBER OF THE GENERAL STAFF (*entering, goes to the telephone*):—Hello, well, do you have the report on Przemyśl ready?—Not yet? Ah, you're still a little sleepy—well, get at it, or else you'll be late again for the partying. Now listen—what, did you forget it all again? You really are— Listen carefully. Let me impress on you once more the main points to stress. First of all, the fortress wasn't any good anyway. That's the most important thing—What? You can't—what? You can't make people forget that the fortress had always been the pride—you can make people forget just about everything, my friend! So listen to me, the fortress wasn't any good any more, nothing but an old heap of rubbish— What do you mean, the most modern artillery? I'm telling you, nothing but an old heap of rubbish, understand? Now then, fine. Secondly, pay attention: Not by enemy power but by hunger, understand? But at the same time don't make too big a thing out of the insufficient supply of provisions, you know what I mean—screen out anything about poor organization, any muddle, as best you can. These explanations suggest themselves, but you'll manage all right. Hunger is the main thing. Pride in hunger, understand! Not because of hunger but because of enemy power—uh, what did I say, not because of force but because of hunger. Now then, that should do it—What? That won't work? Because then they'll realize no provisions—what?—and because then they'll want to know why there weren't enough provisions? Okay, fine, just pretend to agree and say: impossible to store as many provisions as necessary because the enemy gets them anyway when he takes the fortress—How would he have taken it then? By hunger? No, of course not, in that case it would have been enemy power—don't ask so many questions. Don't you understand, if he takes the fortress by force and we have the provisions, then he takes the provisions too. That's why we mustn't have provisions, then he doesn't take the provisions, but he takes the fortress by hunger, but not by force. Now you'll manage all right. So long, now—I have to go to the mess hall. I don't intend to surrender to hunger. That's all!

(*Scene change.*)

SCENE 17

Anton Gruesser's* restaurant. Near the entrance, a Gentleman and a Lady. Silently nodding his head, a man keeps moving about from one table to the next. At a table left front, the Grumbler.

WAITER: Have you already ordered, sir?
GENTLEMAN: No, the menu, please. (*Exit waiter.*)
SECOND WAITER: Have you already ordered, sir?
GENTLEMAN: No, the menu, please. (*Exit waiter.*)
BUSBOY: Would you like to order a drink, beer, wine—

* This name means greeter.

GENTLEMAN: No, thank you. (*Exit busboy.*)
THIRD WAITER: Have you already ordered, sir?
GENTLEMAN: No, the menu, please. (*To a waiter rushing by.*) A menu!
SECOND BUSBOY: Beer, wine—
GENTLEMAN: No, thank you.
FOURTH WAITER (*brings a menu*): Have you already ordered, sir?
GENTLEMAN: No. You've just now brought me a menu. What's ready?
FOURTH WAITER: Whatever is on the menu.
GENTLEMAN: On the menu it says, "May God punish England." I won't eat that.
FOURTH WAITER: Perhaps the fresh sausage? Perhaps the gentleman might like—
GENTLEMAN: Do you have roast beef?
FOURTH WAITER: I'm sorry, but today is a meatless day. Would the lady like a nice cutlet or a little rump steak, or maybe, a little goose, the lady?
GENTLEMAN: Let's start with a first course. What on earth is this: taste-bud teasers?
FOURTH WAITER: That's an appetizer.
GENTLEMAN: My appetite's gone already. Well, perhaps— what on earth is that: fish with egg and oil sauce?
FOURTH WAITER: That's fish with mayonnaise.
GENTLEMAN: What's this: puff pastry shell?
FOURTH WAITER: That's a vol-au-vent.
GENTLEMAN: What's this then: mixed dish?
FOURTH WAITER: That's a ragout.
GENTLEMAN: Well, in God's name bring me—wait a minute— what on earth is this: butterflied slice of beef loin in the manner of a field commander with obstacles, with Dutch sauce?

Act II, Scene 17

FOURTH WAITER: That's entrecôte with Hollandaise sauce.

GENTLEMAN: Fifty-two kronen, a bit expensive, just a bit expensive.

FOURTH WAITER: Yes, sir, but the gentleman must not forget, there's a war going on, and today is a meatless day.

GENTLEMAN: Oh, what do I care? Bring us that. (*Exit waiter.*)

LADY: See, we should have gone to Sacher's after all; there it costs only fifty kronen.

FIRST WAITER: Have you already ordered, sir?

GENTLEMAN: Yes.

SECOND WAITER: Have you already ordered, sir?

GENTLEMAN: Yes.

SECOND BUSBOY: Beer, wine?

GENTLEMAN: No, thank you.

THIRD WAITER: Have you already ordered, sir?

GENTLEMAN: Yes.

FOURTH WAITER (*coming back*): I'm sorry, but we're already out of the entrecôte. (*Crosses out practically everything on the menu.*)

GENTLEMAN: But you just—

FOURTH WAITER: Yes, but today, on a meatless day, that's no wonder. But the gentleman can have us make for him a couple of lost eggs, maybe with a spicy sauce, that's still on the menu—

GENTLEMAN: Lost eggs, what on earth is that? For heaven's sake, who lost them?

FOURTH WAITER (*whispering*): Oeufs pochées, we called them before the war.

GENTLEMAN: Ah, and do we believe that we will win the war that way? —No, wait a minute—perfidy noodles—whatever does that mean?

FOURTH WAITER: Well, macaroni!

GENTLEMAN: Oh, yes, right —Scoundrel's salad, what's that?

FOURTH WAITER: Salad with Italian dressing.
GENTLEMAN: Oh, yes, that's perfectly clear. Well—bring us an order of fine home-style giblets, with upside-down potatoes and lost eggs, along with spicy mixed vegetables, and afterward fruit pudding and two orders of Gruesser's Sahnenkuchen.* What did you call that before the war?
FOURTH WAITER: Gruesser's Schaumtorte.†
GENTLEMAN: Why Gruesser?
FOURTH WAITER: After the boss, of course!

(*Gruesser comes to the table, performs a greeting, and moves on.*)

GENTLEMAN: Who is the boss?
FOURTH WAITER: Herr Gruesser, of course! (*Exit.*)
HEADWAITER: Have you already ordered, sir?
GENTLEMAN: Yes.
DWARFLIKE NEWSPAPER BOY (*bobbing from table to table*): Victory after Victory! Extra! Extra! Read allaboutit! Serious Defeat of the Italians! Victory after Victory!
TWO GIRLS (*going from table to table with picture postcards and war-relief buttons*): For war relief, if you please—
BUSBOY: Would you like some bread? May I have the menu back please?
GENTLEMAN (*moving to hand him back the menu*): Oh, I don't have one.
TWO WOMEN (*with picture postcards, from table to table*): For war relief, please—
MALE FLOWER VENDOR (*hurrying up to the table*): Would you like some flowers—?
WOMAN FLOWER VENDOR (*from further back*): Lovely little violets, for the lady?

---

* The German term for cream cake.
† The Austrian term for cream cake.

WOMAN NEWSPAPER HAWKER: Extra! Extra!

A PATRON (*calling the headwaiter who handles the cash*): Hey you, Herr Finance Minister—!

HEADWAITER (*leaning toward a Second Patron*): Have you heard the latest, doctor? What's the difference between a Galician refugee and—(*Whispers the words that follow in his ear.*)

SECOND PATRON (*getting more and more amused, suddenly bursts out laughing*): Fabulous! But do you know the difference between a Red Cross nurse and— (*Whispers the words that follow in his ear.*)

A WAITER (*with eighteen plates*): Your sauce, if you please—! (*He spills some on the Lady.*) Oh, I didn't do it on purpose, I beg your pardon.

THIRD PATRON: Who used the word pardon? Hey, Herr Gruesser, a waiter just used the word pardon in your good German place.

GRUESSER: Herr von Wossitschek, you just wouldn't believe how hard it is now with these people. You say something to one of them and he's off like nothing, says he can get himself lots of jobs. It's a real cross to bear; the better ones are enlisted, and these uneducated elements are what's left over—

THIRD PATRON: Well yes, that's true, but—

GRUESSER: Pardon, Herr von Wossitschek, I must go to greet the patrons. (*Goes on.*)

THIRD PATRON: Oh, pardon me, pardon me. Don't let me keep you.

A STEADY CUSTOMER: Well, Gruesser, how goes it? They've gotten Leberl into the soup all right.

GRUESSER: No wonder, the prices that man charges! And besides, he's not at all well liked. Now me—since I'm a personality around here, I've never had any complaints whatsoever.

STEADY CUSTOMER: Why don't you sit down for a little while, Gruesser?

GRUESSER: Later, I'll be glad to, but I must still go to greet the customers, you know. (*Does it.*)

STEADY CUSTOMER: Oh, sure, see you.

BAMBULA VON FELDSTURM (*bellowing and pounding on the table*): Jesus Christ, will there be no service at all today? At attention, man!

A WAITER: Be right with you, Major!

GRUESSER: What can I do for you, Major?

BAMBULA VON FELDSTURM: Hey, mister, what's going on here? Isn't anybody getting waited on here today at all? Your service sure isn't what it used to be, for about a year now, I've noticed that. Where are all your waiters?

GRUESSER: Enlisted, Major.

BAMBULA VON FELDSTURM: What? Enlisted? How come they are all enlisted?

GRUESSER: Well, because there's a war on, Major!

BAMBULA VON FELDSTURM: But for about a year now I've been noticing it, that you haven't got more than those four waiters! For such a colossal place! I've been noticing that for about a year now.

GRUESSER: Well, yeah, since the war started, Major.

BAMBULA VON FELDSTURM: What! It's a disgrace! Just so you'll know, my friends are all griping about it—they don't want to come here any more if it keeps on like this. They're all up in arms. Captain Tronner, Fiebiger von Feldwehr, Kreibich, Kuderna, Colonel Hasenörl, they're all up in arms. Just yesterday Husserl von Schlachtentreu from the Sixty-sixth was saying, if it keeps up like this—

GRUESSER: Yes, Major, we'd all like it, if it'd all just stop and we'd have peace—

BAMBULA VON FELDSTURM: What, peace—you can just stop

that peace-whining!—I took part in the Emperor's maneuvers—if our Commander in Chief were to hear you. The word for now is to stick it out, my friend—nothing less! (*A waiter rushes by.*) Hey, eyes right! Goddamn the bastard, just wait, I'll see that he gets drafted—now you tell me, what kind of service is this anyhow—?

GRUESSER: What was it you ordered, Major?

BAMBULA VON FELDSTURM: Nothing yet, but I would like some roast beef—but not too lean—

GRUESSER: I'm sorry, but today is a meatless day.

BAMBULA VON FELDSTURM: What? Meatless? What kind of new fashion is that?

GRUESSER: Well, there's a war on, Major, and so—

BAMBULA VON FELDSTURM: Don't you talk nonsense with me. I'd just like to know what running out of meat's got to do with the war? It was not that way before either.

GRUESSER: Yes, but right now there's a war on, Major.

BAMBULA VON FELDSTURM (*jumps up, hopping mad*): O.K., you don't have to keep rubbing it in. You and your war. I've swallowed enough of that! You're not going to be seeing me and my friends around your place from now on—we'll be going to Leberl's! (*Dashes out.*)

GRUESSER: But Major— (*Shaking his head.*) Strange!

THIRD PATRON (*to a waiter*): Isn't there anything left at all? Not even some pastry?

FIRST WAITER: There are Viennese turnovers, anise wafers, English—

THE PATRON: What? You've got something English, even with the war on?

FIRST WAITER: They're left over from before the war.

THE PATRON: You can kid somebody else. My check!

FIRST WAITER: Check!

SECOND WAITER: Check!

THIRD WAITER: Check!
FOURTH WAITER: Check—
A BUSBOY (*to himself*): Check.
GRUESSER (*stepping up to the Grumbler's table, bows to him and begins to speak, leaning toward him with a fixed stare so that he resembles the Angel of Death, and only gradually becoming livelier*): According to the latest mineralogical analysis the weather appears to be clearing up and business may get brisker again—you were probably away, very good, very good—yes, everybody nowadays has his job to do, my God—the war, the misery—you can't help noticing everywhere in the business world how the middle class is suffering—you just can't foresee all the effects—the gentleman from the newspaper, and a Ph.D. who is the right-hand man at the Ministry said it himself—strange—hm—but it seems to me—little appetite today?—today of all days, too bad, front-cut, all our guests praise it, well, but next time as a special treat, a patron's slice from the Gruesser cake—Poldl, clear up here—the good-for-nothing's asleep again—so it's been an honor, an honor—

(*The Gentleman and the Lady have fallen asleep.*)

FIRST WAITER (*dashing by*): I'm sorry, there's nothing left to serve.
GENTLEMAN (*startled from his sleep*): Re-jec-ted?—oh, so. Well, we'll just go then. (*Gets up with the Lady.*) Adieu.
FIRST WAITER: Pardon me, if I may remind you for next time, we are a German place and speaking French is forbidden here. (*Wipes his forehead with his table-wiping cloth.*)
GENTLEMAN: Yes, well—
GRUESSER (*behind them*): It's been an honor. Have a good day. Always at your service. Come again soon.

(*Scene change.*)

SCENE 26

The Subscriber and the Patriot conversing.

PATRIOT: Well, what do you say now?
SUBSCRIBER: What should I say? If you're perhaps referring to Sir Edward Grey's eye trouble, well then I say, they should all have it so bad!
PATRIOT: True, but what do you say to the muzzling of public opinion in England?
SUBSCRIBER: Sure, I know about that, the publisher of the *Labour Leader* was called up before a magistrate because certain disclosures in his paper violated the Empire Security Act. Just imagine!
PATRIOT: And in France, what's happening there—isn't it something? What do you say about France? Do you know what's going on there?
SUBSCRIBER: Jail sentences for spreading the truth in France. You mean the lady who said—
PATRIOT: That too, but now a man's said—
SUBSCRIBER: Of course. A man said that France didn't have any ammunition, and for that they gave him twenty days! He said the Allies were in a bad way and that Germany was armed for war—
PATRIOT: Please, could you explain that to me—for I don't understand these cases. Is it untrue then to say that Germany was armed or is it true to say that Germany wasn't armed—
SUBSCRIBER: Well, was Germany armed?
PATRIOT: So how—?
SUBSCRIBER: Now keep this in mind once and for all. It's a

known fact that Germany was suddenly attacked—as early as in March of 1914 Siberian regiments were—

PATRIOT: Of course.

SUBSCRIBER: Germany was then completely armed for a defensive war, which it had long wanted to wage, and the Allies had long wanted to wage an offensive war, for which, however, they weren't armed.

PATRIOT: Now you see, the apparent contradiction is clearing up for me. Sometimes a person is ready to think something is true and yet it isn't.

SUBSCRIBER: In the papers it's often easy to get a good overview from two columns running right next to each other. This arrangement has the advantage of clearly indicating the difference between us and them.

PATRIOT: Well, did you read this? Plunder and devastation by Italian soldiers! In Gradisca they took no less than five hundred thousand kronen out of one safe and, besides that, twelve thousand from another!

SUBSCRIBER: I read that. A band of thieves! What do you have to say about the colossal success of the Germans?

PATRIOT: Didn't read that, where was that?

SUBSCRIBER: What a question! Right in the next column! It doesn't seem to me that you read in an orderly fashion—

PATRIOT: Right in the next column? I must have just skipped over it. Where was this success?

SUBSCRIBER: At Novogeorgievsk. "Gold in the Booty from Novogeorgievsk" was the headline.

PATRIOT: Well, what was the story?

SUBSCRIBER: The story was that there were two million rubles in gold in the victory booty at Novogeorgievsk.

PATRIOT: Fabulous! Whatever those Germans touch—!

(*Scene change.*)

SCENE 29

The Optimist and the Grumbler conversing.

OPTIMIST: All right, what then would be your idea of a hero's death?

GRUMBLER: A calamitous act of chance.

OPTIMIST: If the fatherland thought that way, it would be in trouble.

GRUMBLER: The fatherland does think that way.

OPTIMIST: What? It calls a hero's death a calamity? An act of chance?

GRUMBLER: Just about that. The fatherland speaks of it as a "cruel blow of fate."

OPTIMIST: Who? Where? There is no military obituary that does not say it is a privilege for a soldier to die for the fatherland. There's never a death announcement in which even the most unassuming private individual does not proclaim plainly and proudly that his son died a hero's death. Even though under other circumstances that same man would talk about a son's death as a "cruel blow of fate." For instance, look at this in today's *Neue Freie Presse*.

GRUMBLER: I see it. But turn back to this page. Here the Chief of Staff, Conrad von Hötzendorf, thanks the mayor for his condolences "on the occasion of the cruel blow of fate" that fell upon him when his son was killed in the line of duty. He used the same language in the family's announcement of his son's death. You are quite right that every neighborhood shopkeeper whose boy has fallen in action assumes the officially dictated posture of a hero's father. The Chief of Staff renounces the mask and reverts to expressing the plain old-fashioned sentiment that is more justified here than in the face of any other kind of death and that is still alive in this conventional phrase. A Bavarian princess congratulated a relative of hers on the occasion of his son's heroic death. At such social heights there exists a certain obligation to behave like one of the furies. The Chief of Staff not only accepts condolences, but time and again he laments the cruelty of fate. The man who is a bit closer to this kind of fate than the entire cast, that is, closer than the soldiers who may be its victims, closer than the fathers of the soldiers who may lament it, he who is author of this drama of fate, and if not that, its producer, or, let us say, its director, and if not that, at least its stage manager—it is precisely this man who speaks of the cruel blow of fate. And he tells the truth, and all the others are compelled to lie. Stricken by his personal grief, he has discarded the obligation to be heroic and, as is only right, has returned to reality. The others remain imprisoned—they must lie.

OPTIMIST: No! They are not lying. People respond to a hero's death with deeply felt sorrow. The prospect of dying on the field of honor often enraptures the sons of the common folk.

GRUMBLER: Unfortunately it also enraptures the mothers who have renounced their power to save the age from this disgrace.

OPTIMIST: It's just that they have not gotten to the level of your kind of subversive thinking. The fatherland is even further from it. That the top people must think so goes without saying. The incident you mention was an accident. Baron Conrad simply used a conventional phrase. He allowed it to slip out—

GRUMBLER: Yes, his feelings showed.

OPTIMIST: In any case, it proves nothing. Something else I

want to show you proves more—it proves everything about my point of view. It will be proof even for you—
GRUMBLER: Of what?
OPTIMIST: Of the sheer magical unity of this closing of ranks in shared sorrow, in which all classes vie with each other—
GRUMBLER: Come to the point!
OPTIMIST: Here it is—just wait. I must read this aloud, so that I am sure you don't miss a word. "A proclamation of the Ministry of War. The Telegraph Press Bureau reports: The Ministry of War of the Austro-Hungarian Monarchy grants permission for the entire labor force employed by such plants as are engaged in the production of ammunition and in the development and production of army supplies to be given a special holiday on the eighteenth day of August. The Ministry of War sees fit to use this occasion to emphasize the extraordinary sense of duty and the indefatigable hard work of all members of the labor force, who have, through the sweat of their brow, helped our incomparably brave soldiers to reap the laurels of glorious victory in death-defying valor." Well? (*The Grumbler remains silent.*) You seem to be speechless. The social-democratic press prints it under the headline: "Workers' Contribution Acknowledged." Nevertheless, many of these workers may be unhappy that as their reward they got just a day off, even if that day is the Emperor's birthday—
GRUMBLER: Surely—
OPTIMIST: —instead of being granted the satisfaction of finally being taken out of the factory—
GRUMBLER: How true.
OPTIMIST: —and of permitting them the opportunity of using at the front the ammunition that back here they are merely called upon to produce. These brave men are certainly inconsolable because it is only through working with their

hands that they are allowed to manifest their solidarity with their fellow countrymen and class comrades, and not also through joining them in their turn in death-defying bravery. The opportunity of getting to the front, this highest honor that any mortal—

GRUMBLER: Mortality seems to be the primary prerequisite. You believe then that being sent to the front is considered the highest reward—by the recipients?

OPTIMIST: Yes, I do.

GRUMBLER: That may well be so. But do you also believe that it is bestowed as the highest reward?

OPTIMIST: No doubt about that! The matter seems to have left you speechless.

GRUMBLER: It has. And that's why, instead of using my own words, I can reciprocate only by the text of an official proclamation. I shall read it aloud to make sure that no word escapes you.

OPTIMIST: From a newspaper?

GRUMBLER: No! It could hardly be published. In place of it there would be a blank space. But it is displayed in those industrial plants which, enjoying the benefit of having been placed under government protection, have managed to rid themselves of any dissatisfaction in the work force.

OPTIMIST: But you heard yourself that the workers are enthusiastically behind the common effort and that they are at worst dissatisfied because they can contribute in no other way. When even the Ministry of War acknowledges the dedication—

GRUMBLER: Seemingly, you are ready to compensate for my speechlessness by jumping into the breach. Why not give the Ministry of War a chance to have its say. "June 14, 1915. It has come to the attention of the Ministry of War that the conduct of workers in numerous industrial plants which have been requisitioned in accordance with the War Production Law is extremely unsatisfactory in terms of discipline and morale. Insubordination, impertinence, refusal to obey foremen and supervisors, passive resistance, wanton destruction of equipment, unauthorized absence from the place of work, and the like are offenses against which in many cases even criminal prosecution proves ineffectual—"

OPTIMIST: The men are obviously impatient to get to the front. This reward is withheld from them.

GRUMBLER: No, it is offered to them. "For this reason the Ministry of War feels it incumbent upon itself to decree that in such cases penal law must absolutely be invoked. The penalties provided in the present context are severe and can be made more so by appropriate intensification. Furthermore, those found guilty draw no wages while serving their sentences so that in such cases court convictions should be a highly effective deterrent and inducement to reform—"

OPTIMIST: Well yes, those are severe penalties—such individuals have also forfeited the chance of ever being sent to the front.

GRUMBLER: Not quite. "Able-bodied workers of military age who are found to be ringleaders punishable by law shall, after the completion of the court proceedings and after they have served the sentences imposed upon them, not be assigned to the plant. Instead, it shall be incumbent upon the military commander of the plant involved to refer them to the nearest District Recruitment Center for induction into the relevant military contingents. There such men are immediately to take their basic training and shall be included in the next unit sent out to the front. If a worker so inducted is classified as fit for guard duty only, provision is to be made that after the completion of his basic training, he be assigned to a guard unit stationed in an area of military activity or in the immediate vicinity of such an area. For the Minister of War. Signed by his own hand, Major General Schleyer."

(*The Optimist is speechless.*)

GRUMBLER: You seem to be the one who is speechless now. You see that men who crave the blessing of being sent to the front are instead punished by being sent to the front.

OPTIMIST: Yes—even to intensify punishment!

GRUMBLER: Yes, indeed. The fatherland considers the opportunity of dying for the fatherland a punishment, the most severe punishment to boot. The citizen thinks of it as the highest honor. He wants to die a hero's death. He wants to enlist, but he is enlisted instead.

OPTIMIST: I cannot believe it—a punishment!

GRUMBLER: There are gradations of punishment. First disciplinary measures. Second, court proceedings. Third, intensification of jail sentence. And fourth, as the most severe intensification, the front. The incorrigibles are sent to the field of honor. The ringleaders! The repeat offender is sentenced to die the death of a hero. The hero's death is for the Chief of Staff a cruel blow of fate if his son suffers it, and the Minister of War calls it a punishment. Both are right. In both cases, the first words of truth that have been spoken in this war.

Act III

SCENE 2

In front of the Austrian artillery positions.

SCHALEK: Isn't that a simple man standing there, one who is nameless? He will be able to tell me in plain words about the psychology of war. It is his job to pull the cord on the mortar—seemingly a simple operation, and yet, what incalculable consequences are tied to this moment. Is he aware of it? Does he spiritually measure up to the sublimity of this task? Of course, those back home, who know nothing more about cord except that it threatens to run out, have no idea what kind of heroic opportunities are offered precisely to the simple man on the battle line who pulls the cord on the mortar. (*She turns to a Gunner.*) Just tell me, what kind of feelings do you have when you pull the cord? I mean, what are your thoughts when you fire the mortar? (*The Gunner looks startled.*) Well, what are your thoughts? Look, you're surely a simple man who is nameless. You must— (*The Gunner, taken aback, keeps silent.*) I mean, what do you think about when you fire the mortar? You must think of something. What is it you think about?

GUNNER (*after a pause, sizing her up from head to toe*): Nothing at all!

SCHALEK (*turning away in disappointment*): And he names himself a simple man. I'll simply not give the man's name.

(*She continues on down the front line.*)

(*Scene change.*)

SCENE 5

Hermannstadt. In front of a locked German bookstore.

PRUSSIAN RIFLEMAN (*banging on the door*): Open up, or we'll knock your shop down—we Germans are hungry for books!

GERMAN BOOKSELLER (*opening the shop*): I bow to this threat out of joy, not out of fear. It is my ambition as a German bookseller to be able to supply a good many German brothers with German books, because for us Germans the best is just about good enough. What, you German brothers are astounded to find a shop full of good German books so far away from the German fatherland! Feel free to satisfy your genuinely German hunger for education while I report this German experience to the German book-trade journal.

(*Scene change.*)

SCENE 13

Appeal proceedings before criminal court at Heilbronn.

PROSECUTOR: —in June of this year, the accused gave birth to a child fathered by a French prisoner of war. The Frenchman, a waiter by profession, became a prisoner in 1914.

Act III, Scene 13

From the end of 1914 until 1917 he was on her estate, where he was occupied with various kinds of labor, especially attending to the fields and gardens. The accused baroness herself participated regularly in this work. In the proceedings at the first trial the accused attempted to charge her child's French father with rape. Of course, her story did not gain the court's credence, since it was advanced only after she became a defendant. Her deposition is ineffectual simply because the captive Frenchman remained employed on the estate a full six months after inception of pregnancy. The court thus found the accused baroness guilty. She was given a prison sentence of five months. Because of a suspicion that she might attempt escape, her immediate arrest was ordered. In the argument substantiating the verdict it was stressed that the form of defense favored during the trial (accusing the war prisoner of having committed rape), as well as the social position of the accused and her education, were to be considered as aggravating circumstances, while her hitherto absolutely unblemished record and her ignorance in sexual matters were cited as extenuating circumstances.

Your Honors! In view of the judgment's outrageous mildness, I may forgo a lengthy speech. Materially, the facts of the case, the unnaturalness of intercourse with a prisoner of war, have been sufficiently established. It is not necessary to characterize the immoral effect that flows from so shocking an example. I do not doubt that this criminal court shares my feeling that we are standing at the edge of an abyss from which offended morality can save itself only by considering the following: What would become of the fatherland if every German housewife were to sink so low! (*Movement in the courtroom.*) Because of this, I beg the high court to reject the defense's plea that the verdict be set aside; instead, I request that the sentence be increased to two years.

(*The court withdraws for deliberation.*)

A Spectator (*handing the newspaper to the man next to him*): Colossal successes of our bombers northwest of Arras and behind the Champagne front. Altogether, 25,823 kilograms of bombs were dropped during the last three days and nights.

Neighbor: The moral effect was surely no smaller than the material one.

(*Scene change.*)

SCENE 14

The Optimist and the Grumbler conversing.

Optimist: The development of weaponry encompassing gas, tank, U-boat, and 120-kilometer cannon has brought things to the point—

Grumbler: —that the army should be dishonorably discharged from the armed forces on the grounds of cowardice before the enemy. Out of the concept of military honor alone, the world ought to attain peace for all time. For the one thing still incomprehensible is what a chemist's inspiration, which by itself dishonors science, has to do with bravery, and how battle glory can be owed to a chlorious offensive without choking to death in its own infamous gas.

Optimist: But does it really matter what weapon it is that does the killing? How far do you go along with the technical development of weaponry?

Grumbler: If development is unavoidable, then not one step further than the crossbow. Of course, if mankind deems it indispensable to life that men kill one another, it makes no difference how it is done, and mass murder *is* more practical. But the romantic yearning of men is foiled by technical development. That yearning, after all, looks for satisfaction only in the encounter of man and man. The courage that accrues to a man from his weapon may enable him to cope even with a multitude. This courage degenerates into cowardice when the man is no longer visible by the multitude. And this cowardice becomes downright baseness when even the multitude is no longer visible to the man. That's how far we've gotten! But by the devil's counsel, which can be researched in laboratories, this process will be carried further. Tanks and gases will yield the field to bacteria, after the adversaries have continuously outdone one another, and we shall no longer resist the bright idea of utilizing epidemics as instruments of war rather than seeing them as consequences as heretofore. But since men still will be unable to dispense with romantic pretexts for their wickedness, the men in command, whose plans the bacteriologist will implement, even as the chemist is doing today, will still wear uniforms. The glory of the discovery, I suspect, will fall to the Germans; the wickedness of perfecting it to the others. Or the reverse—whichever seems more hopeful to you.

OPTIMIST: The high degree of sophistication of their weapons technology has enabled the Germans, after all, to prove—

GRUMBLER: —that Hindenburg's wars of conquest and victory campaigns do compare favorably with those of Joshua. The objective of destroying and exterminating the enemy fits the modern method more adequately, and a breakthrough prepared by "gassing" three Italian brigades surpasses one of those decisive military miracles of Jehovah.

OPTIMIST: Do you then claim that there is a similarity between the contemporary German drives of conquest and those of the ancient Hebrews?

GRUMBLER: Up to the similarity of their gods! Among the

peoples who have played a world-historical role, these two are the only ones that deem themselves worthy of the honor of having a national god of their own. While today all the peoples opposed to one another on this crazy earth share only the delusion of striving to conquer in the name of one and the same god, the Germans—like the Hebrews of old—have in addition appropriated to themselves a separate god of their own, to whom they present the most dreadful sacrificial offerings. The privilege of being chosen clearly appears to have devolved upon them, and among all the nations whose brains have been singed by the notion of being a nation, the Germans are the ones who most frequently identify themselves by incessantly calling themselves German and, indeed, consider "German" to be an adjective capable of taking the comparative and superlative forms. The connection, however, between the all-German and Hebraic ways of life and their expansionism at the expense of the lives of others can easily be proved more conclusively. The only difference is that the ancient Hebrews, to the higher glory of God, at least paid lip service to their "thou shalt not kill," and thereby came into conflict with the ethical law of Moses, a hideous conflict that was time and again acutely felt and regretted. Contemporary Germans by contrast bluntly proclaim Kant's categorical imperative as the philosophical justification for "Up and at 'em." In Prussian ideology also, to be sure, the Lord of Hosts has, in line with the conceptual concatenation practiced in that country, degenerated into the super-supreme commander-in-chief and superior of Wilhelm II.

OPTIMIST: Strictly speaking, He is just his ally. But who except you would have the weird notion of discovering a spiritual link between Hindenburg and Joshua?

GRUMBLER: Schopenhauer, who long ago saw as common the Germans' and Hebrews' institutions of a national God who gives or "promises" neighboring lands which then must be acquired by plunder and murder—the national god to whom the vital possessions of other peoples must be sacrificed. And Kant, who censured the victor's invocation of the Lord of Hosts as a true Israelite custom, thus placed what should have been a silencer on Wilhelm, who conceived the idea of invoking Kant and the Lord of Hosts in a single breath. I shall explore this juxtaposition showing how this Kantian wants to rely with bombproof certainty on his ally up there and how Kant exhorts him to desist from such doings, which so greatly contradict the moral idea of God's fatherhood of all men, and rather to call upon God for forgiveness for the great sin, the barbarity of war—I shall test the effect of this devastating contrast in the near future in a Berlin auditorium under the title "A Kantian and Kant."

OPTIMIST: It could then happen that you would be deported as an undesirable alien.

GRUMBLER: That I remain here at home, too.

(*Scene change.*)

SCENE 15

A Protestant church.

PASTOR FALKE:* —this war is one of God's punishments for the sins of the nations, and we Germans, together with our allies, are the executors of divine judgment. There can be no doubt but that the kingdom of God will be immensely furthered and strengthened by this war. And one has to

---

* This name means falcon. The pastors' names in the two subsequent scenes mean raven and vulture, respectively.

confess here, clearly and definitively, that Jesus gave the commandment "love your enemies" only for commerce between individuals, but not for relationships among nations. In the battle of nations, love of the enemy has no place. On this issue, the individual soldier must have no pangs of conscience at all! While combat rages, Jesus' commandment to love is totally revoked. It does not apply in the hour of combat. For us the commandment to love your enemy no longer has any meaning on the battlefield. To kill in this case is not a sin, but a service to the fatherland, a Christian duty, nay, even a service to God. Service to God it is, and a sacred duty to punish all our adversaries with frightful force and, if necessary, to destroy them! And thus I repeat unto you, as long as the cannons thunder in this world, Jesus' commandment "love your enemies" no longer has any validity. Away with any misgivings of conscience! Look at it this way: Why were so many thousands of men wounded and crippled? Why did so many hundreds of soldiers become blind? Because God thereby wanted to save their souls! And, therefore, look around you and pray in the presence of the miracles of the Lord: Guide us, O Lord, into Paradise!

(*Scene change.*)

SCENE 16

Another Protestant church.

PASTOR RABE: —therefore, put more steel into your blood! And to the fainthearted let it be said, it is not only one's right, but under certain conditions one's duty toward the nation, when war breaks out, to consider treaties and the like as scraps of paper to be torn to pieces and thrown into the fire, if one can save the nation by doing so. War is nothing but God's last means of bringing the nations back to reason by use of force, if they no longer desire to be guided any other way and to be led onto the God-ordained road. Wars are God's trials and God's verdicts in the history of the world. Therefore, it is also God's will that the nations make full use of all the strength and all the weapons that He has given to them to pass judgment among the nations. And therefore, put more steel into your blood! Even German wives and mothers of heroes killed in the war can no longer tolerate a sentimental approach to the war. While their loved ones fight at the front or die in the war, they do not want to hear plaintive lamentations. God now wants to educate us to an iron energy of will and to the utmost display of strength. Therefore, once again, put more steel into your blood!

(*Scene change.*)

SCENE 17

Another Protestant church.

PASTOR GEIER: —and look around you: Splendid achievements of the German thirst for action are strung together like pearls on a shimmering chain of precious jewelry. This mind created the miracle of the submarine. It produced that fabulous piece of ordnance whose missile rises up into the ether regions of space carrying destruction over more than a hundred kilometers into the enemy lines. But the German mind not only provides weapons; it also works unceasingly on the philosophic aspects of our offensive and defensive preparedness. As I can inform you today, Schulze in Hamburg, on behalf of the Foreign Office, is at work on a fundamental scientific project dealing with "the desecration of corpses and graves by the British and French," a study which will be distributed for international propaganda purposes, and which should win us the sympathies of the neutral countries. From the bottom of our hearts we must wish that it find an echo in those of our neighbors who still harbor doubts about the justice of our cause. Everywhere in German lands the spirit is awakening, ready to speak out for our just cause, to stir up the sluggish, to convert the renegades, and to win us new friends. Our government, in wise anticipation, has recognized that Switzerland is to be considered not only as a transit station for the transport of our bombs, but that it should also be thankful for sharing in the knowledge, by word and picture, of the methods of our warfare. The sinking of innumerable tons of foodstuffs by our submarines, as shown in the newsreels, has such a powerful effect on the audiences in neutral countries—especially the women, who are particularly sensitive to the loss of such treasures—that they simply faint. Gradually, recognition forces its way into people's awareness that the damage we inflict upon our enemies is virtually immeasurable! And in this battle, the written German word by no means remains in the rearguard. "The Battle of Champagne" is the title of a brochure published by the secretariat of the Social Students Council in Stuttgart and designed primarily for Swiss intellectuals. Take to your hearts the words which I found in a magnificent poem, the soldier's prayer, printed in a splendid propaganda pamphlet. Our government has already shipped it to neutral countries in order to enlighten them about German individuality, to awaken understanding for the German character, and thus to contribute to a gradual decrease of the hatred by which we are pursued.

And, therefore, look around you and pray in the presence of the miracles of the Lord: Guide us, O Lord, into Paradise!

(*Scene change.*)

SCENE 18

Pilgrims' chapel.

SEXTON: Here you see an interesting offering for our shrine presented by two soldiers from Lana. It is a rosary made up of beads shaped from Italian shrapnel balls. The material used in fashioning the links is derived from barbed wire. The cross was carved from the driving band of an exploded Italian shell and has appendages consisting of three Italian rifle bullets. The body of Christ was formed from shrapnel balls. On the back of the cross it says in engraved letters: "Out of gratitude. In remembrance of the Italian war, Cima d'Oro, July 25, 1917. A. St. and K. P., from Lana." This rosary weighs more than two pounds. For prolonged prayer it requires a strong hand. Would the ladies and gentlemen perhaps want to try?

ONE OF THE SIGHTSEERS (*having a try*): Gosh! I can't do it.

(*The bell rings.*)

SEXTON: Listen! For the last time! In a minute it will be taken down. Rosaries are made from shrapnel balls, and guns in turn from church bells. We render unto God what is the Kaiser's and unto the Kaiser what is God's. We help one another as best we can.

(*Scene change.*)

SCENE 21

A physician's consulting room in Berlin.

PROFESSOR MOLENAAR (*to patient*): Yes, you have a heart ailment. With that, you're hardly likely to be found fit. Fine situation! You see, that comes from smoking. Despite all the prohibitions of the army command in the borderlands, the smoking goes on. There can be no doubt that immoderate smoking in general, and the premature puffing of our young people in particular, has so far cost us at least two army corps in this war. It's frightening how many men have heart conditions at a relatively early age and thereby are excluded from military service, marriage, and procreation. In the interest of troop replacement, a law against smoking in our country is urgently desired. Death in the service of the fatherland, as we know from experience, removes many young people from military service; it is therefore most deplorable, especially in the interest of troop replacement, and of procreation serving that purpose, that the habit of smoking contributes further to it. You, a young man, have contracted a heart ailment; there is hardly a chance you will be found fit. Don't take it to heart. After all, you may get better. There will always be wars. Your lungs don't seem to be in good condition either. Take a deep breath!

(*Listens.*) No, won't do. At most, rear echelon forces. You owe twenty marks.

(*Scene change.*)

SCENE 22

Office of a command post. A Member of the General Staff. Two old Generals. A War Correspondent.

MEMBER OF THE GENERAL STAFF (*telephoning*): —Hello, well, do you have the report on Przemyśl ready? —Not yet? Ah, you're still a little sleepy—get at it, or else you'll be late for the partying. Now listen—what, did you forget it all again? Listen carefully, here are the main points: While it was hunger through which our garrison, as we all know—now something quite different—the enemy has yielded to our power—that is, by no means overwhelmed by hunger, the enemy was never starving! You understand. Only us! The Russians always had enough provisions—but, of course, could not hold their own against the élan of our fine troops —the power of our attack—furthermore: Fortress absolutely intact, retaken in perfect condition—most modern artillery —what? You can't make them forget? An old heap of rubbish? But no, not any more now, of course not! Just get this straight now, don't make a jumble of it! You can make people forget just about everything, my friend. Most modern fortress—Austria's old pride—retaken intact. Not by enemy power but by hunger. Oh God, what am I saying, not by hunger, but by power. Well, you'll manage all right—as long as our good people find it convincing—now there's really nothing to it—so long then. (*Hangs up.*) That's all. (*Exit.*)

(*Two old Generals enter.*)

FIRST: Yes, those Germans! Now they've given Falkenhayn a doctor's degree. That sort of thing just isn't in the cards for one like us.
SECOND: But you will agree that Borevitsch—
FIRST: I know, I know, but for men like you and me that sort of thing just isn't in the cards.

(*A War Correspondent passes by.*)

FIRST: My compliments, sir!
WAR CORRESPONDENT: Oh, your Excellency, delighted to see you, you're just the man I need. What is the situation with Brody?
FIRST: Brody? What should be the matter?
WAR CORRESPONDENT: Well, the battle at Brody?
FIRST: Is there really a battle at Brody? You don't say!
SECOND: Holy Mother of Christ!
FIRST: Well, then, a battle, what do you say to that! Well, and now you want to know— (*After some reflecting.*) You know what—we'll manage.
WAR CORRESPONDENT (*hastily*): I may report then, that Brody is still in our possession? Or, rather, you know what? I think I'm going to report that Brody is as good as relieved. (*Exit.*)

(*Scene change.*)

SCENE 37

The Subscriber and the Patriot conversing.

PATRIOT: No bathroom at 10 Downing Street! What do you say to that!

SUBSCRIBER: What can I say? The walls are crumbling.

PATRIOT: No bathroom at Downing Street!

SUBSCRIBER: Well now, to whom do we owe this remarkable discovery? To him,* of course!

PATRIOT: Of course, but actually it was Mrs. Lloyd George who made this disturbing discovery, one has to admit that.

SUBSCRIBER: Well yes, that is true. But it was he who printed it.

PATRIOT: Well, and you know what follows then, with inescapable logic?

SUBSCRIBER: He writes expressly that the British Prime Ministers who have resided at 10 Downing Street for more than a century have either forgone the luxury of bathing or have been obliged to go to a public bath.

PATRIOT: Serves them right, those filthy people, I relish it.

SUBSCRIBER: And mind you, not the way it is here, because of the war—no, for more than a century they put up with that piggishness!

PATRIOT: Asquith lived there with his family for nine years.

SUBSCRIBER: That means he did not take a bath in nine years, neither he nor the whole family.

PATRIOT: Well now, one can't say that. Perhaps they went to a public bath.

* Moriz Benedikt.

SUBSCRIBER: I beg your pardon, nothing of the sort has ever been reported. Or did you ever read—
PATRIOT: Not that I can remember.
SUBSCRIBER: Well, there you are.
PATRIOT: But you know what is still possible? All right, there is no bathroom at Downing Street. All right, it is proven that they never went to a public bath—but from this it doesn't follow they never took a bath at all in a hundred years?
SUBSCRIBER: How come? Seems to me you're something of a skeptic!
PATRIOT: Look here, Mrs. Lloyd George discovered it, he writes, when they moved in. Now then, if she discovers such a thing—what will she do in the future?
SUBSCRIBER: Do I know? It's not my worry!
PATRIOT: She will do, I suppose, what most probably Mrs. Asquith also did.
SUBSCRIBER: Well, what did she do?
PATRIOT: What did she do? She did, I suppose, what most probably all of them did who lived there for a hundred years.
SUBSCRIBER: Well now, what did they do?
PATRIOT: What did they do? Well now, is there a bathroom at Schönbrunn?
SUBSCRIBER: At Schönbrunn? What do they have instead?
PATRIOT: Well—I have been told—I shouldn't be saying this —but let's suppose—well, has the Emperor not taken a bath for a hundred years or do you believe that he goes to the Central Baths?
SUBSCRIBER: Fine patriot you are! But what has that got to do with this—you better tell me what they did at Downing Street.
PATRIOT: What they did? Even a simple layman must realize

what they did. They told the shiksa to get water for them and they sent her for a tub. And there in the tub, they took their bath.

SUBSCRIBER (*stops his ears*): I can't bear to listen to such a thing. You're taking the last illusion away from a person.

PATRIOT: Pardon me, I'm just supposing. I believe he is right —they either did not take a bath at all then or were obliged to go to a public bath.

SUBSCRIBER: And I'm telling you they did not take baths at all. And that's all there is to it. Poincaré's position is shaken and Lloyd George humiliated. Englishmen and Germans will meet in Stockholm.

PATRIOT: What does this mean? What has that got to do with this? You almost strike me as if you were Old Biach.

SUBSCRIBER: Come on, that is something you really ought to know. That's how a lead article ends.

PATRIOT: Of course—I do know! You know what I think? The walls are crumbling.

SUBSCRIBER: You're telling me! In all the Allied countries, I've been told there are no bathrooms.

PATRIOT: No, that's exaggerated. Didn't you read about the tsarina in her bathtub?

SUBSCRIBER: Well yes, but as everybody knows, she had to share it with Rasputin.

PATRIOT: You know what I'm eager to know?

SUBSCRIBER: What? I'm eager to know.

PATRIOT: Whether there's a toilet at Downing Street. Or whether for the last one hundred years they were obliged to forgo the luxury or to utilize a public convenience. May God punish England!

SUBSCRIBER: We shall see what we shall see. (*Exit.*)

(*Scene change.*)

SCENE 40

The German spa Gross-Salze. In the foreground, a children's playground. View into an avenue. At its entrance, on the left, a sign: "No Wounded Soldiers Allowed." On the left the villa of the Wahnschaffes, a building decorated with crenelations, battlements, and little towers. A black-red-and-gold and a black-white-and-red flag flutter from the gable. Under the gable in a niche is a bust of Wilhelm II. Above the entrance the inscription: "With Heart and Hand for God, Kaiser, and Fatherland!" A skimpy little front yard, in which ornamental deer and gnomes stand; in the center, an old suit of armor. In front of the entrance on the right and left, two dummies of mortar shells, one with the inscription "Up and at 'em," the other with "Stick it out!" The gothic windows facing front have bullseye panes. Frau Auguste Wahnschaffe, wife of Ottomar Wilhelm Wahnschaffe, appears with her children, who run off immediately for the playground to engage in a war game.

FRAU WAHNSCHAFFE: I have only two children, and unfortunately they are not yet eligible for military service. And, to make things even worse, one of them, to our sorrow, is a girl. So I have to make do by fantasizing that my boy has already been at the front, and has, naturally, already met a hero's death. I would die of shame if the situation were otherwise, if, by chance, he had come home to me unscathed. In no event could I tolerate his being assigned to the rear echelons, although a bullet might easily stray

Act III, Scene 40

even that far. This illusion is the best consolation that I have; I affirm it against every doubt by effortlessly suppressing these doubts. I fortify it during the time when my dear Ottomar is at work. Actually, I am always busy except for the half hour when my husband, who just now went to work, takes time to eat. So far as our food is concerned, since I am an efficient housewife, I have to make do with imagination here, too. Today we were well provided for as far as that goes. There were all kinds of things. We had a wholesome broth made with the Excelsior brand of Hindenburg cocoa-cream soup cubes, a tasty ersatz false hare with ersatz kohlrabi, potato pancakes made of paraffin, and home-style puréed fruit, all of it, of course, prepared on an Obu brand skillet. For dessert we had ersatz ladyfingers, which tasted fine to us.

A German housewife knows what she owes her husband in this serious but great time. To be sure, my husband made a fuss because he did not get his yummy homemade noodles. Nothing doing, he'll have to learn to do without. In the beginning we really missed ersatz margarine, but now that we have Obu brand, we lack for nothing. In the housewives' association meeting we recently decided unanimously that nutritive mineral yeast, whose protein content is primarily extracted from urea, is the equivalent of brewer's yeast in its nutritive value, and should therefore no longer be exclusively distributed to welfare kitchens. It is the fashion today to cater to the broad masses of the population. This one-sided favoritism has to come to an end. The middle class also wants to live. The killjoys, who have something against even this, object that mineral yeast smells like herring and tastes like petroleum and is thus capable of arousing nausea. We German housewives know better and hope that these strange properties will completely disappear in the cooking process. Actually, we are convinced that nutritive mineral yeast lends a fine, pleasant taste to foods.

As soon as lunch is over, I have to start worrying again about supper. For tonight's supper there's a casserole, as always, and, for a change, liverwurst made from starch paste and vegetables artificially colored red. And, as a substitute for cheese, Berlin curds with ersatz paprika. Today we're also going to try the much-praised hodgepodge with Yolktex brand of ersatz egg made from carbonite of lime and baking powder, and a bit of Saladfix, a delicious additive that I prefer by far to Salatin as well as to Saladol. Because for the German family table the best is just good enough, and there's nothing lacking; it's not as it is with poor people.

Yesterday for our bedtime snack we tried Deutscher's Teafix with rum aroma and were quite pleasantly surprised. To be sure, the kiddies raised a ruckus because they didn't have their candy rum grenades, the brand with the motto "Our Fighting Men Are Always the Best." My husband had his acorn water, which is almost as good as the Trench brand of tutti-goody-coffee, which we're out of just now. But unfortunately, we had to get along without ersatz liquid sweetener, so the dispenser sat there alongside, empty. I was tempted to follow a sudden inspiration and fill it with ersatz mineral water in order to preserve my husband's illusion. But that would mean deceiving one's husband, and once one step is taken from the straight and narrow path, the second will soon follow. So I didn't do it. The lovely times are now past when one still had it easy, when it was only necessary to squeeze the dispenser in order to sweeten his wartime ersatz coffee. But since otherwise we would not know that we are being called upon to stick it out now, we'll gladly accept such small sacrifices as part of the bargain. All the more so, since one can't bargain for anything else now, so we simply have to put aside all that money my husband earns.

The dubious peace will come soon enough; then you will spend money on trifles again. But let's hope the war will last long enough so that in this, too, there is a change for the better. At the last convention of the Fatherland Party, my husband proposed that the war, which was forced upon us by British envy, French thirst for revenge, and Russian rapacity, should be continued even after the conclusion of peace. An overwhelming majority supported this proposal. Now the word is to stick it out, and the longer, the better. We'll manage it. Not a day goes by without bringing some news that lifts one's heart. How did Emmi Lewald put it then? "Three thousand dead Englishmen at the front! No symphony could sound more beautiful to me now! How pleasantly that runs through the nerves, merrily awakening hope. Three thousand dead Englishmen at the front!—it reverberates in my dreams and runs in my mind like a cajoling melody." I feel that way, too. And how I love that wonderful Anny Wothe, who has her splendid soldier's wife inform her husband of the birth of a healthy son with the words: "Thanks be to God, another soldier! The boy shall be called Wilhelm. Someday he shall become as staunch as our Kaiser and slash away so that one can see the pieces fly. The other boys pray every day that you strike a good many Frenchmen dead. I pray, too, but not for your life. That's in God's hands. I pray that you will do your duty properly, that you won't tremble if the bullet comes, and that, if it must be, you will die composedly for our fatherland and our Kaiser, and that you won't trouble yourself about us. And if you have the chance to save the life of your captain, don't consider us either. The five boys add their greetings to mine. They want to sing 'Hail to You with the Victor's Crown' at Wilhelm's christening. With that, I remain, your faithful wife"—Oh, God knows, the only reason I, too, can't write to my husband in such a fashion is that he, unfortunately, is not in the field, for, as luck would have it, he is indispensable.

And besides, I have only one son, for the youngest is, as I said, unfortunately a girl. Commercial successes have to be our compensation for the sacrifice of not being able to make a sacrifice for the fatherland. Wahnschaffe has just created a really interesting war novelty that is already patented in Germany and in Austria-Hungary, which is fighting with us shoulder to shoulder. Distribution rights will be given to aggressive salesmen getting a high commission. It is "Hero's Grave in the House," at once a reliquary case and a photograph stand. Thus, it provides not only a pretty decoration for the home but also religious elevation. I wistfully regret that, unfortunately, we ourselves have no use for so appropriate a memorial to the dead. My children are not yet old enough to die for our Kaiser or to sacrifice themselves for the fatherland in some other way. They also have the unfortunate disadvantage of having been born before the outbreak of the war. Otherwise, I would have called the boy Warsaw and the girl Wilna, or Hindenburg and Zeppelina, respectively! True, the boy was named Wilhelm, for even before the war that was a matter of course; I don't see any particular expression of patriotic hommage in it. Oh, here they come now, the cute little kiddies! What's the matter now? Aren't you playing World War?

LITTLE WILLY (*crying*): Mommy, Marie won't stay dead!

LITTLE MARIE: We played encirclement, then World War, and now—

LITTLE WILLY (*crying*): But I only wanted a place in the sun, then—
LITTLE MARIE: He's lying!
LITTLE WILLIE: I successfully bombarded her position, and now she won't stay dead!
LITTLE MARIE (*crying*): No, it's not so, it's an enemy lie, just like a Reuter's dispatch. First he took my forward position, and now he attacks from the flank! I effortlessly repelled the attack and now he says—
LITTLE WILLY: Marie is lying! Her counterattack collapsed under our fire. Now the very last pockets of English resistance are mopped up. Five of our men did not return.
LITTLE MARIE: At Smorgon, heightened battle activity.
LITTLE WILLY: We took prisoners.
LITTLE MARIE: We brought in a certain number of prisoners. The waves of attackers broke under our fire and had to recede in disorder, leaving many bodies behind on our terrain.
LITTLE WILLY: That is the merciless method of the Russians, who drive great numbers forward during their offensives. The positions remained in our hands. We achieved direct hits.
LITTLE MARIE: I took the offensive.
LITTLE WILLY: I am preparing myself for a third winter campaign.
LITTLE MARIE: That'll be the day! You high-handed pup!
LITTLE WILLY: Just you wait, I'll fight to the last drop of blood!
LITTLE MARIE: You colored Englishman and Frenchman, you!
LITTLE WILLY: The Russians succeeded in achieving a foothold in our first line of trenches, but our counterattack at daybreak—
LITTLE MARIE: —threw them back out.

LITTLE WILLY: Several counterattacks attempted by the enemy during the course of the afternoon—

LITTLE MARIE: —were thwarted by a daring surprise attack in hand-to-hand combat. (*She hits him.*)

LITTLE WILLY: She's lying! Besides, those are the initial successes that are typical of every offensive. (*He hits her.*)

LITTLE MARIE: One must refrain from exaggerating the optimistic outlook for the offensive.

LITTLE WILLY: During the last air attack on fortress London—

LITTLE MARIE: —I immediately exercised reprisals. Karlsruhe—

LITTLE WILLY: Yes, three civilians are dead, among them, a child. The military damage is insignificant. It's always the same.

FRAU WAHNSCHAFFE (*up to this point, listening with shining eyes*): Marie, darling, now you just be still. Father said you might play World War, but that you have to stay within humane bounds. Little Willy wouldn't hurt a fly; he is defending his possessions as best he can. He is waging a holy defensive war.

LITTLE WILLY (*crying*): I did not will it so.

LITTLE MARIE: Who did then?

LITTLE WILLY: Up and at 'em! (*He hits her.*) I have achieved a direct hit.

LITTLE MARIE (*hits him*): Just try and get into my blocking position!

FRAU WAHNSCHAFFE: Now stop it, dolly!

LITTLE WILLY: Just you wait—I'll get my flame thrower!

FRAU WAHNSCHAFFE: Kiddies, you can play, but stay within bounds! If Willy keeps being so good, Daddy will bring home the iron cross for him from the office.

LITTLE WILLY: Hurrah! There you have my Belgian pawn, in this fist! (*He jumps on Marie and beats her up. Marie cries.*)

FRAU WAHNSCHAFFE: Willy, darling, always be humane! Don't forget your good upbringing! (*She goes to Marie with a handkerchief.*) Now, children, go back to your positions, but first let me clean off your nose.

LITTLE MARIE (*crying*): The little brat is firing on my sugar factory and using poisonous gases! (*She gets up and puts Willy to flight.*)

LITTLE WILLY: The retreat is only strategic. (*While running.*) In expectation of this attack, the evacuation of this sector, which is exposed to encirclement, has been considered for years and was implemented in the last few days. Therefore, we did not fight the fight through to a decisive conclusion but carried out the proposed movements, which the enemy could not hinder. (*From the distance.*) Hurrah, I shall take up the Siegfried Line.

(*Two Invalids hobble by in the direction of the avenue.*)

FRAU WAHNSCHAFFE: Now I must see to my chores. We're going to do the cleaning today with the War Child brand of ersatz soap preparation. (*She notices the Invalids.*) Again! That's really too annoying! If they don't pay attention to the warning sign, I'll report them to the local magistrate.

(*Both stop in front of the sign and turn around.*)

FIRST INVALID: Where to then?

SECOND INVALID: Back to the front. There's where you're allowed to go. (*They hobble off.*)

(*A Governess comes along with a three-year-old boy, who is picking his nose.*)

GOVERNESS: Fritzy, aren't you ashamed of yourself? Just wait, I'll tell Hindenburg on you!

(*Fritzy pulls back his finger, terrified.*)

(*Hansel meets Trudy.*)

HANSEL: May God punish England!
TRUDY (*staunchly meeting his gaze*): He should!

(*August and Guste enter.*)

GUSTE: In two months England will have been forced to her knees.
AUGUST: Do you think so? I'm no scaremonger, but what do you have to say about America?
GUSTE: Oh, we know those customers!
AUGUST: Our mood is serious, but—
GUSTE: —confident! (*Exeunt.*)

(*Klaus meets Dolly.*)

KLAUS: We were encircled. These days every child knows that.
DOLLY: British envy, French thirst for revenge, and Russian rapacity—we surely know the score. The question of war guilt is clear enough. Germany wanted a place in the sun.
KLAUS: Europe was a powder keg.
DOLLY: The Belgian treaty was a scrap of paper. (*Exeunt.*)

(*Jochen and Suse enter.*)

JOCHEN: What we need are overseas colonies. I tell you, if we don't make headway with world trade, Germany is going to come off badly in this war.
SUSE: Old tales! We have to annex land on the continent. We need Belgium as an air base and also, for instance, the ore basin of Briey, besides that—
JOCHEN: You're speaking of the bare minimum. (*Exeunt.*)

(*A Mother with her little Daughter, beside them a Gentleman.*)

MOTHER: Well, Elsbeth, don't you want to play?
DAUGHTER: No.
MOTHER: Do go ahead and play, child.
DAUGHTER: No.
MOTHER: What a strange child! Why won't you?
DAUGHTER: It's in just this that we are superior to the English and therefore they are envious of us.
MOTHER: Oh, just listen to her—what then, child? Why are the English envious of us? Now go ahead and tell the gentleman, Elsbeth!
DAUGHTER: The English are jealous of us because we are in the process of climbing upward, whereas they are going down. This comes from the fact that after work, the Germans work still some more, whereas the English enjoy themselves with sports and games.
MOTHER: Golden words, Elsbeth. Such a child puts one to shame.
GENTLEMAN: Out of the mouths of babes.
MOTHER: I want to report this to the *Berliner Tageblatt*.
GENTLEMAN: No, better yet, save it for the collection *The Child and the War: Children's Comments, Essays, Descriptions, and Drawings*. (*Exeunt*.)

(*Scene change*.)

SCENE 41

The Optimist and the Grumbler conversing.

OPTIMIST: The *Neue Freie Presse* underscores with justification how noble it is of Count Berchtold* to go out to the

* Austrian Foreign Minister.

front himself now, saber in hand, in order to meet eye to eye with that sworn enemy who caused the greatest difficulties to his foreign policy.

GRUMBLER: You mean the treacherous treaty partner Conrad* has been wanting to attack for years? So far as Berchtold is concerned, it really is decent of him, and indeed, a change in our favor could set in, although, as you know, I am very pessimistic about the possibility of employing sabers in this war.

OPTIMIST: I see. You remain true to your wont: to tear everything down, doing it even in the face of the heroic paragons of our martial epoch. Here you have it in *Die Woche*, Count Berchtold in field uniform. This picture—

GRUMBLER: —is the cause of the war.

OPTIMIST: In what way? But the picture was taken later than the ultimatum—

GRUMBLER: To be sure. The Serbs could not accept the ultimatum because this photograph appeared to them in their mind's eye. Austria's fear that they might just perhaps accept the ultimatum was completely groundless. Austria had hoped for a "localization" of the war because she hoped to crush Serbia without interference from the world, but that, too, was inconceivable.

OPTIMIST: Once again, I don't understand you. So this photograph tells you—

GRUMBLER: —that a race-track dandy led the world to its death!

OPTIMIST: Now I am beginning to understand you. But he was not fully aware of what he was doing.

GRUMBLER: No, or else he wouldn't be a race-track dandy, and then he wouldn't have done it. The devastating thing is that

---

* Conrad von Hötzendorf.

he was indeed not fully aware of it. And that this argument is an extenuating circumstance for statesmen and heads of state who even by law cannot be taken to account for their actions. None of them were fully aware of what they were doing. Austria can't be blamed for it! She merely let herself be encouraged by Germany to drag Germany into the war. And Germany drove Austria into a war that she did not want. Across the border they are all innocence, accusing us, and we, of course, are the merest little lambs. Neither of us can be blamed for the war.

OPTIMIST: This face truly speaks for a good conscience. This photograph—

GRUMBLER: —is taken from the criminal files of world history and will render good service when the instigators of the war are identified before the world sitting in judgment. The subject of the picture will, naturally, be acquitted because of unaccountability or diminished responsibility.

OPTIMIST: How could that be proved?

GRUMBLER: It will be established, among other things, that a harmless owner of racing stables concealed among racing programs Grey's offer to the Austro-Hungarian monarchy that it be allowed to occupy Belgrade and, in addition, a number of other Serbian towns as the compensation it allegedly wanted. For England really did want the "localization" that Austria, in a different way, was hoping for, and for this they called the only honest man in this war "lying Grey." This photograph will contribute to the exoneration of the perpetrator, but also to all his countrymen being found guilty. In its perfect shamelessness the photograph vindicates the aggressive intentions of our enemies in case we really had waged a holy defensive war. For even if it were proved that we had a right to lay hands on Serbia because Hungarian swine were keeping Serbian swine out of the market, this document would still stand up and bear witness against us.

OPTIMIST: I beg you—a photograph! A chance snapshot! But consider, Berchtold is not responsible—

GRUMBLER: No, only we are, for having made it possible for such playboys to escape responsibility for their games. We are responsible because we tolerated a world that wages wars for which no one can be held responsible. Responsible for the one thing for which one really must be acccuntable: disposition over the life, health, freedom, honor, property, and happiness of our fellow men. Yet greater cretins than our statesmen are—

OPTIMIST: —the statesmen of our enemies?

GRUMBLER: No, we ourselves. We have in common with our enemies only the stupidity of holding one and the same God responsible for the outcome of the war, instead of ourselves for the decision to wage it. So far as enemy statesmen are concerned, they can't be any more stupid than our own, for that does not occur in nature.

OPTIMIST: As to ours, at any rate, one can make the observation—

GRUMBLER: —that we would spare ourselves wars if we would send them to the front, which is where Berchtold and his ilk will never go. But still farther away than they are from the front are we from an institution of political life such as the one known to the Spartans, who, as we know, were also out-and-out stick-it-outers. They put their cretins out on Mount Taygetus, whereas we put ours at the head of the state and in responsible diplomatic positions.

(*Scene change.*)

SCENE 42

During the Battle of the Somme. Gate in front of a villa. A company of front-line soldiers, wearing their death-defying countenances, marches by into the foremost front-line trenches.

CROWN PRINCE (*at the park gate, in a tennis outfit, waving to them with his racket*): Do a good job!

(*Scene change.*)

SCENE 43

The Ministry of War. A room fronting on the Ringstrasse. A Captain sits at a desk. In front of him stands a Civilian in deep mourning.

CAPTAIN: Well, then, what more do you want? An up-to-date report is an impossible thing in such cases. After all, we can't know whether a man is dead or wounded and captured. You will have to go to the Italian ministry of war, my dear fellow! Well, now then! What—in addition to everything else are we supposed to do? It is simply unbelievable what people expect of us!
CIVILIAN: Yes—but—
CAPTAIN: My dear sir, I can tell you no more. Besides it is almost three o'clock—you must have some understanding. Office hours are over. That's really splendid—well, what is it now? —Now then, off the record, I can tell you one

thing: you have heard nothing from your son now for six weeks; so confidently assume that he is dead.

CIVILIAN: Yes—but—

CAPTAIN: No but's about it. Where would we be if in such cases we—you can surely imagine that things like this occur a thousand times! There's a war on now, my dear sir! So the citizen must also do his part! Look at us who sit here! We stand here at our posts! And besides that, dear sir—as surely you do know—but again I say this to you privately and completely without any commitment on my part—that for a soldier there can be no higher ambition and no more beautiful reward than to die for the fatherland. So, it has been an honor—an honor—

(*The Civilian bows and leaves.*)

Act IV

SCENE 2

The Optimist and the Grumbler conversing.

OPTIMIST: Are you going to Switzerland again soon?

GRUMBLER: I would love to, though you are always sure to run into the same crowd there that you try to get away from here. Well, at least I will not completely lose sight of the social scene when I work on the drama of Austria's collapse. In Berne one might as well be in Vienna; a rotting empire exports the products of its putrefaction—cheats and diplomats, profiteers and scribblers who can travel unhampered as a matter of course, and who in addition act as propagandists in Switzerland for this hateful miscreation of a state that outrages the world. But for people like myself, it's not so easy, and the formalities required to get away are restrictive.

OPTIMIST: Yes, those passport affairs. One ministry doesn't know what the other one requires. But, after all, war is—

GRUMBLER: War. —We know that. But being granted permission for something by this state is even more annoying than being denied permission. And furthermore, you have to give a valid reason.

OPTIMIST: Well, and haven't you any?

GRUMBLER: Plenty. I would rather not stress as a reason the prospect of getting some bread and butter in Switzerland, but rather the quintessence of all the reasons—the constant awareness of living in Austria. If, instead, one had to give a valid reason for staying in Austria, the authorities would save themselves a lot of paperwork. The mere question of whether or not one has a valid reason is in itself a valid reason to pack up and go. It is indeed a valid reason not merely for crossing the border—

OPTIMIST: But?

GRUMBLER: For emigrating.

OPTIMIST: You'll easily find a reason. With your skill in dialectics, what couldn't you find a valid reason for?

GRUMBLER: For returning.

(*Scene change.*)

SCENE 3

A railroad station near Vienna. A docile crowd of five hundred has been waiting in front of the closed ticket window for the last two hours.

A VIENNESE: It will be here in ten minutes.

A SECOND (*to the Ticket Taker*): Pardon me, when will the train be in?

TICKET TAKER: Well, it often gets in around seven.

A THIRD: But it's already a quarter to eight!

TICKET TAKER: That's right! What do you know! But it's two and a half hours late today. That's been posted anyway.

GRUMBLER: Can one rely on that?

TICKET TAKER (*irritated*): How would I know? All they know is a lot of crap, and if they do know, they certainly are not going to let the public in on it.

Act IV, Scene 3

GRUMBLER: But why won't they?

TICKET TAKER: Because crap is all they know.

GRUMBLER: But yet it's been posted.

TICKET TAKER: Posted, posted, but for all that it will still be late.

GRUMBLER: Is that the rule?

TICKET TAKER: I wouldn't say the rule, but it would be an exception if it came punctually late the way arrivals are posted.

GRUMBLER: But then, why is the delay posted?

TICKET TAKER: Just because nobody can know nothing anyway. Up the line they don't report anything, and in here they don't announce anything.

A FOURTH: I may be wrong, but I think it's coming.

TICKET TAKER: There now, see, it's nothing but pure accident.

GRUMBLER: Yes, but how come?

TICKET TAKER: No use grumbling, mister! Ask somebody else. That's the way the delays work. In here we don't get no report, and out there they don't say nothing. With all that traffic, there is nothing we can do. There's a war on.

A FIFTH: The train's coming!

A SIXTH: The guy behind the ticket window is asleep!

VOICES: What's the matter? Open up! (*The Grumbler hits the window with a cane.*) Good for you!

(*The ticket window opens. The typical Austrian Face appears. It is extremely undernourished, yet besotted with satanical relish. An emaciated index finger, moving back and forth, seems to take away all hope.*)

THE AUSTRIAN FACE: No tickets! No tickets!

(*Muttering, rising to a tumult. Groups form.*)

AN INSIDER: Come with me, I'll show you a back door. There

we won't need no tickets. (*Everybody leaves through the back door.*)

(*Scene change.*)

SCENE 5

Two Poets conversing.

THE POET STROBL: —And all that green interlaced with moonlight spilling over into the distance to far-away white-shining houses and dark mountains. Like Eichendorff's most lovely poem, *Midsummer Night*—(*He lapses into dreaming.*) As I stepped from the dark hall onto the terrace again, the cadet was holding his big pocketknife in his hand, slicing off a piece of smoked sausage. And he remarked just casually, and in an offhand manner: "With this knife I slit the throats of a couple of Dagos." (*After a pause, pensively.*) He was a good kid!

THE POET ERTL: What an experience! I envy you. (*Lost in thought.*) I have a plan. I am going to suggest that we call our seventh war bond issue the Truth Issue.

THE POET STROBL: What a sweet idea! But why call it that?

THE POET ERTL: Because our victory must and will help Truth to triumph in the end! Because Truth must be the prerequisite for successful peace negotiations. In other words: official rectification of all the lies and slanders by which unworthy men in power and journalists in the Allied camp have betrayed the world and their own people, poisoned their minds and misguided them. (*Strobl silently shakes Ertl's hand. They stride onward.*)

(*Scene change.*)

SCENE 6

Students' drinking bout. Hindenburg celebration.

AN UPPERCLASSMAN: —Beer-honest souls! Take to your heart what the German fraternity newsletter urgently recommends to you. (*He reads aloud.*) "It is also necessary to have a chance to drink our fill and to make others drink their fill as well. If we forbid drinking all one can hold, any frosh who can hold his beer well may at any time drink under the table any of our upperclassmen who is less able to take it. And then all authority is gone, we do away with beer-honesty, and with it the basis for any drinking jollity. If we can't pump the froshes full of beer, we'll be giving away an educational tool." (*Shouts of "That's right." "Let's have the stuff now!"*)

I ask you not to quote my words out of context. Our life within the fraternity should represent a succession of educational endeavors. And any fraternity brother will agree that never again in all his life will he get to hear the truth so plain, so unvarnished, so incredibly coarse. And how do you explain that he puts up with it? Ridiculous as this may sound, it's all due to the beer halls. The beer hall is for us what the much-maligned close-order drill and the parade are for the soldier. (*Shouts of "Hurrah!"*) Just as there the command "deep knee bend," repeated a hundred times, overcomes laziness, indifference, obstinacy, rage, listlessness, and fatigue, and discipline is attained from a feeling of helpless impotence and total surrender to one's superior (*shouts of "Hurrah!"*)—with us the command "Bottoms up!" affords the upperclassman an opportunity to show his absolute superiority to the freshman, to mete out punishment, to keep one's distance, to preserve the atmosphere that is an absolute requirement for the ongoing educational work of the fraternity if we don't want to become just a club. (*Shouts of "No, not at all!"*)

But, then, "Bottoms up" is, of course, not always appropriate, not appropriate to everybody, but it must hover over the beer cellar just like the "deep knee bend" over the barracks!

ALL: Hurrah! Hurrah! (*Clinking of steins.*) "Bottoms up!"

(*Scene change.*)

SCENE 7

Physicians' meeting in Berlin.

PSYCHIATRIST: —gentlemen! This individual is the strangest case I have ever had. It was my lucky star that brought him to me from protective custody. Since it is obviously impossible to be sentenced to as many years of hard labor as this man would have to expect for his crimes, we had, whether we wanted to or not, to turn to psychiatry. Here for once we have a case where we need not ask whether the criminal is subjectively responsible for his crime; the deed itself is proof of his lack of responsibility. In order, gentlemen, to enable you to perceive fully the patient's irresponsibility for his actions, I need but mention that he voiced in public the opinion that the food situation in Germany was unfavorable! (*Restlessness.*) More than that: the man doubts Germany's final victory! (*Commotion.*) But, as though that were not enough, the man insists that unrestricted submarine warfare, and indeed submarine warfare altogether, does not fulfill its purpose. It immediately became clear to me that he rejects this weapon as such, and this not merely because he believes it does not fulfill its purpose but because he regards it as downright immoral! (*Shouts of excitement.*)

Gentlemen, we as men of science have the duty to maintain cool heads and to face the object of our indignation only as an object of investigation, *sine ira* although *cum studio*. (*Hilarity.*) Gentlemen, I comply with the sad duty of sketching out for you a full picture of the mental confusion of the patient, and I must ask you to refrain from placing the burden of responsibility on the shoulders of this unfortunate individual or on mine, as I am no more than the accidental demonstrator of a loathsome form of insanity. His responsibility is canceled through his illness, mine through science. (*Calls of "Right you are!"*)

Gentlemen, this man suffers from the fixed idea that Germany is being driven toward an ultimate catastrophe through a "criminal ideology," this being the term he uses to refer to the sublime idealism of our country's rulers. He believes that we are lost unless we declare ourselves beaten, although we are at the pinnacle of our victorious course. He believes that it is our government, that it is our military rulers—certainly not those of England (*shouts of "Hear, hear"*)—who bear the blame for the fact that our children will have to die! (*Cries of "For shame!"*) The mere assertion that our children will have to die, implying that our food situation is unfavorable, alone suffices to demonstrate beyond a shadow of a doubt the man's mental derangement. (*Shouts of "That's right!"*)

I have presented this case to you, my highly esteemed colleagues from internal medicine, so that you, gentlemen, may attempt to exert an influence on the patient by conveying to him your experiences with regard to the state of health of the German population in wartime. From the manner of his response I hope to obtain a rounding-out of the clinical picture, if not its rectification, toward an orientation in which criminal responsibility can perhaps still be demonstrated, since we must leave nothing untried—I hope then that the patient, under the impact of your authoritative exposition, will let himself be carried away into making such utterances that will make it easier for us to reach a decision in one direction or another. (*A voice from the audience:* "*We'll swing it!*")

MENTAL PATIENT: If there is among you one of *the* ninety-three intellectuals,* I shall leave the hall! (*Shouts of "What insolence!"*)

PSYCHIATRIST: I trust, gentlemen, that you will take this outbreak less as an insult than as a symptom. I myself, as you all know, have signed that protest that will live on in the annals of our country as a milestone from a great age, and I am proud of it. I now ask our revered colleague Boas to undertake an experiment on the patient.

PROFESSOR BOAS (*stepping forward*): I have stated repeatedly and confirm once again that the health of our people has not been impaired by the restriction of available provisions. (*Shouts of "Hear, hear!"*) We can take it as an established fact that we have been getting along on no more than one-half the protein ration used before, without an adverse effect on our strength or fitness to work and, indeed, that we have even been able to increase our weight and to improve our physical well-being.

MENTAL PATIENT: You probably provide for your needs on the black market! (*Shouts of excitement.*)

---

* Refers to the leading German intellectuals who, at the beginning of the war, signed a proclamation supporting Germany's war aims.

PSYCHIATRIST: Gentlemen, consider the mental state of the man. Professor Boas, permit me to raise the question of infant mortality, which is a point that keeps coming up time and again in the imagination of our patient.

PROFESSOR BOAS: We have found that there can be no question of the food situation exerting an unfavorable influence on infant mortality.

MENTAL PATIENT: You mean, there *must* be no question— (*Shouts of "Shut up!"*)

PSYCHIATRIST: What do you anticipate, Professor Boas, from a continuation of the war?

PROFESSOR BOAS: With our increasing affluence and the concomitant increase in superabundant nutrition, we were squandering our national health. Now millions of our countrymen, under the pressure of privation, have learned to find the way back to nature and a simple way of life. Let us take care, gentlemen, that the lessons we are learning today in wartime will not again be lost to future generations. (*Shouts of "Bravo!"*)

MENTAL PATIENT: The man is quite right—the Kurfürstendamm crowd gorged too much before the war. But they are still eating too much. It is quite true that for them the food situation has not worsened at all. But as for the future generation of the rest of the population, those circles that do not consult Boas for obesity—for the future population of Germany I foresee children born with rickets! Children as invalids! Blessed are those who died during the war: those born during the war wear artificial limbs. I prophesy that the insanity of sticking it out and the miserable pride in the enemy's losses, which is as characteristic of German men as is the ardent eagerness of German Megaeras to have their sons die a hero's death—that this perverse state of mind of a society that breathes an air of organized glory and feeds on self-deception will leave behind a crippled Germany!

(*Shouts of "For shame!"*) As for this Boas, I challenge him to deny that up to now about 800,000 persons among the civilian population have died of starvation, that in 1917 alone some 50,000 more children and 127,000 more old men and women died than in 1913, that in the first six months of 1918 more Germans—approximately seventy percent more—died of tuberculosis than during the twelve months of 1913! (*Shouts of "Stop it! Stop it! Infamy!"*)

PSYCHIATRIST: You see, gentlemen, what condition this man is in. I thank our esteemed colleague Boas and will now call on our colleague Zuntz to undertake an experiment. I ask him to give his opinion on whether the German fitness to work, that most precious national asset, has suffered even in the minutest way as a result of nutrition.

PROFESSOR ZUNTZ: A reduction in the fitness to work, attributable to present nutrition, is out of the question. It is true that malnutrition has been brought about in wide circles of the population through the fact that the people don't like to ingest sufficient amounts of the less-concentrated vegetable foodstuffs.

PSYCHIATRIST: If I understand our esteemed colleague correctly, the population has itself to blame, for objectively there is no cause for malnutrition.

PROFESSOR ZUNTZ: No, there is none.

PSYCHIATRIST: But malnutrition, insofar as it is brought about or, let us say, if it is brought about at all, has no adverse consequences?

PROFESSOR ZUNTZ: None.

PSYCHIATRIST (*to the Mental Patient*): To this you have probably no answer?

MENTAL PATIENT: No, I don't.

PSYCHIATRIST: He has something insolent to say about everything, but here he is startled and holds his tongue! I thank our esteemed colleague Zuntz and now call on Rosenfeld-Breslau, whom it is our honor to welcome as the guest of the Berlin faculty, to undertake a test.

PROFESSOR ROSENFELD-BRESLAU: With all the malnutrition, our population has become healthier, and the great fear concerning the effects of malnutrition has proven to be unfounded. On the contrary: overeating in peacetime represents a greater danger to life than the food restrictions of the war years. Statistics have shown that almost all illnesses among the female population have resulted in fewer deaths during the war years than in peacetime. In any event, we can sum up our observations to the effect that wartime nutrition has not in any discernible measure reduced the people's resistance to the overwhelming majority of diseases, to illness, and to exertion.

MENTAL PATIENT: Except to the mendacity of professors!

(*Vigorous shouts of indignation.*)

FIRST VOICE: Don't make a nuisance of yourself!

SECOND VOICE: Let's throw him out!

THIRD VOICE: We should get the police here!

CHAIRMAN OF THE SOCIETY OF PHYSICIANS OF GREATER BERLIN: I shall use the occasion of this scandal to raise my voice in a strong appeal. Colleagues: Each of you is the father confessor of your patients, it is your patriotic duty, by word of mouth and through any other form of action, in an enlightening and informative way, to encourage them to stick it out! You must take a most decisive stand against the fainthearted! Reject unfavorable and unfounded rumors that are often spread maliciously or thoughtlessly! We on the home front can, should, and will stick it out! Colleagues! The simple way of life, simpler food, moderation in the ingestion of proteins and fats, has proven conducive to the health of many.

MENTAL PATIENT: To profiteers and to physicians! (*Shouts of "Disgraceful! Out with him!"*)

CHAIRMAN: School physicians have incontestably established—

MENTAL PATIENT: —that Germany has successfully been bombarded with lies! (*Shouts of "For shame!"*)

CHAIRMAN: —that our children do not manifest impairment of health compared with former times!

MENTAL PATIENT: The increase in mortality amounts to only thirty-seven percent! (*Shouts of "Shut up! The man without a fatherland!"*)

CHAIRMAN: Infant mortality has declined. Only recently a leading authority has showed that the newborn have never done so well as now. (*Shouts of "That is correct!"*) The hospitals are less crowded than they were in the past.

MENTAL PATIENT: Because all are dead! (*Uproar.*)

VOICE: The fellow should prove that!

MENTAL PATIENT: The reports of many institutional physicians have a desperate ring when they describe the hunger of the inmates who try to devour thrown-away cabbage stalks and all sorts of indigestible refuse just in order to relieve their hunger pangs. A report requisitioned from a hospital reads laconically: All the inmates have died. —But those who are alive and assembled here have been ordered to issue expert opinions and will find the courage to speak the truth only after the unavoidable collapse of the lies, and of the Reich. But then it will be too late, and no confession will spare them the contempt of the rest of the world. For German science is a prostitute. Our men of science are its pimps! Those assembled here in order to deny—in the service of the General Staff's great lie—the dying of children and to make black look white bear a greater burden of blood guilt than those whose hands are bloody. Those ninety-three intellectuals who cried out "It is not true!" and "We protest!" opened the door to impassioned lies with their protest against attacks on German honor; and those who joined their ranks have drawn German culture even further away from Goethe and Kant and all good spirits of Germany than those romantic arsonists who forced them to lie.

(*Tremendous uproar. Shouts are heard of "It is not true!" and "We protest!" Several of the Professors are about to assault the Mental Patient but are held back by others.*)

PSYCHIATRIST: Gentlemen! We have just witnessed the most violent outburst of hatred of our fatherland, one that cannot possibly have grown on German soil. The patient's reaction to the experiments of our esteemed colleagues, Boas, Zuntz, and Rosenfeld-Breslau, and in particular, to the substantive and pellucid presentation of the esteemed Chairman of the Society of Physicians of Greater Berlin—for which I have to thank our esteemed colleague most warmly—has clearly proven to me that this man is not mentally disturbed but rather that he is in the pay of the Allies.

We are dealing here with an acute case of Northcliffe propaganda, the prevention of whose chronic dissemination is a special obligation of the medical profession of Greater Berlin. Even now the poison of pacifism has penetrated healthy brains, and the exaggerated idealism of the opponents to war encourages weaklings and draft dodgers to assume attitudes that must be seen as one of the worst evils from which the German national body suffers. If this is coupled with criminal propaganda, a condition is soon created that is apt to paralyze our initiative at a moment when ultimate victory is in sight. It is the spirit of defeatism that strengthens the enemy's backbone and lames our wings in a defensive war that has been forced upon us by

British envy (*a voice in the audience: "The British spirit of shopkeepers!"*), French thirst for revenge (*a voice in the audience: "And Russian rapacity!"*), and Russian rapacity.

Here for once we have a typical case before us. I cannot but emphasize that the man looked suspicious to me from the outset, and I have now come to the conclusion that we are dealing here with a real criminal. No mental patient speaks that way, gentlemen; he talks like a criminal enemy of the fatherland! I am in a position, gentlemen, to disclose, furthermore, that the man, through his unrepenting attitude during his protective custody, when he continued his outrageous attacks on everything that is sacred to us Germans and indeed allowed himself to be carried away to the point of speaking disapprovingly about the Wolff News Agency (*unrest*)—aroused the attention of the highest circles and that a personage venerable to all of us (*the audience rises*), our Crown Prince, voiced his opinion that this fellow should be punched in the nose. (*Shouts of "Hurrah!"*) It will depend on the decision of the respective highest authority as to whether such a remedy can be put to use, a remedy that possibly could be taken under advisement as an intensification of his punishment. It is incumbent upon us, gentlemen, to declare this matter outside of our province, since medical science has nothing to do with this case, and to refer the man to the care of the appropriate criminal agencies. (*Opens the door and calls.*) Officer!

POLICEMAN BUDDICKE (*entering*): In the name of the law—okay, come along now.

(*Exit with Mental Patient. The assembled physicians rise and intone "The Watch on the Rhine."*)

(*Scene change.*)

SCENE 11

A divisional command.

COMMANDER: Your Excellency, because of inadequate artillery support, this operation was hopeless. It was almost like target practice for the enemy to hit the pontoons we let down and their crews. Hundreds of bodies sank in the San that day, and then we had to give up the drive to cross the river anyway. We're facing the same situation now.

KAISERJÄGERTOD:[*] You must hold your ground at any cost.

COMMANDER: Your Excellency, the troops are freezing to death in trenches filled with icy ground water.

KAISERJÄGERTOD: How high do you estimate your probable losses?

COMMANDER: Four thousand.

KAISERJÄGERTOD: Your orders are to sacrifice the troops.

COMMANDER: When they come out of there, they'll be wading knee-deep in snow, and in addition, they are supposed to attack a superior enemy position.

KAISERJÄGERTOD: My God, don't you have any chaplain who could fire up the morale of the men? The offensive must not be delayed under any circumstances.

COMMANDER: Your Excellency, there's so much snow on the ground that a whole regiment will be wiped out.

KAISERJÄGERTOD: One regiment? What do I care about one regiment?

COMMANDER: These men are standing with empty bellies up

---

[*] Based on the name of the Kaiser Jäger Regiment; the added syllable means "death."

to here in water! They're fighting desperately against the powerful, uninterrupted assaults of the Russians.

(*Kaiserjägertod is called to the telephone.*)

KAISERJÄGERTOD: What? Relief or reinforcements? Colonel, you have to stand your ground to the last man; I have no troops at my disposal, and the word retreat doesn't exist for me, cost what it may! What? They want a day's rest to dry their clothes? What are you saying? Your poor brave Tyroleans are lying out there, shot to death and floating in the water? (*Bellowing.*) They're there to be shot! Period! —That's it, and I have nothing else to say to you. The troops absolutely must stick it out in their positions, my career is at stake! (*Exit.*)

MAJOR (*to the Commander*): There's nothing you can do, sir, His Excellency usually sends his crack troops in for the most difficult assignments exactly because of their outstanding qualities. His Excellency is an extremely energetic, purposeful, impulsive general who, himself brave and sternly demanding, requires unquestioning sacrifice from his subordinates.

(*Scene change.*)

SCENE 20

Sofia. A banquet for German and Bulgarian editors.

GERMAN AMBASSADOR COUNT OBERNDORFF (*rising*): Honored guests! Every time I find myself in this house, with the black, white, and red banner flying overhead, I delight in being fortunate enough to see German and Bulgarian friends united for a congenial exchange of ideas. But today I am especially delighted. For, esteemed gentlemen of the German and Bulgarian press—allow me to welcome you as colleagues.

SHOUTS: Bravo! Three cheers for our colleague!

GERMAN AMBASSADOR: Yes, even though we may find fault with one another now and then, as can happen among fellow professionals, diplomacy and the press are closely linked together.

SHOUTS: Bravo! Bravo!

GERMAN AMBASSADOR: There is no good journalist without diplomatic sensibility, and no competent diplomat who has not been anointed for his profession with a good thick drop of printer's ink.

SHOUTS: Splendid!

GERMAN AMBASSADOR: I say profession: the word is too modest. It is an art, a high art, which we practice, and the instrument upon which we play is the noblest imaginable, it is the peoples' soul!

SHOUTS: So it is!

GERMAN AMBASSADOR: What can be achieved by the united efforts of diplomacy and the press has been demonstrated by this world war.

SHOUTS: Yes, sir!

GERMAN AMBASSADOR: We should learn from the enemy. If we let the Allied diplomatic celebrities file past the mind's eye and hear names such as the *Times* and *Reuters, Le Matin, Havas, Novoye Vremya*, not to mention the minor satellites in Rome, Bucharest, and Belgrade, then we have to admit that here we are dealing with the appearance of a coalition which can point to successes. Successes in falsification and stultification.

SHOUTS: So it is!

GERMAN AMBASSADOR: Hate and rage such as the world has never seen before. Yes, it is a powerful coalition, and fearful to observe, yet it is only an artificially inflated colossus that will one day surely burst. For it lacks that life-giving, sustaining spirit—truth. And truth fights on our side.
SHOUTS: Right you are!
GERMAN AMBASSADOR: Gentlemen of the Bulgarian and German press! We are fighting with truth as a weapon and in defense of truth, in the proud realization that every success achieved by truth also signifies a success for our common cause. Yes, on that day when the mote finally falls from the eyes of those peoples who are being driven into a futile struggle against us, on that day when they recognize how strong our position is—
SHOUTS: Hurrah!
GERMAN AMBASSADOR: —how invincibly fortified both from within and from without, on that day the war will end! (*Takes his seat. General clinking of glasses.*)
SHOUTS: Hurrah! To your health! —To the Count!
KLEINECKE-BERLIN: Appears to me, my friend, that our Balkan cousins are sitting on their hands. Have you noticed, no lifted voices—!
STEINECKE-HANOVER: Didn't escape me. Oh, well, so what? Oberndorff was splendid.
KLEINECKE-BERLIN: One telling point after another. The man has indeed been anointed with a good thick drop of printer's ink.
STEINECKE-HANOVER: The man is one of the best speakers we've got right now. Truth fights on our side—how simple, unpretentious, and true at the same time!
KLEINECKE-BERLIN: Yes, ever since the day that we could report that French airmen had dropped bombs on Nuremberg. That was the beginning.

STEINECKE-HANOVER: Yes, ever since then we've been at war with the lies of our enemies.

KLEINECKE-BERLIN: What can be achieved by the united efforts of diplomacy and the press has been demonstrated by this war, which British envy, French thirst for revenge, and Russian rapacity have forced upon us. Golden words.

STEINECKE-HANOVER: That reminds me of the pertinent words of one of our great colleagues. How did Ernst Posse put it? The war has revealed what power the modern newsman holds in his hands. Just imagine, if you can, Ernst Posse says, what it would be like if the newspapers disappeared from this international emotional upheaval. Without them, would the war have been at all possible—either in its initial causes or in its realization?

KLEINECKE-BERLIN: How true! Ernst Posse even leaves diplomacy out of it.

STEINECKE-HANOVER: He just speaks as a journalist. Oberndorff is a diplomat, and therefore he gives the press its due.

(*Scene change.*)

SCENE 22

In the Wahnschaffes' parlor.

FRAU POGATSCHNIGG: Well, I can only say that "Hero's Grave in the House" has found very wide acceptance among us Austrians and everyone is enthusiastic.

FRAU WAHNSCHAFFE (*modestly disclaiming the praise*): Oh, but that was only for the dead. But now my husband has invented "Hero's Pillow," the most beautiful gift for our fighting men when they come home to rest up from their deeds. It includes: (1) The meaningful salutation: Victorious Warrior. (2) The Iron Cross. (3) The name of the soldier, encircled by an oak wreath as a symbol of German strength. (4) Miniature German and Austrian flags as a sign of allied loyalty—

FRAU POGATSCHNIGG: Splendid!

FRAU WAHNSCHAFFE: (5) Welcome home! Three marks fifty.

FRAU POGATSCHNIGG: Reasonable. What do you in the Reich have new in children's books and games?

FRAU WAHNSCHAFFE: *We Play World War*, a timely picture book for our little ones. Well, and among children's games as such—well, the forty-two-centimeter buzz bomb, but that's actually from you—wait—oh yes, do you know Dividing up the Booty?

FRAU POGATSCHNIGG: Yes, but we're not particularly satisfied with that; I don't really know why.

FRAU WAHNSCHAFFE: Oh, but it's an enchanting game. My youngsters are overjoyed with it. Yes, for us Germans, the best—

FRAU POGATSCHNIGG: —is just good enough. We in our turn now have Russian Death, something really first-rate.

FRAU WAHNSCHAFFE: That must be nice.

FRAU POGATSCHNIGG: Russian Death, an ingenious invention by Countess Taaffe, is an interesting game of patience for old and young, manufactured by the wounded at the Red Cross Hospital in the old section of Prague Kleinseite, where the Countess, good samaritan that she is, acts as head nurse. In a very tastefully made-up Easter egg, a miniature fortification is represented, complete with barbed-wire barriers and a swamp, in addition to our soldiers and Russian soldiers in battle. The object is, by shaking the egg, to get our men into the fortress and to drive the Russians into the swamp.

Act IV, Scene 22 149

FRAU WAHNSCHAFFE: Serves them right.

FRAU POGATSCHNIGG: Russian Death constitutes a suitable Easter gift not only for young people but also for soldiers in the hospitals, for whom it offers pleasant distraction and exciting entertainment. The Russian Death Easter egg, in very tasteful black-and-gold silk packaging, costs three kronen sixty and is available from the Central Sales Office of the Wartime Social Service Bureau in Prague.

FRAU WAHNSCHAFFE: How lovely. And how nicely that highborn good samaritan took the taste of the wounded into consideration. Yes, the Austrian nobility! Even I must admit that in spite of all their sluggishness, they still have more grace than our German nobility. How did you say that is played, dear Frau Pogatschnigg—you shake the egg and our brave boys must get into the fortress and the Russians into the swamp! That's really very simple.

FRAU POGATSCHNIGG: Since this invention, society people have paid homage to the Countess. And you in the Reich—don't you have anything like that?

FRAU WAHNSCHAFFE: Well, I really shouldn't praise what Wahnschaffe makes—self-praise, you know—but I can't help recommending most warmly to you the new war-game top. This new game should be in every German home, for it affords exciting entertainment to young and old—in every family, in every social gathering, at every occasion. First, each player puts his stake in the bank. Then the top is spun by each player in turn. The letters and numbers mean the following: *R. w. O*: Russia—wins nothing. *E. l. 1/1*: England—loses the whole stake. *F. l. 1/2*: France—loses half the stake. *T. w. 1/3*: Turkey—wins a third of the cash. *A. w. 1/2*: Austria—wins half the cash. *G. w. a.*: Deutschland über alles—Germany wins the whole bank.

FRAU POGATSCHNIGG: Bravo! But if Austria wins half the bank,

can Germany then take all? Does Germany then take also—
FRAU WAHNSCHAFFE: Well now, that's the kind of thing you Austrians don't like—that's the thanks we get for having pulled you out of the mud so often! In the recent offensive you have once again happily mis-succeeded.
FRAU POGATSCHNIGG (*shaking her hand*): You've convinced me. To be sure, Austria only wins half the bank, but, nevertheless—I *am* a German housewife!

(*They leave shoulder to shoulder, singing "Deutschland, Deutschland über alles."*)

(*Scene change.*)

SCENE 24

The Subscriber and the Patriot conversing.

PATRIOT: What do you say to the way the attempted mutiny of three—I say three—German sailors has been exaggerated in enemy countries?
SUBSCRIBER: There's only one answer to that: a great mutiny in the English fleet.
PATRIOT: Where? How come?
SUBSCRIBER: In Spithead in the Nore.
PATRIOT: What? You don't say. There was a mutiny?
SUBSCRIBER: And what a mutiny! Mutiny is not the word for it! The mutiny seized almost the entire fleet of Admiral Duncan. The mutineers blocked the Thames with twenty-six warships.
PATRIOT: Stop, where does it say that—what kind of a mutiny was it?

SUBSCRIBER: The mutiny appeared to be the precursor of a revolution.
PATRIOT: You don't say! What kind of revolution, what kind of mutiny?
SUBSCRIBER: What kind of mutiny? The mutiny of which the esteemed letter writer reminds us!
PATRIOT: Yes, right—but when was that?
SUBSCRIBER: Within the last few years.
PATRIOT: But we never heard anything about it. Now it comes out? Tell me, I ask you, when was this?
SUBSCRIBER: 1797.

(*Scene change.*)

SCENE 28

A movie theater. On the program: "Oh, Amalia, What Have You Done?" and the hit detective film "I Track Down Everybody." The song "Little Dolly, Light of My Eyes" is playing.

MOVIE-THEATER MANAGER (*stepping forward*): There will now follow the first showing of the great film made of the Battle of the Somme. In this film you will get to see the heroes of the Somme, the flower of our youth running forward, side by side with gray-haired men, weatherbeaten and steeled in battle, falling to the ground yet attacking fiercely, fighting between licking flames and the hail of bullets, over shaking ground pulverized by mines, in the all-crushing forge of this howling war. In three parts, scenes of that fearsome battle of fall 1916, unroll before your eyes, that battle with which the enemy's great hope sank into its grave. The tread of innumerable German reservists rumbles impressively. Under fire from their own countrymen, German soldiers gently bring French women, old people, and children to safety. Where once flourishing villages beckoned, where ancient, picturesque cities delighted the eye with their historic beauty—Bapaume and Peronne and whatever they're all called—are now piles of rubble, shattered into debris and dust by the artillery of the Allies. And then, thanks to the unique courage of brave cameramen, four of whom met a hero's death while loyally carrying out their duty during the filming of this sequence, you shall behold in flickering moving pictures a sublime example of purposeful, precise efficiency: "The divisional command has ordered the blasting and assault at 8:30 hours!" —Everything is ready. —The assault troops are in a frenzy. The monsters, the machines of modern warfare, open their blazing muzzles; the most fearful weapons of our technical age swing into action—but behind them stand the human bodies that breathe life into the inanimate machines. Over mine fields and obstacles, through byways of death pregnant with explosives, onward into the heat of close combat! —Hand grenades are cutting them down! —From trench to trench, onward into the enemy main position! Our own artillery draws breath and sprays horror into the enemy reserves; trench after trench is taken. This film ranks with the most beautiful, among the most impressive of the present war.

FEMALE VOICE: Emil, keep your hands to yourself!

(*Scene change.*)

SCENE 29

The Optimist and the Grumbler conversing.

OPTIMIST: So, you've got yourself all worked up about those harmless parodies on Goethe's "Over All Hilltops Is Rest" that are so much in vogue with us and in Germany.

GRUMBLER: I certainly have. To war verse we can reconcile ourselves. As today's beast genially reaches out for death-dealing machinery, he also reaches out for verse in order to glorify it. If nothing else were claimed in Germany's favor but that this poem grew out of its soil, the nation's true prestige will emerge inviolate. After all, this counts more than those transitory prejudices for the buttressing of which wars are waged. Where in all the world could anyone have so little reverence as to mockingly convert the ultimate, deepest breath of a poet into this disgusting claptrap? The debauchery of the idea surpasses every degree of dehumanization that the intellectual home front of this war has produced—it represents the triumph of that trend first initiated by printing on toilet paper quotations from the classics.

OPTIMIST: Do you really believe the war was decided upon by a few wicked men?

GRUMBLER: No, they were only the tools of the demon who led us, and, through us, Christian civilization, into ruin, but we have to hold them responsible, since we cannot seize the demon by whom we are branded. Whatever may happen, to be Austrian was unbearable.

OPTIMIST: The Austro-Hungarian monarchy is an historical necessity.

GRUMBLER: Maybe, because this whole rubbishy conglomeration of ethnic strife that has brought us to cultural ignominy and economic misery has to be preserved in some accursed corner of the earth. But all the revolutions and wars aiming at getting rid of it will diminish this necessity. And if they don't succeed this time, if the Austrian monarchical idea proves itself to be ineradicable for the time being, then there will be new wars. Just for reasons of prestige, this monarchy should have committed suicide a long time ago.

OPTIMIST: If Emperor Franz Josef had been granted a longer life, unity—

GRUMBLER: A reverential shudder makes me shrink in the face of the consequences of this thought before you finished thinking it. You fail to see, as a matter of fact, that a rather long life has been granted him and that nevertheless—

OPTIMIST: But the Emperor died last year—

GRUMBLER: How do you know?

OPTIMIST: I don't understand you—he lived up to—

GRUMBLER: How do you know?

OPTIMIST: Are you alluding perhaps to the joke so popular among the Allies, that in Austria-Hungary a breed of emperors is maintained that always look alike?

GRUMBLER: There may be something to it. You know, even if I could decide to believe in the death of Franz Josef, never could I believe that he ever lived.

OPTIMIST: You can't say that. Can you deny those seventy years?

GRUMBLER: Not at all. They are a nightmare of an evil spirit which, in return for extracting all our life juices, and then our life and property also, let us have as a happy gift the opportunity to become completely idiotic by worshiping an emperor's beard as an idol. Never before in world history has a stronger non-personality impressed his stamp on all things and forms. A demon of mediocrity has determined our fate. Only he insisted on Austria's right to trouble the world with our murderous nationality brawls, a right grounded in the God-ordained bureaucratic muddle under the Hapsburg scepter, the mission of which, it appears, has been to hover above world peace like Damocles' sword.

OPTIMIST: What? The Emperor of peace, in the truest sense, who, in his proverbial affability, has done everything for children, the knightly monarch, the kind-hearted old gentleman in Schönbrunn, who was spared nothing—is this the way you talk about him, and to top it off, now that he is dead?

GRUMBLER: Oh, he's dead? Well, aside from the fact that, even if I knew it, I wouldn't believe it, I must tell you plainly that at the Last Judgment there are absolutely no special privileges, for once there is no political pull and, for that matter, no piety; one can definitely not fix things there, and above all, there death is not an exemption from punishment but rather a prerequisite for sentencing. I would also like to believe that it is more pleasing to God to show veneration for the majesty of death at the graves of ten million youths and men, and hundreds of thousands of women and infants who had to die of hunger, than to bow down before that one casket in the Capuchins' Crypt, that very casket that entombs the old man who considered everything carefully and, with a single scratch of the pen, brought it all about. One day this cipher who was spared nothing, and just for this reason didn't want to spare the world anything—just to spite them, one day decided on the death of the world.

OPTIMIST: But surely you don't believe that the Emperor wanted the war? He is even said to have stated that he was tricked into it!

GRUMBLER: That's right. Such things happen. I am not thinking of the Emperor who could be tricked into it but of the madness of this world of monarchs that made it possible for him and us to be tricked into this holocaust. He preferred to put an absolute end to his wretched royal-imperial world through the war and our inevitable defeat.

OPTIMIST: But after all, you wouldn't question the monarch's personal qualities—

GRUMBLER: They are of little interest to me. He was probably merely a pedant, not a tyrant, merely cold, not cruel. Had he been that, perhaps even at his advanced age he might have had enough strength of mind not to let himself be tricked, but to know what he could risk. He was an untiring worker and, once, among all the death warrants, he signed one that cut down mankind. He, who was tricked into it, had considered everything carefully. It's simply genuinely Austrian tough luck that the ogre destined to bring about this catastrophe wore the features of a kindhearted old gentleman. He had considered everything carefully, but he can't be blamed for it: and that precisely is the ultimate, cruelest tragedy he was not spared. I've made a song out of it all, one that is as long as his life, an unending melody that I've given him to sing when he steps onto the stage in my world-war drama. I wrote this tragic litany as I did a major part of the drama in the year 1915, that is, while he was still alive.

OPTIMIST: When will your drama appear?

GRUMBLER: When the enemy has been vanquished.

OPTIMIST: What? Then you do believe—

GRUMBLER: —that in a year Austria will have ceased to exist! I had taken the manuscript to the ancestral homeland of the Hapsburgs, to Switzerland—

OPTIMIST: In order to keep it safe?

GRUMBLER: No, in order to work on it. I brought it back again, for I have no fear of the enemy. He has allowed such a muddle to spread in his bloody business that I was able to take this manuscript back and forth over the border twice.

Nevertheless, it can't appear right now. That would undoubtedly cost the author his freedom, and, if our bevy of generals were to work up an appetite for dictatorship before the close of the performance, it might even cost him the head he has managed to preserve despite the assaults of imbecility that have accompanied four years of war. The play will appear when the glorious mischief is over, the mischief that, during the very hour in which we are speaking here, has transformed thousands of human beings into corpses or cripples, and all for nothing, nothing whatsoever. In short, when Schalek has spoken her last word.

OPTIMIST: What do you have against Frau Schalek?

GRUMBLER: Nothing, except that the war makes me overestimate her. Thus, I have to take her for the most peculiar phenomenon of this apocalypse. But when the intoxication of the tragic carnival has worn off, and, in the middle of the morning-after hangover, I happen to meet her somewhere behind the lines, I will believe her to be a woman.

OPTIMIST: You do have an unholy ability for overestimating the most insignificant—

GRUMBLER: Indeed, I do have.

OPTIMIST: And the whole drama has probably evolved from this very trait, from this morbid tendency to link minute phenomena to great events.

GRUMBLER: Quite in keeping with the satanic disaster that has led us from minute events to the immense phenomena of the actual tragedy. You will probably not be remiss in asking me what I have against Benedikt.

OPTIMIST: Nor you in answering.

GRUMBLER: He is only a newspaper publisher, and yet he triumphs over our intellectual and moral honor.

OPTIMIST: To understand this, I'll have to wait for your tragedy. It will be published then—

GRUMBLER: —when the other one is over. Before that it isn't

possible. Also, it isn't completed yet, and so I do need my head.

OPTIMIST: Surely only your freedom would be in jeopardy.

GRUMBLER: As long as Vienna is not a battleground. High treason, abusive charges against speculators in dehydrated vegetables, Archduke Friedrich, and other royal personalities, who can only be the object but never the subject of a crime, and whose profiteering is protected by the lèse majesty section of the penal code—well, after all, the most majestic power in Austria is still the gallows. Only consider that under the supreme army command of Archduke Friedrich alone—I consider him a still more fertile phenomenon than the Schalek woman—11,400 gallows were erected, according to another version, 36,000. And to think that he can't even count up to three.

OPTIMIST: Someday it will be said of you, that a bird—

GRUMBLER: —who tears down his own nest instead of building a stranger's, I know, I know. One would undoubtedly hit the bird on the head with that notion. But unjustly, since he was simply fulfilling his moral obligation to sweep up in front of his own doorway. This filthy world would like to think that the fellow who clears away the filth is responsible for having dumped it there in the first place. My patriotism—quite a different sort from that of patriots—couldn't bear to relinquish this work to an enemy satirist. This has determined my posture throughout the war. I would advise any English satirist, who justifiably found us impossible, to employ his satirical endeavors to affairs of his own country.

OPTIMIST: If you had your way, Austria would have been sentenced to death a long time ago.

GRUMBLER: Unfortunately, that won't happen until she has sentenced the Austrians to death, and not a bit sooner. Right now I am thinking of those Austrians who are still alive and who, because they are subjects of the monarchy, are going to meet a fate which, as a people, they have not deserved. For others, those who resisted the consequences of citizenship or in many cases didn't even go that far—Austria saw to it that their death penalty was carried out before her collapse.

OPTIMIST: And do you believe that similar things have not happened among our enemies? The English have executed those guilty of high treason, too. Think of Casement.

GRUMBLER: I don't happen to have a picture postcard of his execution. Casement was condemned to death by a court of law and then shot; Battisti* was disposed of more summarily. They simply caught and hanged him—to be sure, after forcing him, by way of intensifying the death penalty, to stand at attention to listen to the playing of the national anthem. Aside from all that, at the execution of Casement, which England didn't celebrate as though it were part of a country fair, official photographers were not called in. Pictures that immortalize not only a gallows procedure but also its bestial helpers, pictures that show a beaming hangman encircled by cheerful, even transfigured-looking, officers, could hardly be obtained even in the homeland of black English subjects. I would like to offer an award for the identification of that monstrous clod of a first lieutenant who placed himself directly in front of a hanging corpse and offered his vacuous visage to the photographers, and also for the identification of those low-down coxcombs gathering there, cheerful as if at the Sirk Corner, or rushing by with their Kodaks in order to get into the picture, not only as observers, but in the pose of photographing. And naturally, a father confessor, the so-called spiritual adviser, has to be part of the circle of a hundred expectant participants. For there was not only a hanging, there was also a

---

* Cesar Battisti, who was executed by the Austrians for being an Italian irredentist in South Tyrol.

show; and they photographed not only the executions, but also the observers and the photographers as well. And the special result of our bestiality is then that the enemy propaganda did not need to lie, but only reproduce the truth we provided them with; it didn't even need to photograph our deeds because, to its surprise, it found our own photograph of our deeds at the place of our crime. Thus, we, as a whole, in all our ingenuousness—we did not sense that no crime could so expose us before the world as did our triumphant confession. Ours was like the pride of a criminal who even lets himself be photographed in the act, assuming a friendly expression because he feels such tremendous joy at being caught red-handed. It is not the fact that he had killed, nor that he took a picture of the act, but that he managed to get into the picture himself and that he took pictures of himself taking pictures—that makes his like the imperishable photograph of our culture.

OPTIMIST: But surely Emperor Franz Josef knew nothing about all that.

GRUMBLER: He simply knew that since time immemorial his hangmen have represented the ultimate, the only authentic bastion of central power.

OPTIMIST: He, as a knightly monarch—

GRUMBLER: —had already in his youth turned away the delegation of mothers, wives, and daughters from Mantua who had come, like pilgrims in their mourning clothes, to beg reprieve from the gallows tree for their sons, husbands, and fathers, but afterward had to pay the hangman's fee. To this day that region remembers Austria. Austria itself will have to pay its last hangman's fee.

OPTIMIST: How so? When?

GRUMBLER: After its own execution!

(*Scene change.*)

SCENE 30

A *court-martial.*

MILITARY JUDGE STANISLAUS VON ZAGORSKI (*pronouncing the verdict. One hears the following sentences, which he particularly accentuates*):
—With regard to the fact that the accused Hryb is twenty-six years old and unable to read and write, thus has no education, and whereas, in light of the fact that the guilt of the accused Hryb appears to the military court to be the least severe when compared to the guilt of his codefendants, the court-martial has resolved that the accused Hryb shall be the first to suffer the death penalty imposed upon him in compliance with Army Regulations Article 444.
—The accused Struk shall be the second to suffer the death penalty imposed upon him because, in relationship to the guilt of the first defendant, his guilt is more flagrant.
—In consideration of the fact that the accused Maeyjiczyn has been in contact with the Russians for a protracted period of time, it was the decision of the court that he be the third to suffer the death penalty.
—In the same decision, the court, in weighing the crime with which this indicted man is charged, pronounced that he shall be the fourth in line to suffer the death penalty.
—The accused Dzus shall, in compliance with Army Regulations Article 444, be the fifth to suffer the penalty imposed upon him because his perjured defense indicated that he was fully devoted to the Russians.
—and shall be the sixth to suffer the penalty according to the assessment of his course of action.

—The accused Kowal shall be the seventh to suffer the death penalty.
—Since Fedynyczyn has been charged with two punishable offenses, he shall be the eighth to suffer the death penalty.
—In consideration of the seriousness of the deed with which Fedor Budz has been charged, he shall be the ninth to suffer the penalty.
—Petro Dzus, in consideration of the severity of his offense, shall be the tenth to suffer the penalty imposed upon him.
—the military court has decided that his guilt is the greatest, and that therefore he shall be the last to suffer the death penalty. The court is adjourned.

(*The convicted men are led out.*)

FIRST OFFICER: Congratulations. That was juicy. One just senses right away that you're a lawyer. Say, how many death sentences do you actually have behind you?

ZAGORSKI: There were exactly one hundred—so this makes the hundred and tenth.

SEVERAL OFFICERS: Congratulations! That calls for a celebration! Why didn't you say so?

ZAGORSKI: Thank you, thank you! And I have personally attended each execution; I can say that with pride. And how often have I assisted at the implementation of death sentences imposed by other judges!

SECOND OFFICER: But you are overexerting yourself! You are much too conscientious.

ZAGORSKI: Yes, it is a grueling job!

FIRST: You can see that he studied law; this work's not just nothing—

ZAGORSKI: No indeed, a death sentence must be painstakingly substantiated—it is not a pleasure.

SECOND: By golly, we had some trouble on this before, with

the colonel! He was a sworn enemy of court-martials. He always said it was pigheaded judicial sophistry. Simply cut them down, that's what he said.

FIRST: Well, you know that's nothing compared to Ljubicic, when I was in the eleventh corps. He was under Wild; as I remember, in 1914, between Christmas and New Year's Day, Wild had twelve men, political suspects, hanged, six on one day alone. He said that he did not need any legal verdict. He also had quite a few bayoneted.

SECOND: And then there's Lüttgendorff! He also always said he didn't need any court: instead, he said, he had a shortened procedure. Once he had a corporal bayonet three fellows because they were drunk. That was in Schabatz, on His Majesty's birthday; I remember it as if it happened today. There were beautiful bastinadoes and lovely evacuations. And the fires we set, they were really great! You know that time in Syrmia, how they burned down every other house! That time he wanted to set an example, so they picked a village to be wholly wiped out, you know, with pregnant women and so on; they all had to walk all the way to Peterwardein. Whether or not they massacred them all afterward, I don't know. At any rate, the ones who weren't killed—that is, relatives and others who were spared—had to spend the night with those who had been massacred. You know, the Hungarian rural-police sergeants and the commanders of the raiding parties have always liked to streamline disciplinary procedures: they left them all lying, the corpses of the teachers, clergy, village notaries, foresters, and all the rest.

FIRST: Have you ever had a Nazarene?

SECOND: What's that? There's no such thing any more!

FIRST: Yes, there is. Nazarenes, you know, are the fellows who, for religious reasons, refuse to carry a rifle. Well, you know the story. I had a fellow like that once; he was a farmer and was used as a driver. His previous conduct had been good. So, according to his conduct record, he was above reproach, and, except for the fact that he didn't want to carry a rifle in the lineup, there was actually nothing to charge him with. It was simply that by the way he stood there in front of us, he made a highly unfavorable impression on me. In fact, when he already knew that he was going to be sentenced to death, he explained—but, you know, without showing the least repentance—he simply explained that he wouldn't carry a gun even if he'd be shot for not doing so. So with such stubborness there were naturally no circumstances permitting clemency. Well, Stöger-Steiner authorized it, naturally, because of the highly unfavorable impression the man made.

ZAGORSKI: My most interesting case was in Munkacs; that was in the fall of 1914—we still believed in the war with heart and soul. There were three Galician deserters—a pastor, Roman Beresowszkyi, a certain Leo Koblanskyi, and Ssemen Zhabjak—whom I of course sentenced to death and then set up the execution—

SECOND: Did you arrange that one so nicely too—in proper sequence—?

ZAGORSKI: Not at all. They could all three read and write, and aside from that, they were all equally guilty—that is, if one wants to be exact, they were all innocent.

FIRST: Innocent—they were! How so?

ZAGORSKI: Yes, that's exactly what made it so interesting. The case was taken up again by the military court in Stry, and there it turned out that they were innocent.

OFFICERS: What tough luck.

ZAGORSKI (*laughing*): How so? The Ukrainian National Diet registered a complaint about me with the military supreme command! Well, you can just imagine—

First: Oh, I see! What were you at the time?
Zagorski: First lieutenant.
First: And when did you become a captain?
Zagorski: Well, when it turned out that they were innocent!
Second: You believe then that there was a direct relationship —that they wanted you to get it as a kind of satisfaction?
Zagorski: I wouldn't exactly want to maintain that, they're not that sensitive at headquarters—but the complaint did call their attention to me, and then they saw what sort of worker I was. Well, and then—if a politically suspect nation complains about one of us! You understand, if a Ruthenian can hurt us, he doesn't hurt us by his complaints, but at most by just being still alive.
Third: So do you believe after all that the eleven that we sentenced today were also innocent? Because if one wants to be exact, it was actually only proved—
Zagorski: —that they are Ruthenians. Well that will be sufficient! It's one o'clock—let's go to the mess hall.

(*Scene change.*)

SCENE 32

Kragujevac, military court.

Presiding Military Judge (*calling out*): Let them go hang! (*To the clerk.*) Have you made a fair copy of the three death sentences? I mean the ones for the three young fellows from Karlova who had guns.
Clerk: Yes, but (*hesitating*)—here—I would like to call at-

tention to something here—I've made the discovery—that they are only eighteen years old—

PRESIDING MILITARY JUDGE: Well, and—? What are you trying to say?

CLERK: Yes—but then according to the military criminal code—they may not be executed—in that case—the sentence—must be altered to imprisonment at hard labor—

PRESIDING MILITARY JUDGE: Give it to me! (*He reads.*) Hmm. We won't change the sentence, we'll fix the ages. They're strapping young fellows anyway. (*He dips his pen in the ink.*) We'll just write twenty-one here instead of eighteen. (*He writes.*) So, now we can hang them in good conscience.

(*Scene change.*)

SCENE 34

A police station.

DETECTIVE: Well, here's another one of those syphilitic little sluts. And is she full of lice!

PATROLMAN: Her I know. She did some time for petty larceny and she was also brought in for vagrancy. They've already had her at the clinic.

DETECTIVE: How old are you? Where are your folks?

SEVENTEEN-YEAR-OLD: Papa was drafted, and mother died.

DETECTIVE: How long have you been living this kind of life?

SEVENTEEN-YEAR-OLD: Since 1914.

(*Scene change.*)

SCENE 37

German headquarters.

WILHELM II (*to his retinue*): Morning, gentlemen!
GENERALS: Good morning, Your Majesty!
WILHELM II (*assuming a posture, looking up at the ceiling*): Our Lord unquestionably still has something in mind for our German people. We Germans, who still have ideals, should continue working to bring about better times, to fight for justice, fidelity, and morality. We want to live in friendship with our neighbors, but first the victory of German arms must be recognized. The year 1917 with its great battles has demonstrated that the German people have an unfailingly dependable ally, the Lord of the Heavenly Hosts up there. Upon Him they can rely absolutely; without Him nothing would have worked out. We cannot know what still lies ahead of us. But in these last four years, you have all seen how God's will has visibly reigned, punishing treason and rewarding brave perseverance. And from this we can draw the firm confidence that the Lord of the Heavenly Hosts will also stand with us henceforth. If our enemy does not want peace, then we must bring peace to the world with an iron fist and a blazing sword, by smashing the portals of those who do not want peace. God's judgment is on the enemy. Our total victory on the eastern front fills me with deep gratitude. Once again it allows us to experience one of those great moments in which we can reverentially admire God's working in history. (*With raised voice.*) What a turning point, brought about through the Lord's dispensation! The heroic deeds of our troops, the successes of our great field commanders, the admirable accomplishments of the home

front are, in the last analysis, rooted in the moral powers following the categorical imperative, which have been rigorously ingrained in our people. Should the enemy still not have had enough, then, I know, you will— (*The Kaiser makes a military gesture which calls forth grim smiles on the faces of his liegemen.*) The visible collapse of the enemy was God's judgment. We owe our victory not least to the moral and spiritual values which the great sage of Königsberg gave to our people. God continue to help us until final victory!

(*The Kaiser extends his right hand and the generals and officers kiss it, each in turn. During this procedure he utters, in his excitement and amusement, a sound that resembles the howling of a wolf. Excitement makes his face turn red and take on the appearance of a wild boar; the cheeks are puffed up so that the ends of his moustache stand upright at right angles.*)

FIRST GENERAL: Your Majesty is no longer the instrument of God—
WILHELM II (*snorting and sputtering*): Ha—
FIRST GENERAL: —but rather God is the instrument of Your Majesty!
WILHELM II (*beaming*): Well, that's good. Ha—!
SECOND GENERAL: If we break through with the help of both God and poison gas, then we'll have nothing but Your Majesty's ingenious strategic circumspection to thank for it.
WILHELM II (*stepping up to the strategic map*): Ha— From here to here is a distance of fifteen kilometers—there I shall throw fifty divisions! Colossal—don't you think? (*Looks around the room. Approving murmur.*)
THIRD GENERAL: Your Majesty's strategic farsightedness is one of the wonders of the world!

FOURTH GENERAL: Your Majesty is not only the greatest orator, painter, composer, hunter, statesman, sculptor, admiral, poet, sportsman, Assyriologist, businessman, astronomer, and theater director of all time, but also—but also (*He begins to stammer.*)

WILHELM II: Well—?

FOURTH GENERAL: Your Majesty, I simply feel unable to exhaust the list of fields Your Majesty has mastered with such distinction.

(*Scene change.*)

SCENE 39

In the dugout of the company commander Hiller.

JUNIOR MEDICAL OFFICER MUELLER: Froze to death. Attempts at resuscitation unsuccessful. The most disquieting thing about it is that he received no rations.

HILLER: We'll have to cover our tracks carefully so that word of this doesn't get out—

MUELLER: It's fairly obvious that our men are exhausted and sick. They've got nothing but canned soup and the one we have here is injurious to their health. They are obviously suffering from battle fatigue. People are digging around in the snow and jumping about as if possessed.

HILLER: I'll have to admit myself that hunger, beating, and tying men up no longer suffice to fire up their courage to fight. What is to be done? So far as Helmhake is concerned, I can say that I did everything imaginable. I'll write his father the following:

Dear Herr Helmhake: I herewith fulfill my sad duty of informing you of the sudden death of your son, the Guard Fusilier Carl Helmhake. The physician established a bleeding ulcer of the small intestine as the cause of death. During his short illness your son received the best possible physical and medical care. In the deceased we have lost a capable soldier and a good comrade, whose loss we painfully mourn. His last remains have been laid to rest in the cemetery at Dolzki.

(Scene change.)

SCENE 44

Army training camp at Vladimir Volynski.

A CAPTAIN (*dictating to a stenographer*): All personnel are to be informed on three successive days that venereal disease as a form of self-inflicted disability shall result in court-martial proceedings and, in order to give emphasis to this directive, diseased persons shall in every instance be brought before the Army Corps Group Command. In those recent cases which can be proved to have been artificially produced or intentionally contracted, guilty persons are to undergo punishment, with daily flogging to be administered, beginning with five cudgel blows, and to be continued, increasing by one blow a day, until all symptoms of the disease subside. The first flogging is set for two o'clock today and shall involve the following persons. —Here's the list, just copy it. A man from the military police shall be charged with the execution of this order; two strong men from the army corps of engineers shall be placed at his disposal.

(Scene change.)

SCENE 45

Count Dohna-Schlodien, surrounded by twelve Representatives of the Press.

REPRESENTATIVE OF THE PRESS: We deem ourselves fortunate, Count, to receive from the lips of one of our most immortal heroes an authentic account of the glorious voyage of the *Seagull*, a tale our children and our children's children will tell their offspring, a tale that will live on forever.

(They hold their pencils ready.)

DOHNA: Gentlemen, I am a man of action, and a man of few words. You may take down the following essentials. On the basis of the intelligence reports received, I had sketched out a fairly definite plan. And, indeed, on the very first day I had the good fortune of sighting a large steamer. This, as you know, was the steamer *Voltaire*. I let the night go by before I edged near to her.

A VOICE FROM THE GROUP: Bravo!

DOHNA: Later, I was able to put the *Voltaire* out of commission. Thereafter, I cruised the North Atlantic for some ten days, but was unable to sight another ship for the first three days; later, however, I was able to finish off about a ship a day. All the ships carried valuable cargo, part of it war matériel; one of them was carrying twelve hundred horses.

REPRESENTATIVE OF THE PRESS: Real live horses? Twelve hundred horses, Count?

DOHNA: Twelve hundred—! (*He gestures to indicate sinking.*)
REPRESENTATIVES OF THE PRESS (*simultaneously*): Great guns!—Real live horses!—Hurrah!—Record achievement!—Brilliant!

Act V

SCENE 2

The Optimist and the Grumbler conversing.

GRUMBLER:
O gods! Who is't can say: "I am at the worst"?
I am worse than e'er I was
And worse I may be yet: the worst is not
So long as we can say "This is the worst."*
Children whose faces suggest that they've already been starving a lifetime—and still no end! But the worst is contained in this report on a mental asylum. One fellow sits there in his blue-striped smock, and with his incurable depression pays for the glory of Asiago, where he was buried alive by a grenade. Another still has a bullet lodged in his head; in order to escape the maddening pains, he had to become addicted to morphine. Evenings he howls in despair for the nurse, and the whole ward begins to cry with excitement. A brain-damaged baby weeps. He was born two months after his father's hero's death, a death his pregnant mother had feared. One woman, whose sons came back unscathed, didn't wait it out—she lost her mind before they returned. Yet who dares say it can't get any worse?

* King Lear, IV, i.

OPTIMIST: Yes, it can't be denied, the war affects the personal life situation of every single individual. How long do you think this can go on?

GRUMBLER: In any case we will keep lying up to the last breath of both man and beast. Whether we can keep fighting, too, is another question. It appears that we would like to break away from German pressure by means of a little Nibelung un-troth. Through a bit of treachery we will revenge ourselves on Germany because she didn't prevent us from driving her into the war. Yet who would not prefer every disgrace for the fatherland to the disgrace which each minute of a continuing war heaps upon mankind! Fortunately, instead of being prolonged by our victories, it is being shortened by our defeats. Didn't I tell you once that the postponement of the collapse, which we owe to the breakthrough at Gorlice, would be paid for by millions of lives? At that time the statement seemed a paradox, but now it has been corroborated by the greatness of this time.

(*Scene change.*)

SCENE 6

The base at Fourmies.

MILITIAMAN LUEDECKE: Well, even though the alarmists come at us from two sides, both from the front and from back home, we at the base still won't let the war be spoiled for us. Here we booze and whore to our heart's content; there's nothing here that points to a peace in which we will abandon our war aims. The Crown Prince has a regular harem going; the other day he got a splendid addition, which didn't please her folks much, so he just had them deported. We're getting the job done in the west. And after all, what do they want back home anyhow? We send them everything we can. I hear that the booty from Lille is already being sold at Wertheim's. I'd better write home and tell them how well off we are here now. (*He writes.*)

> May 8. Dear Pal, I've been assigned to a requisition detail for the base at Fourmies. We take all the lead, brass, copper, cork, oil, etc., chandeliers, and cookstoves away from the French people, and whatever we scavenge from far and wide finds its way to Germany. It's often awfully unpleasant to take wedding presents away from young brides, but the necessities of war force us to it. One of my buddies and I made a beautiful catch the other day. In a walled-off room we found fifteen musical instruments—a whole orchestra—a brand-new bicycle, one hundred and fifty bed sheets and hand towels, and six copper chandeliers that total twenty-five kilograms all by themselves; in addition, we also found a whole bunch of other stuff. You can just imagine how mad the old witch who owned the stuff was. I had a good laugh. All in all, it was worth more than ten thousand marks. Some bales of wool and many other items. The commander was very pleased. We are even supposed to get a reward. Perhaps we'll even get the Iron Cross besides. And then we have young girls here who are ripe for plucking. Regards—

(*Scene change.*)

SCENE 7

Busch Auditorium (in Berlin). Mass rally in favor of a German peace.

REVEREND BRUESTLEIN (*arm outstretched*): —In the west: Longwy and Briey! And the Flemish coast will not be given back again! (*Clamorous applause.*) In the east that notorious line of fortifications, which must never again threaten East Prussia, has to remain in our hands in one way or another! (*Lively applause.*) Courland and a part of Latvia will not be given back again! (*Thunderous applause.*) Bound up with Courland are Livonia and Estonia. (*His right hand extended.*) The distress signal is being flown out there! That's where our help is needed.

(*Cries: "Hurrah! Hurrah! Hurrah!" Speaker steps down. The group begins to sing the hymn "A Mighty Fortress Is our God."*)

MANAGING EDITOR MASCHKE: My esteemed fellow countrymen! I shall be brief. There's only one thing I want to say, something that inspires us all: Away with the so-called world conscience! (*Cries of "Hurrah!"*) Away with the spirit of "world brotherhood!" Let the German conscience, the self-assurance of power, alone be our commander and our leader! Its rallying cry rings out: More power! More German power! Whoever is moved by his "world conscience" or his sense of responsibility toward mankind to speak or write anything but that which is dictated by the language of power, the power of the German sword—that man is and shall remain a wretched political dreamer, a pitiful visionary with his head in the clouds. (*Clamorous applause.*)

A MALCONTENT: I want to give this honored assembly just one thing to think about. Recently the Minister of Finance tried, by pointing to the brilliant victories of our army, to gloss over the damage done by this war to the people's morality. Yet it says in the Bible: "For what shall it profit a man if he shall gain the whole world and lose his own soul!" This biblical view is identical with one held in our own day—namely that the moral disintegration of the body politic through deceit, theft, and fraud can never be gilded over by the glory of arms. Great national institutions, such as the Postal Service, have become dens of thieves; whole segments of the population have been hurled into the bottomless abyss, all because of this insatiable greed for profit— (*Cries: "Get that fellow out of here!" The speaker is thrown out.*)

PROFESSOR PUPPE: Esteemed members of the audience! I shall be brief, since the guidelines for a German peace stand out so clearly before the eyes of all of us that we can touch them with our hands. Effecting a reconciliation with France through kindness is impossible. (*Cries: "Impossible!"*) We must render France so powerless that she can never attack again! (*Booming applause.*) To that end it is necessary that our western border be pushed further out; the ore deposits of northern France must be ours! (*Lively applause.*) What was formerly Belgium must never again be let out of our hands, neither militarily, politically, or economically! Furthermore, we need a great colonial empire in Africa! (*Clamorous applause.*) And in order to insure its security we need naval bases! An indispensable prerequisite is the expulsion of England from the Mediterranean, from Gibraltar, Malta, Cyprus, Egypt, and her recently conquered bases in the Mediterranean! (*Cries: "May God punish England!"*) In addition to that, naturally, there will have to be war idemnities (*a hurricane of applause*)—specifically, our enemies will have to be forced to place at our disposal a considerable portion of their merchant fleet in order to supply us with gold, foodstuffs, and raw materials. (*Cries: "Hurrah!"*) In addition—

(*Scene change.*)

SCENE 11

General war conference of the Social Democratic Party caucus for the giant voter precinct Teltow-Beskow-Storkow-Charlottenburg of Greater Berlin.

COMRADE SCHLIEFKE (*of Teltow*): —As general spokesman for the general war conference of the Social Democratic Party caucus for the giant voter precinct Teltow-Beskow-Storkow-Charlottenburg of Greater Berlin, I hereby summarize the situation: If Prussian Social Democrats accept this invitation into the Department of the Interior, and if the Kaiser participates in this conversation, this represents no violation of Social Democratic principles. In addition, Comrade David acted properly when he accepted the invitation of the Crown Prince. The Social Democratic Party is a revolutionary party (*cries "Aha!"*) —it must therefore, when changing conditions demand it, also break with old traditions—

A HECKLER: At the Kaiser's court?

COMRADE SCHLIEFKE: —I mean with its own traditions! It must revolutionize within its own ranks. It is for that very reason a revolutionary party through and through! (*Lively approval.*)

(*Scene change.*)

SCENE 14

A battlefield near Sarrebourg.

CAPTAIN NIEDERMACHER:* Our boys keep hesitating. For a long time each of them has known that General Ruhmleben, when discussing the battle situation, gave precise orders to use rifle butts or revolvers to finish off all prisoners of war, whether or not they're wounded, and to shoot the wounded in the field, just as the false enemy propaganda claims we do.

MAJOR METZLER:† Ruhmleben is being faithful to the old maxim of our supreme commander: No pardon, no prisoners! Moreover, His Majesty has ordered the sinking of hospital ships, so we on land must not let ourselves be outdone!

NIEDERMACHER: The brigade order concerning the finishing off of war prisoners was spread through the company by word of mouth. But these rascals keep hesitating.

METZLER: We'll see about that; here's an opportunity. (*He prods an apparently dead French noncommissioned officer with his foot.*) Well now, he can still open his eyes. (*He gestures to two soldiers to come over. They hesitate.*) Aren't you familiar with the brigade order? (*The soldiers shoot.*) There's one squatting over there—it looks to me as if he's even drinking coffee! (*He gestures to a soldier to come over.*) Look here, Niedermacher, you can take care of this matter here; I must see to it that matters in my own bailiwick are being properly attended to.

(*Exit. The wounded man falls to his knees in front of Niedermacher and holds up his hands, begging for mercy.*)

* This name means one who mows down.
† This name means one who massacres.

NIEDERMACHER (*to the soldier, who is hesitating*): We do not take prisoners!

SOLDIER: I just bandaged him up and made him feel a little better, captain—

NIEDERMACHER: He'll repay you by poking out your eyes and cutting your throat. (*The soldier hesitates. Niedermacher is in a rage.*) They shoot treacherously from behind and above. Shoot them from the trees like sparrows, the general said. Everything must be mowed down, the general said. Do I have to order you to do it, man? Twenty men have been killed today, and a fellow like you has second thoughts? You will be held responsible for this! Does everything have to be done for you shitheads?—There—see how it's done! (*He shoots the kneeling wounded man.*)

(*Scene change.*)

SCENE 17

The Subscriber and the Patriot conversing.

SUBSCRIBER: What do you say about the rumors?

PATRIOT: I'm worried.

SUBSCRIBER: The rumor circulating in Vienna is that there are rumors circulating in Austria. They're even going from mouth to mouth, but nobody can tell you—

PATRIOT: Nobody knows anything specific, but there must be something to it if even the government has announced that rumors have been spread.

SUBSCRIBER: The government explicitly warns against believing the rumors or spreading them and calls upon each individual

to participate most energetically in suppressing them. Well, I do what I can; wherever I go, I say, who pays any attention to rumors?
PATRIOT: Well, the Hungarian government has also been saying that rumors have been spread in Budapest that rumors have been spread in Hungary, and it too warns against them.
SUBSCRIBER: In other words, it definitely appears that rumors have been spread throughout the monarchy.
PATRIOT: I think so too. You know, if you only heard about it by way of rumor—but the Austrian government explicitly says it's so, and so does the Hungarian government.
SUBSCRIBER: There must be something to it. But who pays any attention to rumors?
PATRIOT: Exactly. If I meet somebody I know, I first ask him whether he's already heard about the rumors, and if he says no, I tell him not to believe them but to refute them as immediately and energetically as possible. That's the least you can ask—the first duty of loyalty!
SUBSCRIBER: There must be something to it, otherwise the three Representatives who are always seen together would not have turned up at the Prime Minister's and called his attention to the rumors going around.
PATRIOT: Well, you see! But the Prime Minister said that he was well aware of the particular rumors in question that were going around.
SUBSCRIBER: Well, there you are! You know what I think? I'll tell you in confidence—the rumors have to do with the tradition-hallowed, roy— (*He covers his mouth with the newspaper.*)
PATRIOT: What, you don't say! I can tell you even more. Those who spread such rumors want to poison the people's faith in the roy—
SUBSCRIBER: What, you don't say! And it's even being reported

that in each case the rumors were heard in totally different places at the same time, which is why—
PATRIOT: —one is justified in assuming that one is up against organized rumor-mongering.
SUBSCRIBER: So they say! But after all those are only rumors. Who can have established that so precisely—I ask you, at the same time in different places!
PATRIOT: Don't say that! The government can do it. Do you know what they're saying? They're saying that the spreading of rumors might be a new sign of enemy-inspired attempts to sow confusion among us. But they're wasting their energy!
SUBSCRIBER: I've heard that one, too. They're even saying that the rumors are part of the enemy arsenal; they'll bypass no means of shaking the structure of our monarchy and of loosening the bonds of love and reverence, namely toward the tradition-hallowed, roy— (*He covers his mouth with the newspaper.*)
PATRIOT: What, you don't say! Well, here they'll be running into a stone wall!
SUBSCRIBER: You know something?
PATRIOT: Well—?
SUBSCRIBER: I'd like to know what's behind all those rumors!
PATRIOT: I can tell you: absolutely nothing, and the best proof of it is that people don't even know what sort of rumors they are. Do you know what?
SUBSCRIBER: Well—?
PATRIOT: I'd like to know what sort of rumors they are!
SUBSCRIBER: Well, what sort of rumors would they be anyway! Fine rumors, they are; they're going from person to person, but not a soul can tell you—
PATRIOT: We've got nothing to go on but rumors!

(*Scene change.*)

SCENE 18

The Optimist and the Grumbler conversing.

OPTIMIST: What do you say to the rumors?
GRUMBLER: I am not aware of them, but I believe them.
OPTIMIST: Don't say that. The lies of the Allies—
GRUMBLER: —are by far not as dubious as our truths.
OPTIMIST: The only thing that could by some chance lend nourishment to the rumors would be—
GRUMBLER: —that we have none.

(Scene change.)

SCENE 33

The Optimist and the Grumbler conversing.

OPTIMIST: In order to gain insight into the emotional life of those fighting in the war one needs only—
GRUMBLER: —read a letter from the field—particularly, one from somebody who was able to slip it past the censor.
OPTIMIST: In any case, one would conclude from such letters that each man's greatest ambition is to give a good account of himself on the battlefield, and that his devotion to duty even takes precedence over his yearning for wife and child.
GRUMBLER: Or one would be horrified by the inconceivable crime perpetrated by the scoundrels who engendered the war and who are prolonging it—this inconceivable crime which is terrible enough in its effect on even a single destiny,

but which is inflicted on millions—the tearing apart and trampling of every individual's happiness, the torture of expecting disaster for years, of a tension that trembles at the silence and dreads that it will be broken by a message of death from either the trenches or from the home front. A wife becomes a mother, a mother dies—and the man whom it most closely concerns lies in the mud somewhere for the sake of the fatherland. Now the scoundrels have contrived the ingenious arrangement whereby combat mail, this cursed and yet how much desired invention of Satan himself, is temporarily halted altogether. In such cases the poor wretches know more than enough; for the stillness is that which precedes the storm. And how unimaginable is the mechanism with which the elementary facts of life, birth, and death yield to the unfathomable decree of the general staff! Only love does not knuckle under. (*He reads aloud.*)

"—the common reason for the slowing up of the mail from here is said to be the fact that instead of censoring it they simply hold it back until events have overtaken the letters.

"I try in various ways to make this difficult, terrifying time easier for myself—all without success. If I think about you a lot, then I only get sadder still, and if I try to distract myself, then afterward I'm only still sadder. The best thing to do is to live one day at a time so that the time passes faster. For each day that passes does bring us closer together, we must not forget that!

"I am still overwhelmed by the concern I feel for you today, but I shall shake it off, and give myself wholly up to my hope for good news from you tomorrow. When I think that I could be with you now, see your beloved little face, talk with you about the days to come, days that will seal our happiness still more—and here I am, so far away, and you alone! Truly, this war is so cruel, so unnatural; let's not forget that we're not the only ones who have to suffer—so many, so innumerable are those who are made unhappy by the arbitrariness of a few unscrupulous men.

"But what do the others matter to me—it breaks my heart to think what we two have to go through right now! It is too terrible, hardly to be endured! And in addition one has to fulfill one's duty, difficult, heavy with responsibility, and dangerous as it is; one has to act as an example to one's men of courage and devotion to duty—and whatever else all these hateful virtues are called; each step I take in this whole affair is sickening and repulsive, is contrary to all my innermost convictions. We are required to disavow all our better feelings, and those unable to do so suffer unspeakably and do with disgust whatever is demanded of them, however sickening it may be.

"To think how happy we were, how our lives had become so entwined, so much one being that now one is completely lost without the other. I am so impoverished and small without you, sometimes you would hardly recognize me at all. So many times when I surrender to my thoughts, even when they're not just then flying out to you, I often want just to ask you something, to have you share something with me, to hear your opinion, and I am alone! I don't need anyone else's opinion, it's you I want to hear, it's for you that I think and feel, whatever the situation may be; and without you I am not myself, I am only half a person and destitute. Your love, which radiates out to me from afar, is the only thing that still preserves any joy in life for me.

"Why speak, why should I still exacerbate the wounds that burn so much even as it is. You know that you mean everything to me—or rather that you are the cause of my misery, for, if it were not for the thought of you, everything wouldn't be quite so bad! And sometimes I also think ahead to the future. To complete languor—half alive we shall lie in each other's arms and can do no more for love, love!

"Alas, that I can't be there! I wouldn't have moved from your side during the difficult hours that await you, and it would have been so much easier for you. Don't worry yourself about me. If I could magically spirit you to my side, I would quite calmly take you with me into the trenches.

"Oh, that I can't be with you! It's with you that I belong, and I can't be there. Oh, may God grant that you haven't suffered too badly, that nothing has happened to you, that you have remained well for me and that you will be getting stronger from day to day. Oh, may God grant that today I will get a postcard written in your own hand. By the time you receive these lines, you will, God willing, be all right. Did you feel that I was with you and that I was suffering along with you? Oh, the time will come—it has to come—when we will make it up to ourselves for all the suffering we've had to overcome.

"So far away, so far away from you, in these days! Oh, why, why, can't I sit by you now, to warm you and give you strength with my endless love! I can't help myself, my eyes are so full of tears all the time that I can hardly see what I'm writing.

"Oh God, that I can't be with you! And no hope! Nobody is sent home now or back to the base; they are only sent to some hospital.

"I've gotten so many gray hairs that I can't count them any more. But I love you, whether near or far, love, love, love, unspeakingly, maddeningly—"

OPTIMIST: What then? He'll return home and find a wife and child who are feeling just fine.

GRUMBLER: The fatherland has decreed differently. Here a human being comes into the world, there another falls. I have never read anything so sad or so true as this last letter of a man who became a father when he died.

(*Scene change.*)

SCENE 34

In the village of Postabitz.

A WOMAN (*sitting at a table writing*):

Deerly loved husband,
I let you know that I have slipped up bad. It ain't my fault, deer husband. You'll still love me after everything. Im in

the family way by another one. I know you are good and that you forgive me everything. He talked me into it and he said you wasn't coming home anyway and also I got a week moment too. You know how week a woman is, and you can't do anything better but forgive me, it just happened. I was thinking that something must of happent to you since you didn't write a letter for three months now, I was scared when your letter came and you was still alive. I wish that for you, but forgive me, deer Franz, maybe the baby will dye and everything is swell again. I don't like this man anymore since I know you're alive. Everything costs us so much now, it's good you're not here. At lest at the front food don't cost you nothing. The money you sent me I can use very necessary. I great you again, your unforgettable wife,
         Anna

(Scene change.)

SCENE 37

After the winter offensive in Transylvania. An Austrian rear-echelon drill field. The remnant of a regiment, every man wasted away to a skeleton. With their tattered uniforms, worn-out shoes, and filthy underwear, they appear at first glance to be a batch of sick and ragged beggars. They get up exhausted and practice rifle and salute drills.

FIRST WAR CORRESPONDENT: How they will brighten up when they hear that the Commander in Chief,* who at the moment is visiting his courageous troops at the front, will inspect this victorious regiment.
SECOND WAR CORRESPONDENT: He's still at the front, in Gries

---

* Karl I, who succeeded to the throne in November 1916.

near Bozen, but he'll be here soon. I think that they already know.

A Soldier (*to one of his fellows*): Now he's coming here, the chump!

Second Soldier: Out there where the action is, he wouldn't show his face.

First War Correspondent: The Emperor enjoys the blind trust of his soldiers.

Second War Correspondent: They're happy if he so much as smiles at them, the brave boys.

A Captain: Damnit, spruce up a bit there, His Majesty is going to be here any minute now! Sure, a furlough—you would relish that. Did you think just because you were back for rehabilitation you'd be up for furlough? Up for shit! His Majesty is coming to inspect his glorious regiment and so not one man's to be missing, damn them.

First War Correspondent: Look here, it's interesting to see what's going to happen. They're changing their clothes. They're being newly outfitted from head to toe.

Second War Correspondent: What happens to the old rags?

First: They'll get them back as soon as the Emperor is gone.

Second: The companies are down to an average of fifteen to sixty men; surely, they're going to build them up—?

First: What do you mean going to? They're in the process now—over there—look here how they're building them up. They're not going to show the Emperor losses of twenty-five hundred men. Are you crazy?

Second: What sort of replacements are they bringing in?

First: Oh, shoemakers, tailors, orderlies, cooks, teamsters, stablemen, men on the sick list, and so on—they've all got rifles and are already drilling. If only he were here! This kind of cold—it's not for me.

Second: Look at what they're doing now—what's that?

Act V, Scene 37

FIRST: Oh, that's quite clear; they're pushing the decorated and better-looking men into the first rank; they are changing places.

SECOND: I see that, but what are they doing to their faces?

FIRST: What are they doing to their faces? You don't know that, you dumb greenhorn? They're rubbing snow in their faces so that each man gets some color in his cheeks, even the sick ones.

SECOND: That's a splendid idea! Look there, how rosy they look already! But what's going on now? Something's being handed out.

FIRST: Cards with the picture of the Emperor. For that they'll lose half their bread ration.

SECOND: There'll be many who will be satisfied with the exchange, the brave men—Christ, the cars—don't you hear them?

(*Automobiles come. Heavy figures get out, among them a leaner one, enveloped in a thick fur wrap, with huge earmuffs. One sees hardly anything but a thick underlip.*)

FIRST: What a great experience for you; the Commander in Chief inspects the troops at the front, men who have just come back from victorious combat. He engages in conversation with simple enlisted men.

SECOND: He has a winning personality. Look how their hearts go out to him!

FIRST: Now he electrifies them.

SECOND: If only we could hear what he's saying. What is he saying?

FIRST: Nothing, but he's smiling.

(*As he walks from man to man, from file to file, at regular five-second intervals, one hears either "Ah! Very fine!"*

or "Ah! Very good!" or "Ah! Well done! or "Ah! Keep it up!" This lasts for two hours.)

(Departure of the officers. The cars drive off.)

COLONEL *(to the major)*: The following evening order is to be announced "His Majesty has expressed special praise for the regiment. The morale and the appearance of the troops are outstanding; the courage that shines in the eyes of every individual is incomparable. His Majesty was particularly heartened by the slight losses suffered by the regiment. His Majesty concluded, 'Don't you agree, Colonel, this regiment will, as always in the past, be among the most loyal troops of its Emperor and its fatherland, and, in the impending battles which, although difficult, will nonetheless be victorious, it shall fully stand its ground and thus attach laurel after laurel to its standards.' I answered: "Absolutely, Your Majesty, I promise it.'"

CAPTAIN *(to the soldiers)*: What you have witnessed today you can relate to your children and your children's children, if you think it's worth it! The word for now is: Forward to new battles and victories! And above all, hurry up and get out of those new uniforms!

(Scene change.)

SCENE 38

Hofburg. Press Service.

CAPTAIN WERKMANN *(dictating)*: To the Editorial Office: I would greatly appreciate it if you would, if at all possible, be willing to use in its entirety today's report of His Majesty's troop inspections and of Her Majesty's visit to the field kitchens at Ottakring; neither report is overly long as is. I would like to place particular emphasis upon the description of the homage paid to Their Majesties. I was myself witness to these truly overwhelming welcomes and have certainly not said too much in my report. Extending to you in advance my most appreciative thanks. Yours very sincerely—

(*Scene change.*)

SCENE 40

A side street, a doorway of a building. A Soldier wearing two medals, his cap pulled down over his face. At his side his little daughter who leads him and now stoops to pick up a cigarette butt, which she puts in his pocket. In the courtyard of the house, an invalid with a hand organ.

SOLDIER: I have enough of them. (*He pulls out a wooden pipe, into which the girl stuffs the tobacco from the cigarette butts.*)
A LIEUTENANT (*who has passed by, turning around, harshly*): Can't you see?
SOLDIER: No.
LIEUTENANT: What? —Oh, I see—.

(*He leaves. The Soldier is led by the child in the other direction. The hand organ plays the Hoch Hapsburg March.*)

(*Scene change.*)

SCENE 41

Army command headquarters.

A MAJOR (*to another one*): You really get nothing but trouble from the front lines. Again, such damned reports where you simply don't know what you're supposed to do. If I hand them to Waldstätter, he gets mad; if I don't hand them to him, he also gets mad. What should I do, then? Look here:

"In some regiments an improvement in provisions is urgently needed in order to keep the men going physically. In one division the average weight of the men is not much more than a hundred pounds." You see! —And this:

"Every deserter behind the lines, even if he has to live hidden in the woods to hide himself, is better off than the front-line soldier." Deserter! How can one even write such a word! "As to clothing, no full uniform exists any longer because shirt or underwear, or both, are lacking. One man no longer has sleeves on his shirt, another lacks the back part of his shirt, a third has only half of his underwear or fragments of foot rags. Men with the high fever of malaria must wait naked until their rags are washed and dried." Rags! The tone these men at the front allow themselves to use with people like us—it's really as if we were responsible. How's this for nerve! "In one regiment every third man is without a coat. There are combat guards with helmets but without pants." Well, that must be something to see. "You can no longer speak of a soldier's self-respect, simple human dignity is violated." They shouldn't complain so much. What a tone to take. These people at the front don't realize either the iron necessities of war or how to deal with army headquarters. It is really as if we had started the war! And the kind of ideas people get. Look here:

"In order to raise morale, it might be recommended that younger members of the royal family be assigned to fighting units in more difficult sectors of the front lines." Well, here I must really——. This is no less than an insult to members of the royal family. No, my dear sir, at that price we shall not raise morale—we shall raise the morale of these gentlemen in some other way! That is really pure defeatism——. To send members of the royal family to the front! Such insolence!

THE OTHER MAJOR: Why get excited? Would they go?

(*Scene change.*)

SCENE 53

A deserted street. It is getting dark. Suddenly, from all sides, figures rush into the street, each with a bundle of newsprint, breathless. Corybants and Mænads rage the length and breadth of the street, they roar and seem to call out a murder. The cries are incomprehensible. Many seem to literally groan out the news. It sounds as if the agony of mankind was being drawn from a deep well.

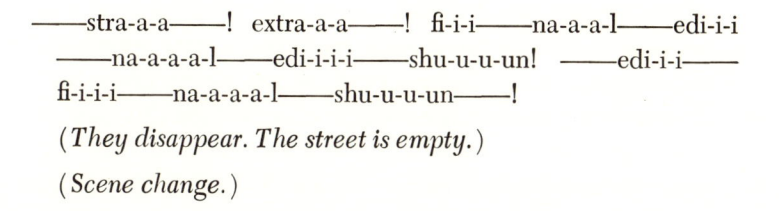

——stra-a-a——! extra-a-a——! fi-i-i——na-a-a-l——edi-i-i ——na-a-a-a-l——edi-i-i-i——shu-u-u-un! ——edi-i-i—— fi-i-i-i——na-a-a-a-l——shu-u-u-un——!

(*They disappear. The street is empty.*)

(*Scene change.*)

SCENE 54

The Grumbler at his desk. He reads:

"The wish to establish the exact time that a tree standing in the forest needs in order to be converted into a newspaper has given the owner of a Harz paper mill the occasion to conduct an interesting experiment. At 7:35 he had three trees felled in the forest neighboring the factory, which, after their bark was scaled off, were hauled into the pulp mill. The transformation of the three tree trunks into liquid wood pulp proceeded so quickly that as early as 9:39 the first roll of newsprint left the machine. This roll was immediately taken by car to the printing plant of a daily newspaper four kilometers away; and no later than 11:00 A.M. the newspaper was being sold on the street. Accordingly, a time span of only three hours and twenty-five minutes was required in order that the public could read the latest news report on the material that stemmed from trees on whose branches the birds had sung their songs that very morning."

(*Outside, from quite far off, the cry:* "*E-e-xtra—*")

GRUMBLER: So it is five o'clock. The answer is here, the echo of my blood-haunted madness. And no longer does anything resound to me out of ruined creation except this one sound, out of which ten millions who are dying accuse me of still being alive, I who had eyes so to see the world, and whose stare struck it in such a fashion that it became as I saw it. If heaven was just in letting this come about, then it was unjust in not having annihilated me. Have I deserved this fulfillment of my deathly fear of life? What's looming there, invading all my nights? Why was I not given the physical strength to smash the sin of this planet with one ax blow? Why was I not given the mental power to force an outcry out of desecrated mankind? Why is my shout of protest not stronger than this tinny command that has dominion over the souls of a whole globe?

I preserve documents for a time that will no longer comprehend them or will be so far removed from today that it will say I was a forger. But no, the time to say that will not come. For such time will not be. I have written a tragedy, whose perishing hero is mankind, whose tragic conflict, the conflict between the world and nature, has a fatal ending. Alas, because this drama has no actor other than all mankind, it has no audience!

So you would have to continue to die for something, which you call Honor or the Bucovina province. For what have you died? Why this scorn of death? Why should you scorn that which you know not? To be sure, one scorns life, which one knows not. You first come to know it when the shrapnel has not quite killed you, or when the beast, acting on orders, foaming at the mouth, not long ago a man like yourself, throws himself on you, and you have a flash of consciousness on the threshold. And now the beast who commands you dares to say of you, you scorn death? And you have not used this moment to shout to your superior that he was not God's superior who could order Him to uncreate what was created? Oh, had you known, at the moment of sacrifice, about the profit that grows despite—no, with—the sacrifice, fattening itself on it! For never, until this indecisive war of the machines, has there been such godless war profit, and you, winning or losing, lost the war, from which only your murderers profited.

You, faithful companion of my words, turning your pure faith upward to the heaven of art, laying your ear in tranquil scholarship to its bosom—why did you have to pass into the beyond? I saw you on the day when you marched out. The rain and the mud of this fatherland and its infamous music were the farewell, as they herded you into the cattle car! I see your pale face in this orgy of filth and lies in this frightful farewell at a freight station, from which the human material is dispatched. Why could you not have died just from experiencing this initiation, one that makes Wallenstein's camp seem truly like the lobby of a palatial hotel! For technological man becomes dirty before he gets bloody. This is how your Italian journey began, you quester after art.

And you, noble poet's heart who, between the voices of the mortars and the murderers, attended to the secret of a vowel—have you spent four years of your springtime beneath the earth in order to test your future abode? What had you to seek there? Lice for the fatherland? To wait, until the grenade splinter came? To prove that your body can better resist the effectiveness of the Schneider-Creuzot works than the body of a man from Torino can that of the Skoda works? What, are we the traveling salesmen of arms factories who are to testify to the superiority of our firms, and to the inferiority of the competition, not with our mouths but with our bodies?

Where there are many who travel, there will be many who limp. So let them turn their sales areas into battlefields. But that they also had the power to coerce higher natures into the service of wickedness—the devil never would have dared to imagine such a consolidation of his dominion. And had one whispered to him that in the first year of the war, the war into which he had chased people, hornbook in hand, in order that they transact his business with more soul, if one had whispered to him that in that first year an oil refinery would reap a one hundred and thirty-seven percent net profit, David Fanto, seventy-three percent, Kreditanstalt Bank, twenty million, and that the profiteers in meat and sugar and alcohol and fruit and potatoes and butter and leather and rubber and coal and iron and wool and soap and oil and ink and weapons would be indemnified a hundredfold for the depreciation of other people's blood—the devil himself would have advocated a peace treaty that renounced all war aims.

And for that, you lay four years in dirt and damp, for that, the letter that wanted to reach you was obstructed, the book that wanted to comfort you was stopped. They wanted you to stay alive, for they had not yet stolen enough on their stock exchanges, had not yet lied enough in their newspapers, had not yet harassed people enough in their governmental offices, had not yet sufficiently whipped mankind into confusion, had not yet sufficiently made the war the excuse, in all their doings and circumstances, for their ineffectuality and their maliciousness—they had not yet danced this whole tragic carnival through to its end, this carnival in which men died before the eyes of female war reporters, and butchers became doctors of philosophy *honoris causa*!

You have lain weeks on end under the assault of mine throwers; you have been threatened by avalanches; you have hung by a rope, three thousand meters high, between the enemy barrage and the machine-gun fire of your own lines; you have been exposed to the ordeal, prolonged a hundredfold, of the condemned; you had to live through the whole variety of death in the collision of organism and machine, death by mines, barbed wire, dumdum bullets, bombs, flames, gas and all the hells of curtain fire—all this because madness and profiteering had not vented on you enough of their cowardly spite. And you out there, and we here, are we supposed to stare still longer into the graves that we had to dig for ourselves by orders from highest quarters—as the old Serbian men were ordered to do, and for no other reason than that they were Serbs and still alive and therefore suspect!

Alas, if one were only—having got out of this adventure unscathed, although careworn, impoverished, aged—if one were only, by the magic of some divine retribution, granted the power to hold accountable, one by one, the ringleaders of this world crime, the ringleaders who always survive, to lock them up in their churches, and there, just as they did with the old Serbian men, to let each tenth one draw his death lot! But then not to kill them—no, to slap their faces! And to address them thus: What, you scoundrels, you did not know, you had no idea, that among the millions of possibilities of horror and shame, the consequences of a declaration of war, if it was so decided in the profiteers' war plans, would also be these: that children have no milk, horses no oats, and that even one far from the battlefield can go blind from methyl alcohol, if it has been so decided in the war plans of the profiteers? What, did you not conceive of the misery of one hour of a captivity that was to last for many years? Of one sigh of longing and of sullied, torn, murdered love? Were you not even capable of imagining what hells are opened up by one tortured minute of a mother's harkening into the distance, through nights and days of this years-long waiting for a hero's death? And you did not notice how the tragedy became a farce, became, through the simultaneousness of a new and hateful nuisance and a mania for fossilized forms, an operetta, one of those loathsome modern operettas, whose libretto is an indignity and whose music is torture?

Act V, Scene 54

What, and you there, you who have been murdered, you did not rise up against this order? Against this system of murder. Against an economic system that for all the future had to condemn life to sticking it out, to drop the curtain on all hope, and to relinquish to the hatred of nations the snatching of even the smallest bit of happiness? Outrages in war senselessly committed and outrages committed against everybody because there was a war on. Poverty, hunger, and shame piled up on those fleeing and those who could still stay in their homes, and all mankind shackled, within and without.

And statesmen in precipitous times called upon to their one duty, to curb mankind's bestial impulse—they have unleashed it! Cowardly hatred of life, inclined even in peacetime to kill animals and children, turned to the machine to ravish all that grows! Hysteria, protected by technology, overpowers nature; paper commands weapon. We were disabled by the rotary presses before there were victims of cannons. Were not all realms of imagination vacated when that manifesto declared war on all the inhabited globe?

In the end was the word. For the word that killed the spirit, nothing remained but to give birth to the deed. Weaklings became strong to force us under the wheel of progress. And that was the press's doing, the press alone, which with its whoring corrupted the world! Not that the press set the machinery of death into motion—but that it eviscerated our hearts, so we could no longer imagine what was in store for us: that is its war guilt! And from the lascivious wine of its debauchery all peoples have drunk, and the kings of the earth fornicated with the press. And the horseman of the apocalypse drank to it, he whom I saw galloping through the German Reich, long before he actually did so.

A decade has passed since I knew that his task was achieved. He is rushing ahead at full speed in all the streets. His moustache stretches from sunrise to sunset and from south to north. "And power was given to him that sat thereon to take peace from the earth, and that they should kill one another." And I saw him as the beast with the ten horns and the seven heads and a mouth like the mouth of a lion. "They worshipped the beast, saying, Who is like unto the beast? Who is able to make war with him? And there was given unto him a mouth speaking great things." And we fell through him and through the whore of Babylon, who, in all tongues of the world, persuaded us that we were each other's enemy, and there should be war!

And you who were sacrificed did not rise up against this scheme? Did not resist the coercion to die, did not resist the last liberty—to murder? All human rights and values traded for the idea of the material; the child in his mother's womb pledged to the imperative of hatred; and the image of this fighting manhood, yes, even of this nursing womanhood, armored bodies with gas masks, like those of a horde of mythical beasts, handed down to the horror of posterity. With church bells you fired on the devout, and before altars of shrapnel, you did not repent.

And in all that, glory and fatherland? Yes, you have experienced this fatherland, before you died for it. This fatherland, from that moment when you had to wait undressed in the sweaty and beery air of the entrance hall to the hero's death, while they inspected human flesh and forced human souls to take the most godless oaths. Naked you were, as only before God and your beloved, before a board of tyrannical martinets and swine! Shame, shame for body and soul should have made you deny yourself to this fatherland!

We have all seen this fatherland, and the luckier ones among us, who could escape it, saw it in the figure of the impudent border guard. We saw it in all shapes of the greed for power of the freed slaves, in the accommodativeness of the tip-greedy extorter. Only we others did not have to experience the fatherland in the shape of the enemy, the real enemy, who with machine guns drove you in front of the enemies' machine guns. But had we seen it only in the likenesses of these hideous generals, who, all through this time of greatness, publicized themselves in fan magazines, as expensive ladies do in peacetime, to show that people are not always only whoring, but are also killing—truly we longed for this blood brothel's closing hour!

What, you there, who were murdered, who were cheated, you did not rise up against this system? You endured the license and luxury of the press strategists, parasites, and buffoons, just as you endured your misfortune and your coercion? And you knew, that for your martyrdom they received medals of honor? And you did not spit this glory in their faces? You were lying in trains that carried the wounded, which the rabble were permitted to write up for their papers? You did not break out, did not desert for a holy war, to liberate us at home from the archenemy who daily bombarded our brains with lies? And you died for this business? Lived through all this horror, only to prolong our own, while we here groaned in the midst of profiteering and misery and the harrowing contrasts of bloated impudence and the voicelessness of tuberculosis.

Oh, you had less feeling for us than we had for you, we who wanted to demand back a hundredfold each hour of these years that they tore out of your lives, we who always had only one question to ask you: what will you look like when you have survived this! When you have escaped glory's ultimate goal—that the hyenas become tourist guides, offering the site of your graves as sightseeing attractions! To be ill, impoverished, dissolute, full of lice, famished, killed in battle in order for the tourist trade to increase—this is the lot of all of us! They have carried your hide to market—but even out of ours their practicality lined their money purse.

But you had weapons—and did not march against this home front? And did not turn around from that field of dishonor to take up the most honorable war, to rescue us and yourselves? And you, the dead, do not rise up out of your trenches to take these vipers to account, to appear to them in their sleep with the twisted countenances that you wore in your dying hour, with the lusterless eyes of your heroic waiting, with the unforgettable masks to which your youth was condemned by this regime of madness! So, rise up, and confront them as the personification of a hero's death, so that the cowardice of the living, empowered to command, might finally come to know death's features and look death in the eye for the rest of their lives. Wake their sleep with your death cry! Interrupt their lust by the image of your sufferings! They were able to embrace women the night after the day on which they strangled you.

Save us from them, from a peace that brings us the pestilence of their nearness. Save us from the calamity of shaking hands with army prosecutors who have returned home and of meeting executioners in their civilian occupations.

Help me, you who have been murdered! Come to my aid, so that I do not have to live among men who, out of ambition or self-preservation, gave orders that hearts should stop beating and that the heads of mothers turn white! As sure as there is a God, without a miracle there can be no salvation! Come back! Ask them what they have done with you! What they did, as you suffered through them, before you died through them! What they did during your Galician winters! What they did that night when telephoning command posts got no answer from your positions. For all was quiet on the front.

And only later they saw how bravely you stood there, man by man, rifle ready to fire. For you did not belong to those who went over to the enemy or to those who went behind the lines and who, because they were freezing, had to be warmed up with machine-gun fire by a fatherly superior officer. You held your positions and were not killed while stepping backward into the murderous pit of your fatherland. Before you the enemy, behind you the fatherland, and above you, the eternal stars! And you did not flee into suicide. You died, neither for, nor through, the fatherland, neither through the ammunition of the enemy, nor through ours—you stood there and died through nature!

What a picture of perseverance! What a Capuchins' Crypt! Arms-bearing corpses, protagonists of Hapsburgian death-life, close your ranks and appear to your oppressors in their sleep. Awaken from this rigor! Step forth, step forth, you beloved believer in the spirit, and demand your precious head back from them! And where are you, you who died in the hospital? From there they sent back my last greeting, stamped: "No longer here. Address unknown." Step forth to tell them where you are, and how it is there, and that you never again will let yourself be used for such a thing.

And you there, with the face to which you were condemned in your last minute, when the beast, acting upon orders, frothing at the mouth, maybe once a man like you, plunged into your trench—step forth! Not that you had to die—no, that you had to experience this is what henceforth makes all sleep and all dying in bed a sin. It is not your dying, but what you have lived through that I want to avenge on those who have inflicted this on you. I have formed them into shadows. I have stripped off their flesh! But to their stupid thoughts, to their malicious sentiments and the frightful rhythm of their nothingness, I have given body and now make them move.

Had one preserved the voice of this era on a phonograph, the outer truth would have been in conflict with the inner truth and the ear would not have recognized either of them. Thus, time makes the essential truth unrecognizable and would grant amnesty to the greatest crime ever perpetrated under the sun, under the stars. I have preserved this truth, and my ear has detected the sound of their deeds, my eyes the gestures of their speaking, and my voice, when it only quoted, did so in such a way that the fundamental tone remains for all time.

> And let me speak to the yet unknowing world
> How these things came about: so shall you hear
> Of carnal, bloody, and unnatural acts,
> Of accidental judgments, casual slaughters,
> Of deaths put on by cunning and forced cause
> And in this upshot, purposes mistook
> Fall'n on the inventors' heads. All this can I
> Truly deliver.

And should the times hear no more, so surely will hear a being above them! I have done nothing but abridge this deadly quantity, which, in its immeasurability, may try to exonerate itself by pointing to the fickleness of time and the press. All their blood after all was only ink—now the writing will be done in blood! This is the war. This is my manifesto. *I have considered everything carefully.* I have taken it upon myself to tell the tragedy, which breaks down into the scenes of mankind breaking down, so that the Spirit, which has compassion for the victims, would hear it, even had he renounced for all future time any connection with a human ear. May he receive this era's fundamental tone, the echo of my madness haunted by blood through which I, too, am guilty of these sounds. May he accept it as redemption!

(*From outside, quite far off, the cry: "E-e-xtra, E-e-xtra!"*)

(*Scene change.*)

SCENE 55

Love feast at a corps command. The wall of the hall opposite the audience is covered by a colossal mural, "The Time of Greatness." A suckling pig is being served. The band plays "Good Old Noah Knew It Well." The banquet is nearing its end. Officers of the German and Austrian armies are clinking glasses in toasts. In the distance, the thunder of artillery. A Hussar First Lieutenant hurls a champagne glass against the wall.

PRUSSIAN COLONEL (*next to a General, humming and nodding his head*): Good old Noah, he knew it, yes, he knew it— Well, to your health!

AUSTRIAN GENERAL (*getting up amid cheers, clinks his spoon against his glass*): Gentlemen—so—after our officer corps has survived—an unprecedented four-year struggle—against the superior power of the world—so I place confidence in my staff—in that I am convinced—that we shall also furthermore—face up to the challenge—fearless—as best possible. Steeled in battle, our heroic soldiers—these brave men—go on toward new victories—we shall not waver—

we shall know how to hit the enemy, who is already cut to the quick, wherever it may be—and this very day—this very day, gentlemen—shall stand as a milestone—in the history of our glorious army forever more! (*Cheers.*) Up and at 'em!

But I expect of you—upon whom falls the most difficult duty in this unprecedented fight—as well as of our enlisted men, true in need and in death, upon whom the most untiring duty is imposed—so I expect of all of you that you will fulfill your duty to the last breath of man and beast with complete disregard. We face one last, but hot fight, and we know that—the stakes are not small. Indeed! Don't we all stand here, each man—and everyone stands his ground—puts his men at their post to persevere—in that very place—wherever our duty puts the soldier—and wherever His Majesty's service has stationed us (*cheers*)—as is expected of the commissioned officer!

In this hour we think of our beloved ones back home—who are far away and who think faithfully of us. And especially the mothers who have taken the lead in that they, quite true to nature, have with joy sacrificed their sons on the altar of the fatherland! And truly—it is not easy to collect all one's thoughts at this moment—because they always have to be directed toward that one goal. It is essential—I speak this word with full consciousness of my significance—it is imperative to be victorious! Victory, gentlemen—do you know what that means? That is the choice remaining to the soldier—otherwise he must die, covered with glory. To this purpose I shall preclude the expectation that you, gentlemen—in view of and with regard to the maintenance of intimate, heartfelt contact with them—that is, with the enlisted men—for the utmost reduction of personal danger have sacrificed yourselves. (*Cheers.*)

For, gentlemen—we all know—the last thing that an officer, particularly a staff officer, possesses—is (*cries of "His honor!"*)—You have guessed it, gentlemen—his honor! And we won't let them—well, I know all right—there are certain subversive elements—that extend clear into the foremost ranks—but—gentlemen—they aren't a match for us! Oh-ho! Our manpower can still take a punch! (*Cries of "Bravo!"*) —And we, who are blood of their blood, of one mind with them, are—no, and a thousand times no!—the officer feels with the common man, with the simple man, who is the bulwark today, the defense upon which the enemy will bloody his head! And then, they can say whatever they want to, these scribblers—one must not generalize! (*He pounds on the table.*) —Can one really do that? (*Cries of "No!"*) These scribblers—naturally, I don't mean the two gentlemen, the war correspondents, who have honored us with their presence today—we know all too well what the army owes to a well-uniformed corps of war correspondents—the press—which, in fulfillment of its high patriotic duty, eliminates—I mean enlivens—the courage of the homeland—can always depend upon our approval! (*Cries of "Bravo!"*)

I don't mean these gentlemen and thus I hope that the gentlemen have not related this to the gentlemen—in that we give the greatest possible recognition to their activities for the common good. (*Cries of "Bravo!" The War Correspondents take a bow.*) I mean—these anarchists and defeatists—who introduce their discord and by spreading rumors contribute to their dissemination! Those are the elements, the people who first subvert things and then in addition undermine them. And I ask you, gentlemen—do we need that? (*Cries of "No!"*)

In my corps—where all nations are peacefully represented all together—we have on our staff German officers and we have Bohemian officers, we have Poles and Croatians and we have Rumanian officers and some of the Mosaic confession are also there. And do we not also have representatives of our splendid Hungarian cavalry? (*Cheers.*) — Well then, no one here has ever complained! Here we always say—nationalities, take them or leave them. I ask you, gentlemen—can you notice any difference? Well then, therefore I say to you—it's not as bad as it's made out to be. At least not among us! You are showing our allies, whom we see with pride at our table here today (*cheers*)—how total unity prevails among us! Each man fills his station— with complete disregard—for we all know that we have to stick it out and what is at stake—all nationalities without exception, just as we are, here in this struggle that has been forced upon us, this defensive war of the German race against the Slavic! (*Cheers and cries of "Hurrah!"*)

Our weapons in this unprecedented fight are called confidence and discipline! (*Cries of "Bravo!"*) Oh, I think a lot of discipline—but it must be of iron! And we all—we can tell you all about it. Thus, during the last inspection I had to note some abuses in this regard, and, unfortunately, I also had to find fault with the fact that too few officers have been killed out there. I don't want to hurt anyone's feelings, but it is necessary, after all, to show the way by setting a good example. Instead of bringing one's own precious carcass to safety! (*"Bravo, bravo!"*)

Pflanzer-Baltin, my illustrious example, (*cheers*)—coined the phrase, "I'll teach my men to die all right!" I consider that very important. And what do the men really want then? Do they want to live forever? Gentlemen, this is no time for such self-indulgence—the fatherland is in danger; it shall, however, if God so wills—emerge like a phoenix from the tempering bath of this world war! What we need now—is self-discipline. I won't tolerate pampering. When they had the good fortune, that time when His Imperial Highness the Most Serene Archduke Friedrich—(*with emotion*) the father of our soldiers (*cheers*)—advanced clear out to the very front line of the trenches in order to deliver the gracious greetings of His Majesty, our Commander in Chief, to the enlisted men (*cheers*)—that made them very happy, as is only natural. So what more do the men want then? At that time it was still quite quiet out there and not so hectic as now, when they must withstand enemy onslaughts.

But no, they're stirring things up, and there are elements who have succeeded in bringing the men to the point of complaining and protesting—because of the dried vegetables and things—they'd probably like to have their little supper at Sacher just as in peacetime (*laughter*)—and puff pastry rolls with whipped cream three times a day! Now the word is to stick it out. (*"Bravo, bravo!"*) Gentlemen—I thoroughly hate this kind of thing, and wherever I notice symptoms I bear down on them hard!

Discipline—gentlemen, do you know what that means? Discipline means obedience to orders! Submission to authority—which is the soldier's daily bread! If that is undermined, then everything comes to an end! These scribblers—Bismarck, it is true, he was—well, our great ally—coined the maxim "What the sword has annihilated for us—is lost again by the pen!" Gentlemen, don't let us lose sight of that! Let us recall! —But I am astounded by the patience of our high War Ministry. If I had my say, the censors would have to set an example and hang all these people! (*Cries of "Bravo!"*)

Auditor et altera parte! I was fighting against the Dagos before these elements had even been born! (*Cries of "Bravo!"*) —I can say that with pride! But gentlemen—if armchair diplomacy brings this about, then of course—we can't take the responsibility! One must not believe all the enemy lies about us. In our beloved fatherland there is plenty of willingness to sacrifice oneself, but what we lack is devotion, and it is just this that matters! So—we must not let that sort of subversive current spread—because otherwise it could have an undermining effect! If each one of us here remains steadfast, we will thus allow the last decision that the enemy forces upon us to approach us according to plan and with honor!

Who among us is not mindful of the nothing less than unprecedented deeds with which our troops, courageous to the death and proven under every test, have gone on ahead of us—after they have loyally followed our orders in storm and danger! And indeed—the staffs, which often sacrificed themselves, have at all times taken the responsibility upon themselves according to plan and also carried things through in unprecedented fashion! And have we not achieved beautiful successes? Successes that will live on in the annals of our army—after we ourselves have fallen, covered with glory. Have we not achieved successes that arouse the envy of our allies—I mean, of our enemies—so that they want to belittle them?

Truly they have not made it easy for us, gentlemen. Surrounded as we are by nothing but enemies, we are defying a numerical superiority forevermore! Victory after victory, gentlemen! Who would have thought four years ago, in those days when we set out into the unknown in order to trample Serbia—according to plan and to the strains of the "Prince Eugen March"! (*Cheers.*) —And have we not succeeded? Have we not trampled Serbia, gentlemen? We have trampled her! (*Cheers.*) —At that time they used to say: Up to this point and no further! So—sweep them out with an iron hand!

Act V, Scene 55

Gentlemen, one step more and the victory is ours! Russia more and more clearly shows herself to be a colossus with feet of clay! This can be as good as taken for granted. And so far as the Dagos are concerned—well, who among us today still has any doubts about a final, ultimate victory? It is the duty of a soldier, gentlemen, to hold his own, and we have held our own, indeed! These brave ones—who have gone on ahead and have taken all the risks—our thoughts are with them—for they have held high the banner of their regiment and sealed it with their blood as well as they could! Gentlemen—we are living in a great time and invaluable fruits are still growing for our fatherland—its prestige in the world—and above all we have this tempering bath to thank for the tremendous spiritual uplift we have undergone. Is that perhaps nothing? Now there is but one step separating us—and we will have unconquerably attained the laurel wreath! Therefore I say—and this is true for the commissioned officers as well as for the enlisted man—cold courage, cold blood, gentlemen! You are the last ones who matter—remember that! You know why we stand here! For the service of Our Most Gracious Majesty!! (*All stand and cheer.*)—For Our Most Gracious Emperor (*cheers*)—to whom each man should give of his best, in distress and in death, in assaults, dangers, and undertakings of every kind, as is proper for a brave soldier! (*Cheers.*)

God help us further! I drink to the health of our almighty allies—whom we see here under the banner of battle-tested and battle-hardened Nibelung troth, shoulder to shoulder, bound to us for better or for worse! (*Cheers and cries of "Hurrah!"*) His Majesty the German Kaiser and His Majesty, our Commander in Chief, Our Most Gracious Emperor, together with the hereditary ruling house—may they all live long! Viva! Viva! Viva! (*Clamorous cheers and hurrahs. General toasting. He sits down.*)

PRUSSIAN COLONEL: Your Excellency, I'm a man of few words and no longer have the strength—to manage a toast. Your Hungarian wine—is too good for that. (*Laughter.*) But this much I can still say—your words have also spoken to my German heart! Where discipline is lacking, the worst is yet to come. The sloppy spirit prevalent in your Austrian home front would certainly also make the front waver—

(*A Captain has fallen under the table. Some movement ensues.*)

GENERAL: It's the fault of the scribblers! What do they want—we are pure litle lambs as it is!

PRUSSIAN COLONEL: Not so. Your peace-whining was improper. In that you sinned against yourselves. Now this spirit threatens to contaminate your front as well.

GENERAL: Do you hear? Discipline must be maintained, there's no other way.

(*The Officer on Telephone Duty comes in, goes to the General Staff Officer on Duty and hands a dispatch to him. The General Staff Officer opens it, staggers over to the General, and whispers something in his ear.*)

GENERAL: Idiots!

PRUSSIAN COLONEL: What's the matter now?

GENERAL: Forward position taken. Back to the second line. Wottawa's to blame for that.

PRUSSIAN COLONEL: Awkward situation! Well, were you shouting "Hurrah" on the wrong foot there again? (*The musicians play a Viennese song.*) Ah, delightful! (*He sings along.*) "Let's drink just one more little bottle—drink just one more little bottle—for I still have money in my

pocket—" (*Looking around.*) But I really haven't met some of these gentlemen yet— (*He points to a group of officers.*)
GENERAL (*pointing*): You! You! You! (*The officers stand up.*)
A HUSSAR FIRST LIEUTENANT: Géza von Lakkati de Némesfalva et Kutjafelegfaluszeg.
PRUSSIAN COLONEL: Funny name. A jolly fellow.
GENERAL: That's a red devil.
PRUSSIAN COLONEL: Red devil—dashing! Yes, the splendid Hungarian cavalry men.
A MAJOR: Romuald Kurzbauer.
PRUSSIAN COLONEL: Viennese?
GENERAL: No, he's a Salzburger.
A FIRST LIEUTENANT: Stanislaus von Zakrychiewicz.
PRUSSIAN COLONEL: Croatian?
GENERAL: A Pole, a Pole.
PRUSSIAN COLONEL: Ah, a noble Pole!
A LIEUTENANT: Petričič.
PRUSSIAN COLONEL: Romanian?
GENERAL: No, Croatian.
A FIRST LIEUTENANT: Iwaschko.
PRUSSIAN COLONEL: Bohemian?
GENERAL: Romanian.
A MAJOR: Koudjela.
PRUSSIAN COLONEL: Italian?
GENERAL: Bohemian!
A CAVALRY CAPTAIN IN THE ARMY SERVICE CORPS: Felix Bellak.
PRUSSIAN COLONEL: Aha. (*The men who have introduced themselves sit down. The Chief Staff Surgeon clinks his glass with the Chief Military Judge; the Field Rabbi, with the Field Chaplain.*) Live it up! Always looking snappy! Keep it up!
A MAJOR: He is our gallant anti-sin cannon. (*Peals of laughter, in which the Field Chaplain takes part.*)

FIELD CHAPLAIN: Yes, yes indeed—I do manage to tidy up their iniquities!

(*Sound of artillery.*)

A GERMAN GENERAL STAFF OFFICER: Long live Austrian Gemütlichkeit (*Cheers and hurrahs. Clinking of glasses.*)

CHIEF STAFF SURGEON: Long live German organization! (*Cheers and hurrahs. Clinking of glasses.*)

(*The band plays on. Laughter and singing at the end of the table. The Officer on Telephone Duty hurries in, steps up to the General Staff Officer on Duty and hands a dispatch to him. The General Staff Officer gets up, staggers over to the General, and whispers something in his ear.*)

GENERAL: Such blockheads!

PRUSSIAN COLONEL: What's the matter now?

GENERAL (*reading*): Position—smashed to smithereens. Adjoining areas lie—under—under heavy annihilating fire— These boneheads! They're spoiling one of our most beautiful successes—! (*Lets the dispatch fall.*) Never mind—we won't even ignore it.

PRUSSIAN COLONEL (*picking it up*): Reserves deployed. Reserves for that sector already completely used up. Batteries must be brought back to a rallying point. —Damn it all! (*Strengthened thunder of artillery.*)

AUSTRIAN GENERAL STAFF OFFICER ON DUTY (*to a waiter*): Don't keep filling it up all the time. Today I need—a clear— head.

PRUSSIAN COLONEL: Well, let's hope that Hindenburg will see that things go properly. In the end it will be up to us to pull you out of the mud again!

GENERAL: Gentlemen—we are proud—that we march— shoulder to shoulder with our battle-steeled allies—with gleaming weapons—. Gentlemen, I drink to our Nibelung troth—in this alliance that they've now consolidated (*cries of "Bravo!"*)—and—and—

PRUSSIAN COLONEL: —deepened— (*Cheers and hurrahs. The music plays "The Watch on the Rhine" and "Hail to You with the Victor's Wreath."*) I thank you, gentlemen—I thank you! But now let's drop the festive folderol, if I may ask. Let us postpone our rapturous celebrations for the day of ultimate victory. Now for another of your delightful Austrian songs—one from your splendid Lehar, who has brought us so much joy on the western front. (*Cries of "Bravo!"*)

GENERAL: Play "Call Me Poopsi!"

PRUSSIAN COLONEL: "Poopsi"—what's that anyhow? All right, "Poopsi," fine! (*The band strikes up the song.*)

GENERAL: But where are our field mattresses? They're keeping pretty mum today? How come you're not singing along?

CAVALRY CAPTAIN (*calling across the table*): Nurse Paula—what a backside she's got on her! Terrific. Nurse Ludmilla can't hold a candle to her.

NURSE PAULA (*shrieking*): Ouch! —Stop it—what a dreadful man, he is!

CAVALRY CAPTAIN: What's the matter, can't a fellow hand out compliments any more?

NURSE LUDMILLA: Always making personal remarks!

AUSTRIAN FIRST LIEUTENANT: Well, and those knockers!

PRUSSIAN COLONEL: "Knockers"—? Hey, listen, what funny words you have—what are "knockers"? (*The general explains.*)

CHIEF COMMISSARY OFFICER: The girls ought to sing a duet! (*Cries: "A duet!"*)

FIRST LIEUTENANT: The Field Chaplain and the Field Rabbi ought to sing a duet!

ANOTHER FIRST LIEUTENANT: The Field Rabbi can yodel—and the Field Chaplain can yiddle—no—the other way round— (*Resounding glee.*)

(*The Officer on Telephone Duty dashes in, goes directly up to the General, and whispers something in his ear.*)

GENERAL: What? The miserable—the miserable—these swine in the front lines—!

PRUSSIAN COLONEL: What's the matter now?

GENERAL: I don't understand it. But I had specifically—

PRUSSIAN COLONEL: Now, now, fellows—just don't get weak-kneed now, when we have victory in our pockets. (*To the Officer on Telephone Duty.*) What's the matter now?

OFFICER ON TELEPHONE DUTY (*stammering with great excitement*): The first waves of the retreating divisions have already reached the position of the corps command—the entire artillery was left in the lurch—the roads are blocked by piled-up baggage—the troops demoralized—enemy cavalry in sharp pursuit. (*Exit.*)

(*The Colonel talks to the General emphatically. The others engage in relaxed conversation.*)

A CAPTAIN: You—Koudjela—

KOUDJELA: Yes—

CAPTAIN: The homemade pastry was good! Really very good!

KOUDJELA: Yes—

CAPTAIN: You—Koudjela—

KOUDJELA: Yes—

CAPTAIN: The wine is good! Really very good!

KOUDJELA: Yes—

A LIEUTENANT COLONEL (*to a sleeping Austrian Colonel*): Colonel, colonel!

AUSTRIAN COLONEL (*waking up*): What's happened—

LIEUTENANT COLONEL: Nothing! (*Laughter.*)
A PRUSSIAN FIRST LIEUTENANT: One of the worst things about being at the front is that they give you marmalade every day.
A SECOND FIRST LIEUTENANT: Ah, we've already run out of hero's butter, too. In Russia our men are in an awful fix. In one sector they have a real cholera outbreak. You know, because the guys drank water from a pond where there were Russian corpses.
CAVALRY CAPTAIN: That's not for me—I need champagne! (*Peals of laughter.*)
A THIRD FIRST LIEUTENANT: Well, yes, the Colonel is complaining about the thunder of the artillery. He can't sleep at night. His former quarters were better in this regard. I've always said the situation is unfavorable. Tonight's going to be another one of those nights! Nothing much can happen, but the noise at night is a pain in the neck.

(*Violent detonation.*)

ARTILLERY ADVISER: That was quite a whopper!
A LIEUTENANT: —Scharinger from the Eleventh? He really is a lucky dog! Now he's up for a promotion—
CAVALRY CAPTAIN: —You know, bosom— (*gestures*) first class!
A FIRST LIEUTENANT: But if you only knew what I've got going for me—but wow—!
CAVALRY CAPTAIN: Skirt chaser! In the last issue of *Die Muskete*—
A MAJOR: Long live our supply officer! (*Cheers. Clinking of glasses.*)
A MAJOR GENERAL: Yes, Pschierer! He really shows his mettle. Twelve courses—you've got to admit that he really outdid himself. (*Drinks to him.*)
MAJOR: You know, those humanitarians—I've already gotten a bellyful of them. All I have to do is to see a humanitarian

from a distance, and I get all riled up. Imagine opposing a man such as Stöger-Steiner! Tersztszyansky once made short work of such a trial. That is, he didn't allow any trial at all.

CHIEF MILITARY JUDGE: How's that?

MAJOR: You know, there was one of your humanitarians—one of your close colleagues—

CHIEF MILITARY JUDGE: Hey, there's no need to suspect me!

MAJOR: Oh, come on, I'm only kidding you a little bit. So listen to me—this guy refused to court-martial a fellow. It's only a disciplinary case, he said, just some tomfoolery. Well, in the mess hall—here comes Tersztszyansky in for you, sits down to his soup—you know, I have never ever seen Tersztszyansky so calm! —He says, Captain, says he, we don't need a trial at all for your prisoner any more. How come, the captain asks. Well, look at him out there in the garden—just look at him—he's lying out there. Tersztszyansky had simply told the corporal to cut the fellow down with a bayonet—zappo! You know, because he was so terribly mad at the stubborn fellow.

CHIEF MILITARY JUDGE: At the prisoner?

MAJOR: No, at the captain!

CHIEF MILITARY JUDGE: Oh, yes, naturally! —Play "The Dance Was Beautiful, but They're Not Playing It Now." (*Cries of "Bravo!" The band plays. The officers sing along.*)

(*The Officer on Telephone Duty dashes in, white as chalk, rushes directly up to the General, and says something in his ear.*)

GENERAL: What—? They're mutinying? Mow the bastards down! Let them put a couple of fresh regiments into action! Keep them at it, keep them at it! Hurry!

PRUSSIAN COLONEL: What's the matter now?

(*The Officer on Telephone Duty whispers something else to the General.*)

GENERAL: What? The gas grenades won't work either?! The whole thing's a filthy mess!!
PRUSSIAN COLONEL: Now listen a minute, that just should not—! Among us Germans this could never happen—!
GENERAL: Such an—awful muddle! —Such tough luck! —It just can't be helped—
PRUSSIAN COLONEL: Well, it just mis-succeeded! A little bit weak-kneed, our beloved Austrians, a little bit weak-kneed!
FIRST WAR CORRESPONDENT: Look at the General, so what did I tell you—!
SECOND WAR CORRESPONDENT: Major, can you perhaps tell me how things stand in the battle—?
MAJOR: An enemy offensive has started.
FIRST WAR CORRESPONDENT: Oy vey!
MAJOR: The enemy has pushed in the front-line positions somewhat—
SECOND WAR CORRESPONDENT: His own positions? To what end?
MAJOR: We hope that we will be successful in thwarting this treacherous plan. But please, don't mention my name.

(*The sound of artillery grows weaker and weaker.*)

GENERAL STAFF OFFICER ON DUTY: —But, at Tolmein—
GERMAN GENERAL STAFF OFFICER: Oh, that was long ago. In only one day we gassed far more men there than you did in a whole year! In smoking out the last pockets of French, white and colored Englishmen, and the like. Yes sir—our German hand-gas-grenade type B! With that thing the poisonous substance sprays out and creates suppurating wounds, with a secretion like an honest-to-goodness case of the clap. (*Laughter.*) You don't believe it? It has been scientifically proven incontestably! The man isn't done for until the next day.

(*The sound of the artillery is completely silent.*)

VARIOUS VOICES: Aha! Now what's up? Now what's up?

WAR CORRESPONDENTS: What's the meaning of this?

GENERAL (*leaping up with a fiery red face, pounds on the table*): Good God!! But I specifically—!! This could only happen to us— Didn't I tell the riffraff often enough! (*Roaring.*) If a single cartridge is missing, skin the man alive! —Throw yourself on the enemy with a hearty hurrah! —While still at a short distance burn one in under his nose, then immediately let him have it in the ribs with your bayonet! —Cut down disloyal comrades ruthlessly! —In spite of hand grenade and machine gun, the rifle is always the infantryman's best friend! Officers must be tough and get the best out of their men! —And what have they done—these front-line swine, these dogs—these—these— (*Wailing.*) They spoil everything for you—these scribblers! —Not by the enemy, by hunger! (*Clenching his fists.*) These subversives—hang them all! —I—was the one—I have always seen it coming, the misfortune of our army will—drag even my corps along with it!—This bottomless recklessness—ineradicable—nothing but gorging themselves and hussies—demoral— (*He breaks down.*)

GENERAL STAFF OFFICER ON DUTY (*jumping up*): It's these malingerers who are at fault for all this—out there—these front-line swine—these—

AUSTRIAN COLONEL (*waking up*): What's happened now?

GENERAL: Where—were the machine guns to drive our men forward? What happened to our superior fire power?! — Those scoundrels!! After an unprecedented four-year struggle—against a model—superior power—exemplary—our glor— (*He falls into his chair, whimpering.*) So—in the—end—they're—even going to—come—right in—here—

PRUSSIAN COLONEL: Not so, Your Excellency, keep your head high! Gentlemen, we must not and cannot let our courage

Act V, Scene 55

sink—now before the ultimate victory—we can and must, with heads held high—be assured, gentlemen, that this is only an example of the initial success typical of every enemy offensive—a bluff and no more. This is not the time to panic. What is still open to us is a strategic retreat—and a strategic retreat is always a success! (*Isolated cries of "Hurrah!" and cheers.*) And I have been convinced from the outset that the enemy will not hinder our movements, which were taken into consideration years ago and implemented days ago. Our operations are proceeding according to plan. We have simply detached ourselves from the enemy and are smoothly pulling them along behind us! Up and at 'em! The mood of the troops can't be beat. Gentlemen, we shall not waver, nor shall we yield! The more often we give the enemy the opportunity to advance, the better prospect we have of wearing them down! It's the tactic we practiced at the Somme. It's the tactic that will also succeed for us here at the Piave. Only, no wavering now! God is with us. We will manage it—and even if the world were full of devils! The enemy will—be assured of it, gentlemen—the enemy will come up against us as upon a iron fire wall—

(*The horizon is a wall of flames. Sounds of panic. Many of those present are lying under the table. Many are hurrying or wobbling toward the exit; a number turn back with horror and distorted faces.*)

CRIES: What's happened now? —What's—

GENERAL (*babbling*): They've broken—through—! Keep playing—

(*All the lights have gone out. Outside there is tumult. One hears the explosion of aerial bombs. Then there is silence. Those present are sleeping, lying there in a somnolent state or staring, totally aghast, at the wall where the mural*

"The Time of Greatness" hangs and where now the following apparitions appear in turn.)

Narrow mountain path to Mitrovica. Snow flurries. Among thousands of carts, an incalculable mass of human beings: old people and women, children, half-naked, holding the hands of their mothers, many of whom also carry an infant in their arms. A little boy, at the side of a peasant woman from the Moravian valley, holds out his little hand and says:

Uncle, give me bread—

The scene is supplanted by another picture. The Balkan train is speeding across the landscape. It gradually slows down. One sees the dining car. Both War Correspondents are leaning out the windows; they appear to be drinking to their counterparts in the dining hall. One of them calls out:

Say what you will, there's something beautiful about the war—

Now the first apparition returns. The exhausted refugees, already almost dead of cold, lie on the ice-covered stones. The morning light falls on the hollow-cheeked, pale faces, in which the horror of the past night can still be seen. A cry; a horse plunges into the abyss. Yet another cry, still more piercing: the man leading him has plunged after him. On the edge of the path, a horse, almost dead from exhaustion. Nearby an ox with its intestines hanging out, a man with his skull battered in. The wagon train starts up again. Weakened, tired animals remain behind. They stand, unmoving. Their gaze, deathly mournful, follows the wagon train. A peasant woman with a deathly pale face sits leaning against a fir tree—she is the one from the Moravian valley. In her arms she holds a small lifeless body at whose head, with a flickering light, a tiny wax candle burns.

(*The apparition vanishes.*)

Act V, Scene 55

A garrison. The following scenes take place in rapid succession. Slovak peasants, home from Russian captivity, dressed partly in peasant clothes, partly in Russian uniforms, request extension of their furloughs, because they have to get in the harvest. The company commander orders that the petitioners be immediately assigned to the next unit to go to the front. A room becomes visible in which two young returnees, nineteen and twenty-one years old, are sleeping. They are awakened by the noise of an incident that is taking place outside. A sergeant is distributing uniforms. The men refuse to accept them and demand to be heard by the battalion commander. The corporal strikes several of them and is himself struck in the face. The permanent cadre are alerted, rifles are loaded, the mutineers are driven to the barracks compound at bayonet point and surrounded. The captain appears; all follow his order to line up in ranks. The two young men are among them. The captain receives the report concerning the incident. No one knows who delivered the blow. The captain pulls out every tenth man, has them led off to the guardroom. There they are beaten, lie with shackles on their feet, and are then brought out under garrison arrest. Martial law is declared. Interrogations follow. Six are to be brought before the military court.

The detention compound in the gray hours of the next morning. The judges, the battalion commander, the provost marshal, and two priests appear. A table and a crucifix are brought. The court groups itself around the table with a priest at either end. One of the six prisoners has a heart attack at this sight; he collapses, howling and foaming at the mouth. Others tear their hair, rage, and rip their clothing. The guards try to calm them with the assurance that only two will be sentenced to death. A judge reads the indictment. The nineteen-year-old and the twenty-one-year-old are sentenced to be shot by the firing squad; the remainder are given prison sentences of several years. The nineteen-year-old falls to his knees in front of the presiding officials, shaken by sobs, and begs for mercy. He shows a locket with the picture of his old mother. She will not survive his death; let them send him to the front; he wants to prove that he is a good soldier; he was asleep during the riot; he is completely innocent. The judge has him led away. The other accused stands there, pale as death, but upright. He speaks the words:

God knows that I die innocent!

He lets himself be led away while the others weep for their comrades. The judges move to the mess hall. There one of them says:

It's quite clear that only the one with children could be guilty. But can one shoot a father of six children? The state would then have to support his survivors! So he got six years, as many years as he has children—and the dependents of military convicts can be denied state assistance.

A second says:

Three others are also married—so the only ones who could be shot were the two young fellows. They've most likely done something. If not today, then tomorrow. Innocence here, innocence there—an example must be set.

At night in jail. Behind the barred window, the younger one stands praying, a rosary in his hand. The chaplains appear to administer the last rites to the convicted men. The younger one cries out, asking to see his mother once more. Then they all pray together. The prisoner asks for paper and pencil in order to write to his mother. He writes. It is already 8:45 P.M. He gets up.

Mother!

He collapses. The other says:

Is it for this that I fought, for this that I returned from Russia, so that I could be led to the butcher like a steer to slaughter? —They should truss me up and carry me! —Have I lived to be twenty-one years old only in order to be shot? —Do it quickly!

On the way to the place of execution. He takes leave of the shining August sun. He tears off a green leaf from a tree and kisses it fervently. The younger one does not cease to cry for his mother. At the place of execution, an ancient castle courtyard. Entrance is limited to those showing proof of authorization. Among those present can be seen the chief authorities, high-ranking officers, various other dignitaries, and their wives. The best social circles of the city are represented. The judges, the battalion commander, and the off-duty battalion officers take positions in the middle of the square. The sentence is read. The older of the two says:

If the sergeant is capable of giving such testimony, he deserves to stand here and be shot.

They do not wish to be blindfolded.

I have no more fear of the bullet.

They are blindfolded. They kneel down.

Fire!

Brandishing of sabers. Two corpses in the grass. The captain gives an order for prayer. They all salute. One of the priests, with an officer's cap and a golden insignia on his sleeve, gives a speech, points with his raised right arm to the banner and looks, transfigured, toward the heavens in the direction of the Hapsburg coat of arms above the gateway.

(The apparition vanishes.)

Kragujevac. In each of two parallel rows twenty-two graves have been dug. In front of them are kneeling forty-four older front-line veterans, with hero's medals of all degrees. Bosnian executioners shoot from a distance of two paces. Their hands tremble. The first group rolls to the ground. None of them are dead. Rifle barrels are put to their heads. The scene changes to an officers' mess. The Chief Military Judge lifts his glass and speaks the following words, while he drinks to his counterpart in the banquet hall:

You know, I could have had three hundred of them hanged. The commission of violent acts while drunk cannot be tolerated. As an exception, I granted these men the honorable death of being shot.

(The apparition vanishes.)

Captain Prasch stands in front of his dugout, totally smeared with blood; over his head he holds a head that he has stuck on a staff. He speaks:

This is my first Italian prisoner; I did it with my own saber. As for my first Russian prisoner I had him tortured before. I like going after Czechs the best. Whomever I met in Serbia, I shot down on the spot. Twenty people, among them civilians and prisoners, I killed with my own hands; at least one hundred and fifty I had shot. Every soldier who was tardy when there was an attack or who hid during bombardment, I shot down with my own hands. I always struck my subordinates in the face, either with my cane or my fist. But I also did a lot for them. In Serbia I raped a Serbian girl, but then I turned her over to the soldiers, and the next day I had the girl and her mother hanged from the grating of a bridge. The rope broke and the girl fell into the water, still alive. I drew my revolver and shot at the girl until she disappeared under the water, dead. I have always fulfilled my duty to the last breath of man and beast. I have been decorated and promoted. I was always at my post. The war demands rigid concentration of all one's powers. One must not let his courage fail. Head high! (*He raises his staff higher.*)

(*The apparition vanishes.*)

A lancer first lieutenant has a Russian Orthodox priest tied to the stirrup of a mounted rider. They take off his coat.

You won't need your coat any more.

The rider goes off at a slow trot.

(*The apparition vanishes.*)

Winter in the Carpathians. A man tied to a tree. He is being untied and collapses in a faint. The company leader kicks him with his boot heel and indicates a hole in the ground to which the soldiers carry him.

(*The apparition vanishes.*)

In flight. It is raining. The General who had been at the love feast sits in his automobile and gives the order to take the tenting away from the stretcher of a wounded man and to spread it out over his car. He waves to his alter ego and drives off.

(*The apparition vanishes.*)

Near a beet field in Bohemia. Two children are carrying a child's coffin to the cemetery. They let the coffin drop. They drag the body, which has rolled into the field, back to the coffin and set out again on their way.

(*The apparition vanishes.*)

A pile of garbage, waste matter, and factory debris next to a bakery plant. Half-starved children are looking for bread crumbs. They find an unexploded shell. They play with it. It explodes.

(*The apparition vanishes.*)

Row of gallows in Neusandez. Children swing and twirl the hanging corpses. A woman who has managed to buy potatoes is beaten to death by people for whom nothing was left. They stamp around on the corpse.

(*The apparition vanishes.*)

On a track stands a freight train, the home of a swarm of filthy human beings: they are refugees, among them pregnant women, dying old people, and sick children.

(*The apparition vanishes.*)

In front of a hut in Volhynia. A farmer with his sheep dog. A soldier comes along the road and wounds the dog with a bayonet thrust.

(*The apparition vanishes.*)

Drinking bout of officers. A lieutenant shoots a waitress.

(*The apparition vanishes.*)

Pause in the fighting on the Drina. A Serbian farmer goes for water. A lieutenant stands across from him and takes aim. He shoots him down.

(*The apparition vanishes.*)

Act V, Scene 55

Good Friday in a church in Paris. It is hit by a missile from a 120-kilometer cannon.

(*The apparition vanishes.*)

Easter Sunday. Russian prisoners who have refused to join a work detail on a position under enemy fire say their last prayers.

(*The apparition vanishes.*)

Dying men in the barbed wire in front of Przemyśl.

(*The apparition vanishes.*)

Close combat and the mopping up of a trench.

(*The apparition vanishes.*)

A schoolroom into which an aerial bomb falls.

(*The apparition vanishes.*)

A soldier is pulled up out of a mass of earth. His face is streaming with blood. He spreads out his arms. He has been blinded.

(*The apparition vanishes.*)

A medical depot at the front is hit by an aerial bomb.

(*The apparition vanishes.*)

A mine explosion. A soldier stretches out the bloody stumps of his arms in the direction of the banquet hall.

(*The apparition vanishes.*)

A double apparition: A German officer who shoots down a French prisoner pleading for his life. A French officer who shoots down a German prisoner pleading for his life.

(*The apparition vanishes.*)

Desolate region along the Somme. Swaths of smoke like gigantic mourning flags. Buildings collapse. Wells are blasted by engineers and closed off. Evacuation. Old people are driven out of their houses. People shiver with cold at the assembly points. Women fall to their knees in front of officers. They are transported for forced labor.

(*The apparition vanishes.*)

The Sorel dairy farm at Loison is reduced to ashes and 250 wounded men housed there are burned to death.

(*The apparition vanishes.*)

The sinking of a hospital ship.

(*The apparition vanishes.*)

Longuyon set to the torch with buckets of gasoline, the houses and the church plundered. The wounded and small children burn to death.

(*The apparition vanishes.*)

Flanders. In a plundered hut, a figure in a gas mask sits in front of a kettle. On his lap, a smaller gas mask.

(*The apparition vanishes.*)

A horse, upon whose back the outline of a gun is etched in blood, appears.

(*The apparition vanishes.*)

Winter in Asinara. Prisoners strip comrades who have died of cholera. Starving people eat the flesh of those who have starved to death.

(*The apparition vanishes.*)

Barracks in Siberia. Gray-haired men, starved-looking and barefoot, in ragged uniforms, huddle on the ground, staring into the distance with sunken eyes. A few sleep, a few write, a few exercise with shovels and practice rifle drills.

(*The apparition vanishes.*)

Thousands of crosses in a field of snow.

(*The apparition vanishes.*)

A battlefield. Craters and holes. Walking paths through the barbed wire, which is still standing. Luxury automobiles arrive. The tourists scatter in groups, photograph each other in heroic positions, parody gun salvos, laugh and emit cries. One has found a skull, sticks it on the end of his walking stick, and brings it along with a triumphant expression. A mourner steps among them, appropriates the find for himself, and buries the skull.

(*The apparition vanishes.*)

The front lines in the Carpathians. All quiet. In the trenches corpses stand upright, their rifles ready.

THE FROZEN SOLDIERS:
    Cold was the night.
    Who has e'er imagined this death!
    O, you who slept in beds,
    Why do your hearts not break?
    The cold stars do not save us.
    And naught will ever save you!

    (*The apparition vanishes.*)

An old Serbian peasant is digging his grave.

THE OLD SERBIAN PEASANT:
    We stood around our empty chest.
    The soldiers yelled and swore at us.

We had nothing left. They wanted more.
That's why I'm digging now my grave.
We were poor. We were bare.
And so they did lay hold of us.
They put my children against the wall,
Ahead of me they sent them all.
Burned is my house, burned is my land,
My grave I dig with my own hand.
The children are calling. I'm on my way.
Lord, take me in and let me stay.

(*The apparition vanishes*).

Twelve hundred horses emerge from the sea and come ashore. They trot off, water streaming from their eyes.

THE TWELVE HUNDRED HORSES:
We are here; we are here; we are here; we are here.
We are here, the twelve hundred horses.
The horses of Dohna are here, they are here.
We have surged from our grave in the waves.

O Dohna, we're coming to you in your sleep.
From the bottom of the sea did we rise.
We had no light. Too much water can seep
Into twelve hundred pairs of eyes.

(*The apparition vanishes.*)

Count Dohna is surrounded by twelve representatives of the press. In their place suddenly appear twelve horses. They press in upon him and kill him.

An inventor's workshop of former times.

LEONARDO DA VINCI:
. . . wherefore I do not write down my method of staying under water as long as I can; and this I shall not publish

or explain because of man's evil nature, which would lead him to utilize it for committing murders on the floor of the ocean by breaking the bottoms of ships and sinking the same, together with all the peoples in them . . .

(*The apparition vanishes.*)

Sweet strains are heard. Dead calm after the sinking of the Lusitania. Two children's bodies on a piece of flotsam.

THE LUSITANIA CHILDREN:
Bobbing about on the ocean,
We drift and don't know where.
This life is so joyous and merry
We children so happy and gay.

(*The apparition vanishes.*)

Two Army dogs, yoked to a machine gun.

ARMY DOGS:
We're hauling evil freight and yet we haul.
For we are faithful till the day we die.
How good it was when God's sun brightly shone!
The devil becked. The dog obeyed his call.

(*The apparition vanishes.*)

A dead wood. The trees have all been strafed or chopped or sawed down. Bare earth, with a few sickly trees growing here and there. Hundreds of tree trunks, stripped of their branches and sawed into lengths, litter the ground, their bark already half rotten. The remains of a military railroad track cut diagonally across the wood.

THE DEAD WOODS:
Your doings, evil and obscene,
Have turned me gray. Once I was green.

Look at my present sorry sight
A woods was I, a woods was I!

You Christians hear: beneath my dome
The soul found its eternal Rome.
Within my silence was the Word.
But what you do plain murder is.

I curse you as I slowly die,
No longer reaching for the sky.
How old I am! How green I stood!
A woods was I, a woods was I!

(*The apparition vanishes.*)

A colonel orders the arrest of a Dalmatian woman and her blond twelve-year-old son. As the woman is being dragged away, he gives orders for the boy to be shot through the head. He stands by, smoking as the soldiers kneel on the boy's hands and the execution is carried out.

THE MOTHER:
Through all the days your presence stains this planet
May your mind's eye not blot away this scene
And when you've ended your descent to Hell,
This image shall in shame greet you again!
The splinters from the forehead of this child
Shall penetrate your very hearts and brains.
Long life to you! And may this mother's scream
Stay with you always through your every dream!

(*The apparition vanishes.*)

The sound swells into terrible music during the next vision. Monte San Gabriele. A high pile of rotting unburied corpses. A flock of ravens swarms over the carrion, croaking.

THE RAVENS:
  We have always found good pickings
  Whenever men for honor died,
  While you generals flock together,
  We ravens stay well supplied.

  We, who never begged for fodder,
  Have received it—and in plenty.
  Neither you nor we need starve here
  These for you and us have perished.

  You, like us, croak with elation,
  As the piles of dead mount higher.
  For the fools throughout the nation
  Don't resist the calls you utter.

  Army generals, too, are ravens,
  Croaking bombast in the mess-hall.
  Out here lie the dead, unburied.
  There the ravens are the generals.

  Safely you may lose the battle,
  Neither you nor we the ravens
  Should feel shame for any reason;
  You and we from war do profit.

  Full of life and vim and vigor,
  You and we are still quite healthy,
  Happily we bear the hardships
  That the war has forced upon us.

  While you gluttons join in gorging,
  We don't do so badly, either.
  Since we follow all your armies,
  Never have we ached from hunger.

Hunger never would delight us
Yes, the shame of it would kill us.
We're obliged that you have saved us
From a home front plagued by hunger.

Back at home they truly suffer.
Old folks, children, all do perish.
While their men out here are dying
Heroes' deaths to keep us happy.

But your slaughterhouses never
Keep your lined-up shoppers starving
Ravens, since the killing started,
Never have run short of fodder.

(*The apparition vanishes.*)

The music, muted now, accompanies the following scene and dies gradually away. An endless procession of pale women files past, flanked by soldiers with fixed bayonets.

THE WOMEN AUXILIARIES:
To inspire the glorious army
We the troop of harlots followed.
Turn our backs now on you heroes,
We the lost brigade of specters.

Yielding to the heroes' lustings
Your bright courage was contagious.
On our cheeks red roses blossom,
And the syph'lis in our systems.

Blood and semen, wine and weeping,
Flowed in bacchanalian orgies.
Those fine parting gifts you gave us
Home we carry to the clinic.

Act V, Scene 55

We are objects of derision,
Loosely our garments dangle
Drearily we drag our booty
Behind the lines—and homeward.

Yet our ranks grow through the ages
Soon will sweep an army flailing
Crippled mankind, sparing no one
Through a shuddering millennium.

(The apparition vanishes.)

A phosphorescent glow now fills the banquet hall.

THE UNBORN SON:
  Later witnesses of outrage,
  We implore you to abort us!
  Don't permit us to be born!
  We would be your shame's betrayer
  We don't want such hero-fathers
  Gloryless we wish to fade.

  Joy and pain of earthly doing!
  Lovingly that wretch, my father,
  Handed down the clap to me.
  To these realms you must not drag us.
  Offspring are we but of corpses.
  Here the air is noxious-foul.

(The glow dies out. Total darkness. Then, on the horizon, the wall of flames leaps high. Death cries off stage.)

THE END

Critical Analysis[*]

BY FRANZ H. MAUTNER

I

The Last Days of Mankind is a unique phenomenon in the history of the drama. This satiric tragedy is almost eight hundred pages long, and its list of characters includes approximately five hundred figures. It has half of Europe as its stage. Organized in a prologue, five acts, and an epilogue, it begins with the voice of a newsboy and ends with that of God. The cry of the newsboy resounds in Vienna in June, 1914; the voice of God rings out over a battlefield at the end of World War I, at which point the drama has been transformed into a modern Walpurgis Night. From Vienna the drama spreads out over the territory of the Austro-Hungarian monarchy, the occupied territories and war zones, and, from the third act on, into Germany, and onward, everywhere, wherever the armies and merchants of the Central Powers had penetrated.

It takes place in the streets of Vienna and Berlin, in chancelleries and barracks, churches and coffeehouses, places of entertainment and military hospitals, homes and editorial

[*] An abridged version of the article by Professor Mautner entitled "Die letzten Tage der Menschheit" in *Das deutsche Drama*, edited by Benno von Wiese, Volume II, pp. 357–82. The translation is by Sue Ellen Wright.

offices; at the freight terminal in Debrecen and in a gynecological clinic in Weimar; in the rear lines and at the front, in an artillery emplacement high in the Dolomites and on a U-boat. Local color is almost nowhere the object, but rather, emphasis is upon the types of people acting and speaking in each place, their manner of speech, and what is going on in their minds. Among them are hundreds of real-life characters—from literature, finance, and the theater—and invented characters—business, professional, and street types. The last two Austrian emperors and the last German kaiser appear, along with Hindenburg and Ludendorff, Austrian army commanders and archdukes, German professors and politicians, government ministers and restaurateurs, prostitutes and pastors, police and traveling businessmen, local Viennese greats, and, again and again, journalists. The Optimist discusses the events of the war with the Grumbler—Karl Kraus himself.

In a dozen dialects these characters speak everyday German; the voice of the heart, as well as that of the journals, is heard; dashing contemporaries introduce themselves in music-hall ditties; Emperor Franz Josef chants the litany of his life. More and more often, as the drama approaches its end, the voice of its author and the lament of nature, profaned by the war, come to the fore. Wordless apparitions, more eloquent than any words, are among the most heartrending episodes of the work; loquacious scribblers betray their own nothingness through the vanity of their own words.

This drama full of sanguinary jokes has no plot, only a sequence of scenes that become ever more threatening, more farcical, and more terrifying. Its protagonist is European mankind, above all the Germans and Austrians, from 1914 to 1918. Its subject is the disintegration of European culture, especially that of the Central Powers. In 1871 Nietzsche saw the genesis of this disintegration against a German background. In Austria Karl Kraus had seen it coming and had been predicting it since 1910. It is reflected in the drama's incessantly changing stream of episodes, and even more so in the conversations and speeches of its characters. And *how* these things are said is frequently more significant than *what*. Here and there this flow is suspended by the argumentative dialogues between the Grumbler and the Optimist, or by the monologues of the Grumbler. In the latter, Kraus comments in prose and verse upon the meaning of the events in the drama and endeavors to insure that his tragic intent is properly understood. (See Act V, scene 54, "The Grumbler at His Desk.")

Kraus foresaw that those events that were to him a terrifying reality would be incredible to future readers. This foresight, fired by an ethical impulse, was a stimulus to preserve that reality in the text of the drama. Beginning as early as 1915, during the war, he had made parts of it public in dozens of lectures, in his journal *Die Fackel*, and in the volumes of poetry, *Worte in Versen* (Words in Verse). The drama in its entirety could not be published before 1918 and 1919. Only the epilogue, "The Last Night," was produced on the stage during Kraus's lifetime.

II

Die Fackel and the lecture halls in which Kraus had been reading his satiric works for many years were the natural forum for the presentation of *The Last Days*. At first attacking the war of the Central Powers, then opposing war altogether, the drama was essentially nothing but the continuation of Kraus's cultural criticism and satire, intensified to the highest, broadest, and most profound degree. But the suffering and degradation of man during the war had grown so outrageous that these themes themselves gradually became the subjects of his drama.

Kraus saw in the suffering and the atrocities of those four years the evils that had always been prevalent; during the war they had only become distinctly and fatefully obvious. It appeared to him that the responsibility for this state of affairs lay with a society that, motivated by its craving for prestige and profit, idolized power and the machine, a society for which life's means had become life's goal. To Kraus, the substance of true humanity—heart, soul, and spirit—appeared to be threatened by a morally insensitive intellectualism, a pseudoliberalism that he believed was particularly embodied in the Austrian Jews of his time. "Enlightenment," together with the economic drive for expansion, seemed to have destroyed respect for nature, for every mystery, for the femininity of woman, and for the dignity of man. Other symptoms of degeneration were general, associated with no specific group or world view: a hypocritical sexual morality, dominated by the drive itself, but finding it either despicable or amusing, was coupled with an equally hypocritical sentimentality. Kitschy decorate-your-home art in Germany and an equally calloused *Gemütlichkeit* in Austria were disguises for falsehood and a lack of substance.

The incarnation of all these evils was the press, through its nature, through its power—for it generated public opinion, and with it, values. Corrupt in its commercial interests, in its morals, and in its language, it did not present the essence of things but instead accentuated the sensational; it neglected rational substance in favor of social prestige. It pried into the private life of the individual without respect for either the cradle or the grave, prayer or mystery. Whatever it could scrape up, the press printed. Its reporting and argumentation were couched in journalistic phrases and clichés devoid of all imagination, of all capacity for experience. That the press wrote in hackneyed phrases and clichés was an expression of its unnaturalness and its profound falsehood. Its manner of writing became the manner of speaking and thinking of the society, and vice versa.

As a consequence of the war, the role of the press and of the essentially "journalistic" world view that it fostered became more important and more disastrous in its effect. Journalism had its share in unleashing and prolonging the war; it intruded itself between the reader and the fighting, suffering, and dying at the front; in this activity it carried over the irreverence, the practices, and the style that were its wont during peace, a style embellished with the metaphors of a long-vanished chivalric and heroic past, metaphors that were vacuous and hypocritical in the war of machines. What was annoyance became ignominy; what was an inconvenience to private life endangered life itself. Journalism re-created the war in its own image, and the war adapted itself to journalism's forms and needs.

Before the war the locale within which Kraus observed and satirically treated the substitution of genuine ethics and genuine culture with a deceptive façade had been Austria, in particular Vienna—Vienna's society, institutions, and customs. At that time he had preferred Berlin for its organizational competence, unrelated to cultural pretensions, its separation of the matters of civilization from those of culture, and its differentiation between factual and personal criteria. All these aspects he preferred to the peculiar Viennese self-infatuation, a milieu in which automatons "have collective personality, but don't function," popularity substitutes for personality, and genuine personality is stifled. When the war began—brought about, in Kraus's eyes, by Austria—he saw it as a tragedy for mankind, acted out by characters who had the dimensions of operetta figures. For Kraus their phantomlike nature, their thirst for publicity, and the lack of misgivings or conscience with which they exercised the power entrusted to them either to cause suffering or to ease it, brought them into tragic relief against the bloody background of the war and caused its atmosphere to appear tragically grotesque. His drama attempted to reflect this atmosphere as such.

In the Preface, Kraus did his best to affirm the literal authenticity of the grotesque, dreadful, unnerving episodes and dialogue in *The Last Days*. "The most improbable deeds reported here really happened. . . . The most glaring inventions are quotations." The readers of the special issues of *Die Fackel*, in which this drama was first published, encountered here hundreds of documents, reports from the front, and advertisements, all reincarnated in the form of oral speech. These artifacts of the times had previously been offered in *Die Fackel* as they were culled from the news and advertisement sections of newspapers, official gazettes, military orders of the day, and collections of poetry. Those who authored these printed words were now forced to speak them. As Kraus wrote in the Preface: "The document is a dramatis persona; reports come to life as personae; personae breathe their last as editorials."

That Kraus succeeded in utilizing this raw material in such a manner that it took shape as a work of art is an accomplishment that runs counter to all conventional aesthetic laws. The "matter," in the most literal sense, plays a more important role here than it does in any other drama. That so great a part of the text—at least a third of the drama—is identical with its raw material is central to its form. Intrinsic to the idea of the play is the demonstration that these utterances—their content and their form—were possible. The content of that which is being said is in itself already terrible and ridiculous enough; the incongruities between the speakers and what they say render the content still more monstrous or more ridiculous. Thus cultural, ethical, and religious tendencies are transformed into structured satire. Kraus's work is satire in the most radical sense. The primary thing that the satire castigates is apostasy from the true spirit, from true ethos, from pure humanity, the turning away from the idealized origin to the worldly goal. Therefore, the obvious reproach, evoked by some of the Grumbler's dialogues with the Optimist, of "lack of moderation," "exaggeration," and "injustice," is without substance: it stems from the world of the practical, of "reality." Kraus's work, however, originates in the realm of the uncompromising idea.

The pillorying of all the contrasts between illusion and truth is present everywhere in *The Last Days*; the attack against the lie was obviously its reason for being born. Kraus's famous war essay, "In dieser grossen Zeit" (In This Great Time; December, 1914), which has as its thesis the smallness of man in this purportedly great time and the mendacious nature of man's wartime ideology, can be seen by us today to be the generative cell of the tragedy, the theme out of which sprang the polyphony of *The Last Days of Mankind*. The Prologue, set just before the outbreak of the war, is the overture to the drama; many of the drama's voices and motifs are already contained in it.

III

Every plot summary for a work of art does violence to its nature; all the more so where the relationship of the content to the raw material and to its essence is as unusual as it is in this drama. Besides, the literally thousands of factual allusions and subtle linguistic effects, which require a trained ear on the part of the reader, are almost inseparably bound up with its significance. Nevertheless, in view of the length of the drama and its impression of cyclopean formlessness, I will attempt to sketch the progression of the 259 scenes, their interrelation, and their individual characteristics.

The action of the Prologue (omitted in this edition) extends from the day of the assassination of the Austrian heir apparent and his wife on June 28, 1914, until the day their bodies are transported from Vienna to the burial site. In the Prologue three thematic strata unfold in four locations. The locations are the Sirk Corner by the Vienna Opera House, which was the pivotal point of the promenade on the Ringstrasse; Café Pucher, habitual haunt of well-to-do citizens, higher government officials, and a few ministers of state; a chancellery in the bureau of the chief of protocol; and the hall in the South Terminal in which lie the sarcophagi of the heir apparent and his wife. The thematic strata are represented by figures typifying Viennese society in its various guises: the lower middle class, the middle class, the aristocracy, the press, and, at the opposite pole, the retinue of the assassinated Franz Ferdinand.

The cultural physiognomy of traits, tendencies, and situations becomes apparent in the conversations of the loitering masses, in the coffeehouse discussion between two sleepy government ministers, in the telephone conversations of the court official responsible for making the arrangements for the burial rites, and in the flowery speeches of publicity-hungry functionaries and dignitaries. This is the object of Kraus's satire: a flaccid, unprincipled world of make-believe and lies, of pseudowords, pseudovalues, and pseudojoviality. This world is typified by the upper crust of society and the representatives of certain professional classes, by the baptized Jews seeking admission into the aristocracy, and by the members of the court society. This last group, having been relieved of the oppressive presence of the brusque Franz Ferdinand, hated as he was by Emperor Franz Josef, takes heartless revenge on those who belonged to Franz Ferdinand's circle. And, eternally ubiquitous, the representatives of the press are pushy and tactless, greedy for prestige and conscious of their own importance. The solemnity of the consecration of the bodies, the quiet prayer, and the sobbing of the children are interrupted by the loud voice of a reporter who advises a colleague: "Better take notes on how they're praying!"

The first three acts take place almost totally in Austria (the first almost exclusively in and near Vienna) and are peopled by Austrian characters. The fourth and fifth acts include German territory, German types, and German degeneration of the spirit as objects of satire that is equally as merciless as that already bestowed upon the Austrians. Just as in the Prologue, the first scene of each act, on Sirk Corner, presents the almost identical dialogue of the quartet of brainless, loose-living home-front officers, whose thoughts circle about moderate drinking and whoring. Nevertheless, references to events of the time, expressed in their conversations and in those of other characters and in the cries of the newsboys, are enough to allow a sort of historical chronology to evolve: each act roughly corresponds to the occurrences of one of the four and a half years of the war.

The first act demonstrates what has become of culture and morality in Vienna and in Austria during just a few months of war. Viennese street figures of all classes are heard through fragments of their conversations and through their characteristic intonations. Hunger for publicity and greed for profit, the lower instincts of the people, and the spirit of revelry are now patriotically tinged; stupidity and brutality are streaked with wartime hysteria. The first act ends with a short nocturnal scene at the Graben (scene 30). There a newsboy's cry—"Extra Edition, 40,000 Russians Dead in Front of Przemyśl!"—mixes unobserved with the oblivious hit-tune warbling of two tipsy traveling salesmen with their female companions. There are new topics for conversation, which the Austrian character deals with in its usual manner; new themes on which the Viennese press expresses itself in an unchanged fashion; new activities, which Kraus's typical Viennese characters have turned to—but the Austrians themselves have remained the same. And tragic humor—it will become tragic horror—grows out of the contrast between the supposedly great time and its small figures, whoever they may be: young officers or old army leaders, ministers of state or coffeehouse owners, antisemitic petit bourgeois or promising Jewish talents, or representatives of the last two of these groups, such as the boastfully folksy reporter for the conservative *Reichspost* or his obtrusive, shrewd counterpart for the free-thinking *Neue Freie Presse*. They are all united by the phraseology of the time.

Kraus's satire in *The Last Days* directs itself more frequently and more vehemently against the manner of self-expression of Austrian Jewish pseudoliberalism than against that of Christian pseudoconservatism, for he held the former to be more dangerous in its destruction of authentic values than the latter in its rigid preservation of illusory ones. To him, the danger of the influential "liberal" press appeared greater than that of the less powerful, more provincial "Christian" one. Old Biach, a longtime subscriber to the *Neue Freie Presse*, and the imperial councillor, the oldest subscriber to the *Presse*, are harmless old Jews from the mercantile sphere. Both war enthusiasts, they embody the consequences of the linguistic and intellectual poisoning that the paper pours out. Moriz Benedikt, the publisher of the *Neue Freie Presse*, is their God. They speak in the style of his editorials—which they quote constantly—and they feel quite at home with them: "He speaks like one of us, only more clearly. It is hard to say whether he speaks as we do or we speak as he does."

In conscious disregard for the requirements of traditional drama, almost a third of the first act is taken up by the long dialogue between the Grumbler and the Optimist. The latter is a well-meaning patriot. Although striving for objectivity, he is dominated by official propaganda. The Grumbler furnishes commentary on prevailing opinions and conditions and on the war itself. He justifies his attitude, which seems negative to the Optimist, by pointing out that his prewar thoughts have turned out to be prophetic. The war, then, in his opinion, could "be ended not by peace, but rather by a war of the cosmos against this rabid planet." This cosmic war is the subject of the Epilogue, "The Last Night."

In the second act, the horrors and the brutalization of the war become evident on the home front. "Vienna remains Vienna." Middlemen, high livers, and profiteers in officers' uniform "who have fixed things up for themselves" feel molested by war cripples on the Sirk Corner (scene 1). A starving man disturbs the "light eater" and the "heavy eater" during their discussion of the tight food situation (scene 12). In the Wurstelprater, Vienna's amusement park, the first showing of a true-to-life trench, advertised as "showing life in the actual trenches with striking realism," becomes a social event through the attendance of Archduke Karl, who is now the heir apparent (scene 8). An operetta singer reads war reports from the stage between two acts (scene 24). In a family scene (scene 33), court councillor Schwarz-Gelber and his wife hatefully reproach one another for not using their various activities—concerts for widows and orphans, and hospital visits to invalid amputees—to best advantage in order to further his career and her social climbing.

"An older, corpulent gentleman with muttonchop whiskers and a pince-nez, who carries a field marshal's staff in each hand," the senile Archduke Friedrich, supreme commander of the Austro-Hungarian armed forces, sits in a movie theater at headquarters and accompanies each bomb hit on the screen with the word "Zap!" (scene 28). With the same cry of "Zap," a Catholic chaplain fires his gun at the enemy for his own amusement. Jealous, Alice Schalek, a war correspondent for the *Neue Freie Presse* and a nuisance on all fronts, procures permission for herself to do the same and thus draws enemy fire onto the hidden Austrian position (scene 7). And, in the midst of all these Austrian scenes, appears the first scene (scene 14) that is supposed to demonstrate the mentality of the German allies: Herr von Dreckwitz reports in great detail on his "hunting successes in Russia" (that is, shooting down Russians). He concludes: "And now for a jolly hunt in France!" Kraus took this speech directly from the sportsmen's magazine *Wild und Hund* (Game and Dogs).

The period of time encompassed by the third act is the transition from the second to the third year of the war. Romania has declared war: "It's a breach of faith, just like Italy," explains the "politically educated" officer at the Sirk Corner (scene 1). Now the satire concentrates on the German anti-spirit of the Wilhelminian age; more than a third of the scenes in this act pertain to this theme. The rapid capitulation of German culture to the influence of the war is demonstrated. Kraus shows how university faculties embraced the military anti-spirit, how courts succumbed to war hysteria, how pastors accepted "war goals" and unchristian acts, and how poets and literati catered to the crudest mass instincts.

In the long scene at the spa Gross-Salze, through the ditty of the commercial councillor Ottomar Wilhelm Wahnschaffe (this part of scene 40 does not appear in this edition) and the conversation of his wife and children, that which the Grumbler had analyzed and condemned as "new German bourgeois mentality" becomes audible. The Wahnschaffe villa, abounding in kitsch and vulgar patriotic items—among them two imitation mortar shells, one bearing the inscription "up and at 'em"—forms the background for Wahnschaffe's praises of things German in twenty-four nine-line stanzas, sung to a cheap folk melody. The panegyric begins: "Whether under sea or in the air, / Who's not for fighting is a wretch."

The tactless, dashing manner of the tennis-playing Crown Prince Wilhelm, as he waves off the troops marching into the Battle of the Somme (scene 42), and the noisy jokes of young traveling salesmen in the face of the quiet dignity of the Imam in a mosque (scene 19) supplement Karl Kraus's picture of new German behavior in Europe. Nor does he spare Austrian representatives of a mankind for whom the war has become an excuse to release inborn and environmentally fostered inferiority and stupidity. We meet the latrine humor of the brutal first lieutenants Fallota and Beinsteller (scene 3). The German poets Otto Ernst and Richard Dehmel have their counterpart in the Austrian priest-poet Ottokar Kernstock (scene 32), and Wahnschaffe has his equal in matters of artistic sensibility and religion in the sexton who displays a rosary made from Italian shrapnel fragments (scene 18).

In the next-to-the-last scene (scene 45), in a Viennese nightclub, the voices of black marketeers, officers, and military doctors, drunken and brutal, join together singing variety hits and patriotic songs, unperturbed by bad news from the front. Thus, the final scene at the Graben (scene 46), provides a still stronger contrast. It is raining and the monologue of the Grumbler in front of the Plague Column resounds through the deserted silence. One image emerges for him:

> Out of sleep and slime the ancient sloppiness
> Speaks the flaccid, melting dialect
> Of the last Viennese . . .

And for the first time in the drama the certainty of doom is expressed:

> O desolated world, this the night
> That nothing more can follow, save the Judgment Day!

In a side street stands, in a monumentally indecent position, a drunkard, who babbles the words "a pleasure!—a pleasure!"

In the first scene of the fourth act even the impressive description of the promenade on the Ringstrasse has been transformed from a realistically satiric, burlesque tone to one that is transparent and surreal. It shows the mood of the year 1917, the year of heavy losses in both victories and defeats, and the entrance of the United States into the war. The manifestations of the old themes become crasser as a consequence of greater losses, greater need, and the progressive disintegration of conscience. A long dialogue between the Grumbler and the Optimist takes issue with Austrian tradition, that "untidy, sanguinary business" for which the rule of Franz Josef was responsible (scene 29). "A seventy-year-old softening of brain and character . . . is the content of days governed in this fashion, a leveling out, disordering and corrupting of all the noble values of a people that has no precedent in world history."

In dozens of variations, "the typical Austrian face" becomes visible. It is to be seen in its most fearful guise, the visage "of the Viennese hangman on a picture postcard who . . . holds his paws over the head of the executed, while grinning faces crowd in close around the corpse." That photograph became the frontispiece for the book edition of *The Last Days*.

The 11,400 gallows that were erected at the order of the zapping Archduke Friedrich continue the tradition established in northern Italy by Franz Josef in his youth. A subsequent scene shows the sleeping Franz Josef chanting the unending litany of his life and of Austrian history (scene 31). It is brilliantly composed from his own well-known turns of phrase and from other contemporary Austrian ones.

This act includes five scenes that exemplify the new German

war spirit. Kaiser Wilhelm appears with a speech that is also linguistically characteristic (scene 37). He proves himself to be a vulgar, sadistic barbarian in the midst of his groveling Byzantine retinue. The fourth act ends with a scene (scene 45) that shows the suffering inflicted on the most guiltless creature in the war: Count Dohna-Schlodien's U-boat has sunk 1200 horses.

The stage directions at the beginning of the fifth act reflect the mood of the last year of the war: "Evening. Wet and cold . . . Soundless staring of a herd of bucks. The wounded and dead line the streets." It is an atmosphere of the approaching end. The front is on the verge of collapse, which, in turn, will bring about the downfall of the Central Powers. And this collapse will be followed by the end of militaristic, capitalistic mankind, its destruction by God's decree. Disconsolation reigns among the soldiers and their families, the millions of prisoners of war and the cripples. But politicians and journalists, blind to reality, demand a "German peace" and the annexation of Allied lands. War profiteers celebrate, only here and there frightened by rumors of peace; an owner of armament stocks almost dies from a heart attack. The conservative Austrian press tries to keep enthusiasm for the Hapsburg dynasty alive. But Emperor Karl's stature is even less imposing than that of Franz Josef, whom he had succeeded; the old archdukes profit from war contracts, and young ones run around with operetta stars.

For the first time the Optimist concedes to the Grumbler that the expectation of a time of greatness was a chimera. This recognition of illusion occurs in the scene at the Vienna North Terminal when exchanged wounded prisoners arrive (scene 52). In many respects this is a verbatim repetition of the final scene of the Prologue at the South Terminal, when the coffins of the heir apparent and his wife arrived. Again the same journalists and the upper crust of society swagger about, unconcerned about the occasion of their coming together—the arrival of the wounded. They utter the same journalistic clichés as they did four years before.

More often now compassion for nature ravaged by man is impressed upon the reader. It may be a horse, the weight of a piece of ordnance etched in his festered back; a dog destined to be butchered; a tree converted into cellulose and newsprint. A radiant snow landscape with a deep-blue sky provides the background for "two gigantic fat balls," the Berlin profiteers Gog and Magog, who wallow out of the car of a Swiss funicular railway (scene 50). "Now, as the group moves, it is for a moment as if the giant silhouettes of a black stain concealed the radiant blue and white cosmos." To Gog's question, "Now what do you say to *that* sun and *that* sky?" Magog answers, content, "Efficient operation! Well, and the snow is also worth the money!"

Again in the fifth act the major motifs of all the preceding acts are brought forward in ever new variations. Once more they are debated dialectically in eight dialogues between the Grumbler and the Optimist and in the Grumbler's desperate monologue at his desk (scene 54). The accusation against Germany and Austria is enlarged to include accusations against monarchy and war. The monologue closes with an explanation and a justification for the drama *The Last Days of Mankind*.

This, the most dramatic of all the Grumbler's monologues, is followed by the most dramatic scene in the drama, the last of the fifth act (scene 55). A disorderly banquet of Austrian and German officers at an Austrian corps headquarters comes to an end when the last of several hardly noticed telephone dispatches makes it fully clear that the enemy has pushed through and that the troops at the front are in wild flight.

The last voice of living figures in the drama falls silent.

There follows a harrowing series of apparitions on the wall of the dining hall in the place where a kitschy tableau "The Time of Greatness" had hung. These apparitions bring before the eye the lamentation of creatures in the war and the wickedness of so many who took part in it. The characters in the early apparitions speak a few words. Those in the later ones are completely silent. The reader's convictions about what is proper to theater may bristle at the primitive nature of this technique, but his emotions succumb to it. The terse prose makes this possible, for it provides nothing much more than titles that remind one of the explanations in silent films. In the last of the apparitions the postwar period is conjured up—noisy tourists photograph each other on a battlefield. Then the apparitions take on a completely unreal dimension. Choirs of battlefield ravens, indulging in horrible word plays, point with satisfaction back at all the annihilated life; the verses of the syphilitic female auxiliaries point forward to the yet-unborn life of the future. The Unborn Son himself turns to the spectators with the request that they never let him come into this world. Darkness and death cries conclude the fifth act.

The Epilogue, "The Last Night" (omitted in this edition), completely in rhymed verse, follows immediately. It takes place during a starless night on the battlefield, in the middle of all the terror of destruction. The transition of the figures from individual to typical and from typical to symbolic is imperceptible. A gas mask representing a female war correspondent—robbed of her individuality and sexless in appearance—her colleagues photographing a dying soldier, and the hussar from the Hohenzollern skull-and-cross-bones regiment all embody again, in the rhythm and phraseology of their speech, the evil powers that have been quoted, mocked, and damned throughout the drama. But the voice of pure nature speaks out in the words of a soldier, mutinying even as he bleeds to death, and in those of a blinded man, creeping along, feeling his way forward. Siegfried Abendrot ("evening's reddish glow") from Berlin presents himself as a chemist who has been completely successful in fusing technology and mythology, science and fairy tale, cruel urge to destroy and true German rhetoric.

Just as repulsive as Abendrot's blaring self-confidence and his commercial, teutonic vocabulary is the assiduousness of the marrowless singsong German, corrupted by Jewish jargon, that the "hyenas with human faces," the Viennese profiteers Fressack ("glutton") and Naschkatz ("nibbling cat"), speak into the ears of the dead soldiers. The tango of the hyenas around the corpses and their ghostlike burlesque song on the delights of forcing up prices are halted by the appearance of the Lord of the Hyenas, Moriz Benedikt, the antichrist. "Three occasional contributors," employing all the clichés that Viennese journalism was accustomed to use when reporting the event of the season, the press ball, describe the waltz that follows Benedikt's appearance on the battlefield.

The social imagery is again transformed into military imagery; the battlefield is overrun by the chaotic flight of the German and Austrian armies. Miracles and signs appear in the heavens, but blaspheming voices take them for their own airmen. The voices laud rains of blood, ashes, and stone as new military tricks, conceived for their own support. But "voices from above" proclaim the "long-awaited counterattack." As total darkness falls, cinema operators demand "more light for 'The Last Judgment!' "

Again a voice resounds from above. It declares war and destruction upon mankind in a speech that is unendingly long and yet powerfully and precisely constructed in a grand and simple style. Alternating between pathos and sanguinary mockery, it gives new meaning to the official and journalistic stock of wartime phrases:

> We have considered everything carefully.
> We have thus determined to eradicate
> Your planet with all its battlefronts . . .

and with it the humans who

> Have defiled the image of creation,
> Tormented the creatures and enslaved the men,
> Honored shame and punished dignity . . .

And thus this sentence, probably the longest in German literature and also the longest catalogue of the sins of the German people, goes on for seventy-two lines of verse. Then a meteor shower sets in, but undaunted, audacious and blasphemous, the battle cries and phrases of the war echo and die away. Then once again we hear the voice from above: "The attack succeeded. The night was wild. God's image is destroyed."

And, after "great silence," follows the last word of the tragedy: the voice of God saying, "I did not will it so." Like the line "We have considered everything carefully," it is italicized in Kraus's text. With the one phrase Kaiser Wilhelm II ushered in the war; the other is from Emperor Franz Josef's war manifesto "To My Peoples."

IV

Setting aside the Prologue, the Epilogue, and the dialogues between the Grumbler and the Optimist, one can venture the rough estimate that the text of about half the drama consists of newspaper reports and documents of all kinds, such as reports from the front, editorials, edicts, court judgments, business advertisements, and letters.

By what means did Kraus form scenes out of documents, a drama out of a plethora of scenes? In addition, what means, be they touching or outrageous, did he employ to imbue the scenes with satire? First of all, he assumed a presentation that conforms outwardly to the dramatic genre. Material quoted from numerous printed sources was assigned to a speaker, usually its author. Through the stage directions it is placed in a specific milieu and thereby into a specific atmosphere. By the fact that the speaker voices his own words in such an atmosphere, he unwittingly becomes an object of satire. The rest of the text is freely invented, but is full of quotations and phrases current in those years. The intertwining of documents, quotations, and phrases with ordinary, freely invented action serves to confirm the factual authenticity of the events.

Here, as in all Kraus's works, language has a religious dimension. It is not only the means of representation, but also the object of representation, the focal point of attention, evidence itself. He believed in a mystical unity between word and sense, between word and essence, resulting in an unconscious revelation of spiritual and moral abuses through corrupted word usage. Language in daily usage appeared to him to be just as mishandled and tarnished as all other cultural possessions. Certain wartime phrases surface again and again in the drama in order to reflect the social or spiritual situation.

Whatever abuses Kraus found he reproduced, and he created linguistic misdeeds, serious and humorous, just as a dramatist lets his characters commit real misdeeds. Particularly he employed word play in order to uncover hidden connections. Accurate reading of Kraus's prose and verse brings to light an inexhaustible abundance of word plays of all varieties. These range from a very few that are inexcusably silly, that derive from the pure joy of the game, through instances that appear less silly at the second glance than at the first, on to those that are very witty and full of emotion, as profoundly penetrating as those in Greek tragedy.

The transformation of document into dialogue and the deceptive dual function of language work together to produce a gripping, structured, satiric drama. Mimesis renders it true to nature; emphasis on contrasts produces the satire. Kraus's various methods can be mixed with elements of pathos, parody, humor, or the burlesque. Finally, the lyrical, didactic verse monologues have the effect of allowing the burlesque elements to be seen from a tragic perspective, and of preventing the intention of the whole from being forgotten.

The textual authenticity of so many scenes lends an unexpected advantage to the poetic form. On the one hand, they have the linguistic genuineness of the milieu from which they spring. On the other hand, the freely invented scenes are written with such a fine ear for the characteristics of every social, professional, and regional group and class, are shaped with such accomplished linguistic mimicry—in accent and grammar, in vocabulary and thought association—that they fuse together with the documentary elements into a unified whole. The reader who is familiar with the respective manners of speech will have the lively experience of recognition accompanied by all the feelings of sympathy or antipathy that are usually evoked in him by a speaker of that idiom. I know of no other literary work that employs the services of so many different modes of speech for mimetic or satiric characterization as does *The Last Days*.

The frequent, often horrifying incongruity between that which is said and the speaker has been mentioned above. One touches the nerve of the drama in observing that an endless variety of incongruities and contrasts, presented in structured form, runs through the drama, constituting the most prevalent stylistic device and means of creating impact. Incongruities are the rule: satire, after all, is in its essence the visual rendering of reality's apostasy from the ideal, the making visible of the contrast between truth and pretension. An example of this is the scorn that Kraus poured forth on a body of metaphors taken from teutonic tradition, metaphors of chivalry and single-handed combat, the phrases of knightly warfare with its banners and swords. All of this was depleted of imagination in an age of tanks and of gas and air attacks, an age in which the goal of war is the creation of new markets.

As the end approaches, the style of the drama distances itself from the realism of the majority of the scenes, a process that becomes more and more frequent with the progression of the tragic events, until, in the transition from the final scene to the surrealistic Epilogue, all semblance of reality disappears. This path is marked by an increased number of the Grumbler's pathos-laden and lyrical verse monologues, the gradual change in the stage directions, and in the giving of names. Even among the names of characters for a given scene realism and expressionistic caricature exist side by side.

Imitation, contrast, exaggeration, and arrangement also govern the drama as a whole and the relationship of the individual scenes to each other. The unity of a vast panorama, spanning the four and a half war years, overwhelms the reader by the abundance of scenes and figures. But it is not the huge numbers and variety alone that give the drama a paradoxical unity. As one reads on, the character of the whole is transformed; it grows ever darker. The suffering represented becomes worse, the people more evil, the fear and the premonition of the coming doom stronger, greed and noisy lust louder and shameless, until the military collapse, the universal conflagration, and the Last Judgment put an end to all this. And the insight and the horror of the imaginary witness—be he author or reader —keeps pace with the tragedy. There occurs a change in the comprehension of the subject and its rendering. The individual case becomes typical, the comic facets become dreadful and distorted; the mournful elements become ghostlike; the wit gains in grandeur; mimicry becomes caricature; dialectical statement becomes hyperbolic pathos; earthly reality becomes unearthly symbol.

The previous characterization of the peculiarity of the drama as "cyclopean formlessness" is then relevant only for the first impression. It is structured through and through. Repetition —both unchanged and varied—of specific phrases, motifs, and episodes contributes to holding the endless succession of scenes together, to pointing both forward and backward as a structural element and a carrier of meaning. If a phrase such as "to draft" governs a scene that has as its theme the destruction of human dignity and then reappears countless other times, then that theme is echoed whenever the phrase is repeated. The unchanged similarity of the comments of the four home-front officers in the first scene of each act shows their nature to be unchanged by the war, but the subtly changed content of their comments indicates the darkening of conditions from year to year. Some motifs share in the gradual internal and external transformation of the tragedy. Quite a number of episodes come up at least three times: as an event, as an apparition in the last scene of the fifth act, and as a subject of conversation between the Grumbler and the Optimist.

The recurring phrases, motifs, and episodes are only one means of holding together and relating to one another scenes that are neither linked by a plot nor subordinated to any strict time sequence. About twenty-five scene sequences, interrelated in their action, form thematic unities that are not always obvious at first glance. They are also mostly governed by the principle of contrast. For example, a sequence of scenes that contrasts the misery of the Austrian soldier to the negligence of duty on the part of glorified members of the imperial house contains at its center a short scene in which an invalid plays the Hoch Hapsburg March on a hurdy-gurdy. Sometimes uniformity characterizes the sequence; occasionally the effect is achieved by means of exaggerated stylization. In IV, 37, the German kaiser is presented as a sadist. In IV, 38, the German company commander Hiller appears in the same light. In IV, 39, a medical officer tries to cover up Hiller's cruelty. In IV, 40, the Grumbler quotes words about human kindness from the opening address that was delivered to the joint medical convention of German and Austrian physicians. And in IV, 41, the last scene of the sequence, a brutal military physician and a martinet-like hospital administrator appear.

In V, 14, French prisoners of war are "taken care of" at German command; in V, 15—the only scene taking place in the enemy camp—Germans are disposed of at French command; and both incidents recur, with exactly the same words, as apparitions in the final scene. In this ultimate scene, Kraus wanted to make clearly visible something that had already emerged in the Grumbler's dialogues with the Optimist: that *The Last Days* has as its subject not only the culture and war-waging of the Central Powers but also war and militarism as such. After the ring of genuine language throughout the drama, the speech of the German-speaking Frenchmen strikes the reader as oddly wooden (yet without being a parody). The scene has something cheap, comic-strippish about it.

The attempts, renewed again and again from act to act, to reinforce the theme of *The Last Days*—mankind's fall and end—flow together into the Epilogue. It is the obvious concentration of the entire drama, climaxing in the listing of the sins of the questionable heroes, recited by a voice from above. After a short, insolent, bombastic, yet unsuccessful resistance, the exact nature of which is left to the imagination, there follows the word of God: "I did not will it so."

As a whole, in its mingling of tragedy and wit, of dialectic and low humor, in its monumentality, in its technique of making a document into a dramatic character, in its multiplicity of style and forms, the drama is comparable to nothing else. In many respects it reminds one of the tragedy of the baroque age, in other respects of Nestroy, here and there of Offenbach and Gilbert and Sullivan. (Perhaps Thomas Mann's comment in 1925 is valid for the work: that for the modern artistic spirit, the categories of the tragic and the comic blend into one another, that the grotesque becomes the style of the age "to the extent that the extraordinary itself hardly appears today other than in the form of the grotesque.") This drama appears to have influenced the expressionist and epic drama. Bertolt Brecht admired it.

In summary, *The Last Days of Mankind* is a unique work of art: unique in the magnitude of its subject matter, which develops out of one idea—that of man's destiny—and in the combination of the gigantic nature of the design with the most subtle art of linguistic detail. This drama is, in many respects, bound to a specific time and place—not in its subject, but in the extent to which the local references can be understood. Perhaps here and there it is not free from errors in taste. Nevertheless, we know of no satiric drama that can approach its greatness.